MEMORIES OF A HOSTESS

MRS. FIELDS

MEMORIES OF A HOSTESS

A CHRONICLE OF
EMINENT FRIENDSHIPS

DRAWN CHIEFLY FROM THE DIARIES OF

MRS. JAMES T. FIELDS

BY

M. A. DeWOLFE HOWE

"I stay a little longer, as one stays
To cover up the embers that still burn"

WITH ILLUSTRATIONS

THE ATLANTIC MONTHLY PRESS
BOSTON

PRINTED IN THE
UNITED STATES OF AMERICA

CONTENTS

ILLUSTRATIONS

(*Most of the photographs reproduced are in the collections of the Boston Athenæum and the Harvard College Library, to which grateful acknowledgments are made.*)

MEMORIES OF A HOSTESS

MEMORIES OF A HOSTESS

I

PRELIMINARY

In the years immediately before the death of Mrs. James T. Fields, on January 5, 1915, she spoke to me more than once of her intention to place in my possession a cabinet of old papers — journals of her own, letters from a host of correspondents, odds and ends of manuscript and print — which stood in a dark corner of a small reception-room near the front door of her house in Charles Street, Boston. On her death this intention was found to have been confirmed in writing. It was also made clear that Mrs. Fields had no desire that her own life should be made a subject of record — "unless," she wrote, "for some reason not altogether connected with myself." Such a reason is abundantly suggested in her records of the friends she was constantly seeing through the years covered by the journals. These friends were men and women whose books have made them the friends of the English-speaking world, and a better knowledge of them would justify any amplification of the records of their lives. In this process the figure of their friend and hostess in Charles Street must inevitably reveal itself — not as the subject of a biography, but as a central animating presence, a focus of sympathy and understanding, which seemed to make a single phenomenon out of a long series and wide variety of friendships and hospitalities.

The "blue books" — more than fifty in number — which Mrs. Fields used for the journals have already yielded many pages of valuable record to her own books, especially "James T. Fields: Biographical Notes and Personal Sketches" (1881), and "Authors and Friends" (1896); also even, here and there, to Mr. Fields's "Yesterdays with Authors" (1871). Yet she left unprinted much that is both picturesque and illuminating: so many of the persons mentioned in the journal were still living or had but recently died when her books were written. There are, besides, many passages used in a fragmentary way, which may now with propriety be given complete.

Into these manuscript journals, then, I propose to dip afresh — not with the purpose of passing in a miscellaneous review all the friends who crossed the threshold of the Charles Street house in a fixed period of time, but rather in pursuit of what seems a more promising quest — namely, to consider separate friends and groups of friends in turn; to assemble from the journals passages that have to do with them; to supplement these by drawing now and then upon the old cabinet for a letter from this or that friend to Mr. or Mrs. Fields, and thus to step back across the years into a time and scene of refreshing remembrance. Many a friend, many a friendship, must be left untouched. In the processes of selection, figures of more than local significance will receive the chief consideration. In passages relating to one person, allusions to many others, sometimes treated separately in other passages, will often be found, for the friendships with one and another were constantly overlapping and interlocking. Bits of record of no obviously great importance will be included, not because they or the subjects of them are taken with undue seriousness, but merely that a vanished society, interesting in itself to those who care for the past and doubly interesting as material for a study in contrasts with the present, may have again its "day in court." When Fields was publishing his reminiscences of Hawthorne, Lowell wrote to him: "Be sure and don't leave anything out because it seems trifling, for it is out of these trifles only that it is possible to reconstruct character sometimes, if not always"; and he commended especially the hitting of "the true channel between the Charybdis of reticence, and the Scylla of gossip." Under sailing orders of this nature, self-imposed, I hope to proceed.

"Another added to my cloud of witnesses," wrote Mrs. Fields in her journal, on hearing, in 1867, that Forceythe Willson had died. Nearly fifty years of life then remained to the diarist, though she continued to keep her diary with regularity for hardly ten. Before her own death the cloud of witnesses was infinitely extended. Yet new friends constantly stood ready to fill, as best they might, the gaps that were left by the old. It is not the new who will appear in the following pages, but those with whom Mrs. Fields herself must now be numbered.

II

THE HOUSE AND THE HOSTESS

The fact that Henry James, in "The American Scene," published in 1907, and again in an article which appeared in the "Atlantic Monthly" and the "Cornhill Magazine" in July, 1915, has set down in his own ultimate words his memories of Mrs. Fields and her Boston abode would be the despair of anyone attempting a similar task — were it not that quotation remains an unprohibited practice. In "The American Scene" he evokes from the past "the Charles Street ghosts," and gives them their local habitation: "Here, behind the effaced anonymous door" — a more literal-minded realist might have noted that a vestibule-door contributed the only effacement and anonymity — "was the little ark of the modern deluge, here still the long drawing-room that looks over the water and towards the sunset, with a seat for every visiting shade, from far-away Thackeray down, and relics and tokens so thick on its walls as to make it positively, in all the town, the votive temple to memory." In his "Atlantic" and "Cornhill" article he refers to the house, in a phrase at which Mrs. Fields would have smiled, as "the waterside museum of the Fieldses," and to them as "addicted to every hospitality and every benevolence, addicted to the cultivation of talk and wit and to the ingenious multiplication of such ties as could link the upper half of the title-page with the lower"; he pays tribute to "their vivacity, their curiosity, their mobility, the felicity of their instinct for any manner of gathered relic, remnant, or tribute"; and in Mrs. Fields herself, surviving her husband for many years, he notes "the personal beauty of her younger years, long retained and not even at the end of such a stretch of life quite lost; the exquisite native tone and mode of appeal, which anciently we perhaps thought a little 'precious,' but from which the distinctive and the preservative were in time to be snatched, a greater extravagance supervening; the signal sweetness of temper and lightness of tact."

There is one more of Henry James's remarks about Mrs. Fields that must be quoted, "All her implications," he says, "were gay, since no one so finely sentimental could be noted as so humorous; just as no feminine humor was perhaps ever so unmistakingly directed, and no state of amusement, amid quantities of reminiscence, perhaps ever so merciful." Mirth and mercy do not always, like righteousness and peace, kiss each other. In Mrs. Fields the capacity for incapacitating laughter was such that I cannot help recalling one occasion, near the end of her life, when an attempt to tell a certain story — of which I remember nothing but that it had to do with a horse — involved her in such merriment that after repeated efforts to reach its "point," she was forced to abandon the endeavor. What I cannot recall in a single instance, in the excellent telling of innumerable anecdotes, is unkindness, in word or suggestion, toward the persons involved in them. Mr. James did well to include this item in his enumeration of Mrs. Fields's qualities.

Through all his lenses of memory and phrase he brought so vividly to one's own vision the Mrs. Fields a younger generation had known that, on reading what he had written, I wrote to him in England, then nearly ending its first year in the war, and must have said that his pages would help me, at some future day, to deal with these of my own, now at last taking form. Thus, in part, he replied: —

July 20th, 1915

Your appreciation reached me, alas, but through the most muffling and deadening thickness of our unspeakable actuality here. It was to try and get out of that a little that I wrote my paper — in the most difficult and defeating conditions, which seemed to me to make it, with my heart so utterly elsewhere, a deplorably make-believe attempt. Therefore if it *had* any virtue, there must still be some in my poor old stump of a pen. Yes, the pipe of peace is a thing one has, amid our storm and stress, to listen very hard for when it twitters, from afar, outside; and when you shall pipe it over your exhibition of dear Mrs. Fields's relics and documents I shall respond to your doing so with whatever attention may then be possible to me. We are not detached here, in your enviable way — but just exactly so must we therefore make some small effort to escape, even into whatever fatuity of illusion, to keep our heads above water at all. That in short is the history of my "Cornhill" scrap.

The time into which Henry James escaped by "pip-
ing" of Mrs. Fields has now grown far more remote than
the added span of the last seven years, merely as years,
could have made it. Remote enough it seemed to him

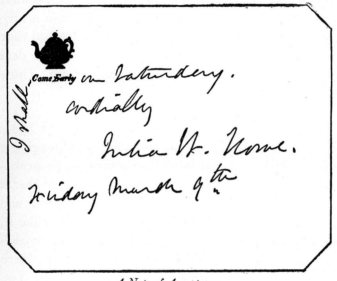

A Note of Acceptance

when, at the end of his reminiscences of the Fieldses, he
recalled a small "feast" in the Charles Street dining-
room at which Mrs. Julia Ward Howe — it must have
been about 1906 — rose and declaimed, "a little quaver-
ingly, but ever so gallantly, that 'Battle Hymn of the
Republic' which she caused to be chanted half a century before and still could accompany with a real
breadth of gesture, her great clap of hands and indica-
tion of the complementary step, on the triumphant

line, 'Be swift my hands to welcome him, be jubilant my feet!'"

Now it fell to my lot that night, as perhaps the youngest of the party, to convoy Mrs. Howe across two wintry bits of sidewalk into the carriage which bore her to and from the memorable dinner-party, and to accompany her on each of the little journeys. Quite as clear in my memory as her recitation of the "Battle Hymn" was the note of finality in her voice, quite free from unkindness, as she settled down for the return drive to her house in Beacon Street, far from a towering figure, and announced in the darkness: "Annie Fields has shrunk." The hostess we were leaving and the guest some fifteen years her senior, and nearing ninety with what seemed an immortally youthful spirit, appear, when those words are recalled, as they must have been before either was touched by the diminishing hand of age; and the house whose door had just closed upon us — a house more recently obliterated to make room for a monstrous garage — came back as the scene of many a gathering of which the little feast described by Henry James was but a type.

Early in January of 1915 this door, which through a period of sixty years had opened upon extraordinary hospitality, was finally closed. Since 1866 it had borne the number 148. Ten years earlier, in 1856, when the house was first occupied by James T. Fields, afterwards identified with the publishing firms of Ticknor and Fields, and Fields, Osgood and Company, it was numbered 37, Charles Street. This Boston man of books and friendships, who before his death in 1881 was to become widely known as publisher, editor, lecturer, and writer, had married, in 1850, Eliza Josephine Willard, a daughter of Simon Willard, Jr., of the name still honorably associated with the even passage of time. She died within a few months, and in November of 1854 he married her cousin, Annie Adams, not yet twenty years old, the beautiful daughter of Dr. Zabdiel Boylston Adams. For those who knew Mrs. Fields toward the end of her four score and more years, it was far easier to see in her charming face and presence the exquisite, eager young woman of the mid-nineteenth century than to detect in the Charles Street of 1915, of which she was the last inhabitant of her own kind, any resemblance to the delightful street of family dwellings, many of them looking out over the then unfilled "Back Bay," to which she had come about sixty years before. The Fieldses had lived here but a few years when, in 1859, Dr. Oliver Wendell Holmes — with the "Autocrat" a year behind him and the "Professor" a year ahead — became their neighbor at 21, subsequently 164, Charles Street. On the other side of them, nearer Beacon Street, John A. Andrew, the great war governor of Massachusetts, was a friend and neighbor. Across the way, for a time, lived Thomas Bailey Aldrich. In hillside streets near by dwelt many persons of congenial tastes, whose work and character contributed greatly to making Boston what it was through the second half of the last century.

The distinctive flavor of the neighborhood derived nothing more from any of its households than from that of Mr. and Mrs. Fields. Their dining-room and drawing-room[1] — that green assembling-place of books, pictures, music, persons, associations, all to be treasured — were the natural resort, not only of the whole notable local company of writers whose publisher was also their true and valued friend, but, besides, of many of the eminent visitors to Boston, of the type represented most conspicuously by Charles Dickens. After the death of Mr. Fields there was far more than a tradition carried on in the Charles Street house. Not merely for what it had meant, but for all that the gracious personality of Mrs. Fields caused it to go on meaning, it continued through her lifetime — extending beyond that of Miss Sarah Orne Jewett, for so many years of Mrs. Fields's widowhood her delightful sister-hostess — the resort of older and younger friends, whose present thus drew a constant enrichment from the past.

It was not till 1863, nearly ten years after her marriage, that Mrs. Fields, who had kept a diary during a visit to Europe in 1859–60 with her husband, and for other brief periods, applied herself regularly to this practice, maintained through 1876, and thereafter renewed but intermittently. She wrote on the cover of the first slender volume: "No. 1. Journal of Literary Events and Glimpses of Interesting People." A few of its earliest pages, revealing its general purpose and character, may well precede the passages relating, in accordance with the plan already indicated, to individ-

---

[1] *A Shelf of Old Books*, by Mrs. Fields (1894), pictures many aspects of the house and its contents.

ual friends and groups of friends. In the first pages
of all, on which Mrs. Fields built a few sentences for
her "Biographical Notes," I find: —

July 26, 1863. — What a strange history this literary
life in America at the present day would make. An
editor and publisher at once, and at this date, stands
at a confluence of tides where all humanity seems to
surge up in little waves; some larger than the rest
(every seventh it may be) dashes up in music to which
the others love to listen; or some springing to a great
height retire to tell the story of their flight to those who
stay below.

Mr. Longfellow is quietly at Nahant. His translation
of Dante is finished, but will not be completely published until the year 1865, that being the 600th anniversary since the death of the great Italian. Dr. Holmes
was never in healthier mood than at present. His oration delivered before a large audience upon the Fourth
of July this year places him high in the rank of native
orators. It is a little doubtful how soon he will feel like
writing again. He has contributed much during the
last two years to the "Atlantic" magazine. He may
well take a temporary rest.

Mr. Lowell is not well. He is now travelling. Mr.
Hawthorne is in Concord. He has just completed a
volume of English Sketches of which a few have been
printed in the "Atlantic Monthly." He will dedicate
the volume to Franklin Pierce, the Democrat — a most
unpopular thing just now, but friendship of the purest

stimulates him, and the ruin in prospect for his book because of this resolve does not move him from his purpose. Such adherence is indeed noble. Hawthorne requires all that popularity can give him in a pecuniary way for the support of his family.

The "Atlantic Monthly" is at present an interesting feature of America. Purely literary, it has nevertheless a subscription list, daily increasing, of 32,000. Of course the editor's labors are not slight. We have been waiting for Mr. Emerson to publish his new volume containing his address upon Henry Thoreau; but he is careful of words and finds many to be considered again and again, until it is almost impossible to extort a manuscript from his hands. He has written but little, of late.

July 28. — George William Curtis has done at least one great good work. He has by a gentle but continuously brave pressure transformed the "Harper's Weekly," which was semi-Secession, into an anti-slavery and Republican journal. The last issue is covered with pictures as well as words which tend to ameliorate the condition of the colored race. Mr. Curtis's own house at Staten Island has been threatened by the mob; therefore his wife and children came last week to New England. I fear the death of Colonel Shaw, her brother, commanding the 54th Massachusetts (colored infantry), will induce them to return home. His death is one of our severest strokes.

July 31, 1863. — We have been in Concord this week, making a short visit at the Hawthornes'. He has just finished his volume of English Sketches, about to be dedicated to Franklin Pierce. It is a beautiful incident in Hawthorne's life, the determination at all hazards to dedicate this book to his friend. Mr. P.'s politics at present shut him away from the faith of patriots, but Hawthorne has loved him since college days and he will not relent.[1] Mrs. Hawthorne is the stay of the house.

To

FRANKLIN PIERCE,

AS A SLIGHT MEMORIAL OF A COLLEGE FRIENDSHIP, PROLONGED
THROUGH MANHOOD, AND RETAINING ALL ITS VITALITY
IN OUR AUTUMNAL YEARS,

𝕿𝖍𝖎𝖘 𝖁𝖔𝖑𝖚𝖒𝖊 𝖎𝖘 𝕴𝖓𝖘𝖈𝖗𝖎𝖇𝖊𝖉

BY NATHANIEL HAWTHORNE.

The Offending Dedication

The wood-work, the tables and chairs and pedestals, are all ornamented by her artistic hand or what she has prompted her children to do. Una is full of exquisite maidenhood. Julian was away, but his beautiful illuminations lay upon the table. The one illustrating a portion of King Arthur's address to Queen Guinevere (Tennyson) was remarkably fine.

All this takes one back into a past sufficiently remote. The 1859–60 diary of travel achieves the more remarkable spectacle of Mrs. Fields in conversation with Leigh Hunt less than two months before he died,

---

[1] About two months later, Mrs. Fields wrote in her diary: "Emerson says Hawthorne's book is 'pellucid but not deep.' He has cut out the dedication and letter, as others have done."

and reporting the very words of Shelley to this friend
of his. They may be found in the "Biographical
Notes" published by Mrs. Fields after her husband's
death. Shelley says, "Hunt, we write *love*-songs; why
shouldn't we write hate-songs?" And Hunt, recalling
the remark, adds, "He said he meant to some day,
poor fellow." Perhaps one of his subjects would have
been the second Mrs. Godwin, for, according to Hunt,
he disliked her particularly, believing her untrue, and
used to say that when he was obliged to dine with her
"he would lean back in his chair and languish into
hate." Then, wrote Mrs. Fields, "he said no one could
describe Shelley. He always was to him as if he came
from the planet Mercury, bearing a winged wand
tipped with flame." It is now an even century since
the death of Shelley, and here we find one of the older
generation of our own time talking, as it were, with
him at but a single remove. Almost the reader is
persuaded to ask of Mrs. Fields herself, "Ah, did you
once see Shelley plain?"

Thus from the records of bygone years many remembered figures might be summoned; but the evo-
cations already made will suffice to indicate the point of
vantage at which Mrs. Fields stood as a diarist, and to
set the scene for the display of separate friendships

III

DR. HOLMES, THE FRIEND AND NEIGHBOR[1]

IF any familiar face should appear at the front of the procession that constantly crossed the threshold of 148, Charles Street, it should be that of Dr. Oliver Wendell Holmes, for many years a near neighbor, and to the end of his life a devoted visitor and friend. Here, then, is an unpublished letter written from his summer retreat while Fields was still actively associated with the "Old Corner Bookstore" of Ticknor, Reed, and Fields, and in the year before his marriage with Annie Adams: —

PITTSFIELD, *Sept. 6th,* 1853

MY DEAR MR. FIELDS: —

Thank you for the four volumes, and the authors of three of them through you. You did not remember that I patronized you to the extent of Aleck before I came up; never mind, I can shove it round among the young farmeresses and perhaps help to work off the eleventh thousand of the most illustrious of all the Smiths.

I shall write to Hillard soon. I have been reading his book half the time today and with very great pleasure. I am delighted with the plan of it — practical in-

---

[1] The greater part of this chapter appeared in the *Yale Review* for April, 1918.

formation such as the traveller that is to be or that has been wishes for, with poetical description enough to keep the imagination alive, and sound American thought to give it manly substance. It is anything but a *flash* book, but I have not the slightest doubt that it will have a permanent and very high place in travelling literature. Many things have pleased me exceedingly, — when I have read a little more I shall try to tell him what pleases me *most*, — as I suppose like most authors he likes as many points for his critical self-triangulation as will come unasked for.

Hawthorne's book has been not devoured, but *bolted* by my children. I have not yet had a chance at it, but I don't doubt I shall read it with as much gusto as they, when my turn comes. When you write to him, thank him if you please for me, for I suppose he will hardly expect any formal acknowledgment.

I bloomed out into a large smile of calm delight on opening the delicate little "Epistle Dedicatory" wherein your name is embalmed. I cannot remember that our friend has tried that pace before; he wrote some pleasing lines I remember to Longfellow on the ship in which he was to sail when he went to Europe some years — a good many — ago.

Don't be too proud! Wait until you get a prose dedication from a poet, — if you have not got one already, — and then consider yourself immortal.

Yours most truly,

O. W. HOLMES

AN EARLY PHOTOGRAPH OF DR. HOLMES

This letter contains several provocations to curiosity. "Aleck, . . . the most illustrious of all the Smiths," was obviously Alexander Smith, the Scottish poet of enormous but strictly contemporaneous vogue, in whom the English reviewers of the time detected a kinship to Tennyson, Keats, Shelley, and Shakespeare. George S. Hillard's new book was "Six Months in Italy," and Hawthorne's, "not devoured, but bolted" by the Holmes children, was "Tanglewood Tales." The "delicate little 'Epistle Dedicatory'" has been found elusive.

From this early letter of Dr. Holmes a seven-league step may be taken to a passage in a diary Mrs. Fields was writing in 1860, — the year following the removal of the Holmes household from Montgomery Place to Charles Street, — before her long unbroken series of journals began. The occasion described was one of those frequent breakfasts in the Fields dining-room, which bespoke, in the term of a later poet, the "wide unhaste" of the period. Of the guests, N. P. Willis was then at the top of his distinction as a New York editor; George T. Davis, a lawyer of Greenfield, Massachusetts, afterwards of Portland, Maine, a classmate of Dr. Holmes, was reputed one of the most charming table-companions and wits of his day: the tributes to his memory at a meeting of the Massachusetts Historical Society after his death in 1877 stir one's envy of his contemporaries; George Washington Greene of Rhode Island was perhaps equally known as the friend of Longfellow and as the grandson and biographer of

General Nathanael Greene; Whipple was, of course, Edwin P. Whipple, essayist and lecturer; the household of three was completed by Mrs. Fields's sister, Miss Lizzie Adams.

Thursday, September 21, 1860. — Equinoctial clearing after a stormy night and morning. Willis came to breakfast, and Holmes and George T. Davis, G. W. Greene, Whipple, and our little household of three. Holmes talked better than all, as usual. Willis played the part of appreciative listener. G. T. Davis told wonderful stories, and Mr. Whipple talked more than usual. Holmes described the line of beauty which is made by any two persons who talk together congenially thus ⌣⌢⌣, whereas, when an adverse element comes in, it proceeds thus ∧; and by and by one which has a frightful retrograde movement, thus /. Then blank despair settles down upon the original talker. He said people should dovetail together like properly built mahogany furniture. Much of all this congeniality had to do with the physical, he said. "Now there is big Dr. ——; he and I do very well together; I have just two intellectual heart-beats to his one." Willis said he thought there should be an essay written upon the necessity that literary men should live on a more concentrated diet than is their custom. "Impossible," said the Professor, "there is something behind the man which drives him on to his fate; he goes as the steam-engine goes and one might as well say to the engine going at the rate of sixty miles, 'you had better stop now,' and so make it stop, as to say it to a man driven on by a vital preordained energy for work." Each man has a philosophical coat fitted to his shoulders, and he did not expect to find it fitting anybody else.

At another breakfast, in 1861, we find, besides the favorite humorist of the day, Dr. Holmes's son and namesake, then a young officer in the Union army, now Justice of the Supreme Court of the United States.

Sunday, December 8, 1861. — Yesterday morning "Artemus Ward," Mr. Browne, breakfasted with us, also Dr. Holmes and the lieutenant, his son. We had a merry time because Jamie was in grand humor and represented people and incidents in the most incomparable manner. "Why," said Dr. Holmes to him afterward, "you must excuse me that I did not talk, but the truth is there is nothing I enjoy so much as your anecdotes, and whenever I get a chance I can't help listening to them." The Professor complimented Artemus upon his great success and told him the pleasure he had received. Artemus twinkled all over, but said little after the Professor arrived. He was evidently immensely possessed by him. The young lieutenant has mostly recovered from his wound and speaks as if duty would recall him soon to camp. He will go when the time comes, but home evidently never looked half so pleasant before. Poor fellows! Heaven send us peace before long!

The finely bound copy of Dr. Holmes's Fourth of July Oration at the Boston City Celebration of 1863, to which the following passage refers, is one of the rarities sought by American book-collectors. It was a practice of Dr. Holmes at this time to have his public speeches set up in large, legible type for his own reading at their delivery. One of these, an address to the alumni of Harvard on July 16, 1863, with the inscription, "Oliver Wendell Holmes to his friend James T. Fields. One of six copies printed," is found among the Charles Street papers, and contributes, like the passage that follows, to the sense of pleasant intimacy between the neighboring houses.

August 3, 1863. — Dr. Holmes dropped in last night about his oration which the City Council have had printed and superbly bound. He has addressed it to the "Common Council" instead of the "City Council," and he is much disturbed. J. T. F. told him it made but small consequence, and he went off comforted. One of the members of the Council told Mr. F. it was amusing to see "the Professor" while this address was passing through the press. He was so afraid something would be wrong that he would come in to see about it half a dozen times a day, until it seemed as if he considered this small oration of more consequence than the affairs of the state. Yet laugh as they may about these little peculiarities of "our Professor," he is a most wonderful man.

In explanation of the ensuing bit, it need only be said that in October of 1863 Señorita Isabella Cubas

BROTHERS OF THE ASSOCIATION OF THE ALUMNI

IT is your misfortune and mine that you must accept my services as your presiding officer in the place of your honored President. I need hardly say how unwillingly it is that for the second time I find myself in this trying position; called upon to fill as I best may the place of one whose presence and bearing, whose courtesy, whose dignity, whose scholarship, whose standing among the distinguished children of the University, fit him alike to guide your councils and to grace your festivals. The name of Winthrop has been so long associated with the State and with the College, that to sit under his mild empire is like resting beneath one of these wide-branching elms, the breadth of whose shade is only a measure of the hold its roots have taken in the soil.

In the midst of civil strife we, the children of this our common mother, have come together in peace. And surely there never was a time when we more needed a brief respite in some chosen place of refuge, some unviolated sanctuary, from the cares and anxieties of our daily existence, than at this very hour. Our life has grown haggard with excitement. The rattle of drums, the march of regiments, the gallop of squadrons, the roar of artillery, seem to have been contin-

Reduced facsimile of first page of Dr. Holmes's 1863 Address
to the Alumni of Harvard

was appearing at the Boston Theatre in "The Wizard Skiff, or the Massacre of Scio," and other pantomimes. "The Wizard Skiff," according to the "Advertiser," was given on the fourteenth.   On the sixteenth, a characteristic announcement read: "At ¼ past 8 Señorita Cubas will dance La Madrilena." The tear of Dr. Holmes at the spectacle may be remembered with the "poetry and religion" anecdote of Emerson, Margaret Fuller, and Fanny Ellsler.

October 16, 1863. — Mr. F. went in two evenings since to find Professor Holmes. His wife said he was out. "I don't know where he is gone, I am sure, Mr. Fields," she said in her eager way, "but he said he had finished his work and asked if he might go, and I told him he might, though he would not tell where he was going."

Yesterday the "where" transpired. "By the way," said the Professor, "have you seen that little poem by Mrs. Waterston upon the death of Colonel Shaw, 'Together'? It made me cry. However, I don't know how much that means, for I went to see the 'beautiful Cubas' in a pantomime the other night, and the first thing I knew down came a great round fat tear and went splosh on the ground. Was n't I provoked!"

The next fragment is neither a letter nor a passage from the diary, but a bit of excellent fooling, in Dr. Holmes's handwriting, on a sheet of note paper. The meteorological records of 1864 would probably show that there were heavy rains in the course of the year.

BOSTON THEATRE

LESSEE AND MANAGER..........Mr WYKEMAN MARSHALL
STAGE MANAGER.......................................Mr J. G. HANLEY

 HER STAR UNDIMNED!

SENORITA ISABELLA

CUBAS

—— IN A ——

CHANGE OF PIECE

INTRODUCING HER TO THE PUBLIC IN

☞ Another Character !

PECULIARLY ADAPTED TO THIS

GREAT ARTISTE.

THE PIECE PRODUCED WITH

NEW SCENES, MUSIC AND STARTLING MECHAN-ICAL EFFECTS !

WOLFO.....................................Mr W. H. EDGAR

Wednesday Evening, October 14, 1863,

Will be performed the Legendary Drama, in 3 acts, entitled the

WIZARD SKIFF!

Or—The Massacre of Scio.

ALEXA............ ....SENORITA ISABELLA CUBAS
WOLFO..Mr W. H. EDGAR
Constantine..............W. H. Whalley | Michael..................W. H Danvers
Count Bergesnoff.........W. H. Hamblin | Anastasius................F. O. Savage
Von Waddledorf.............W. Scallan | Fritz ....Barry
Agassti................N. T. Davenport | Pauline............Miss Blanche Gray
Guards, Greek Sailors and Pirates.

ACT FIRST—GREEK PIRATES' RENDEZVOUS.

ACT SECOND—THE WIZARD SKIFF.

ACT THIRD—TERRIFIC EXPLOSION OF THE WIZARD'S CAVE—Appearance of the Wizard's Skiff, under Full Sail—Rescue of Alexa & Constantine
—Denouement of Victory,

GRAND OVERTURE

Of Musical Selections. Leader, F. Suck.

FROM THE PLAY-BILL OF THE NIGHT OF
DR. HOLMES'S "GREAT ROUND FAT TEAR"

From Dr. Holmes's interest in the tracing of Dr. Johnson's footsteps an even century before his own, it is
easy to imagine his fancy playing about the rainfall of
the century ahead.   I cannot find that this *jeu d'esprit*,
with its entirely characteristic flavor of the "Breakfast
Table," was ever printed by its author.

Letter from the last man left by the Deluge of the year 1964
to the last woman left by the same

MY DEAR SOLE SURVIVORESS : —

Love is natural to the human breast. The passion
has seized me, and you, fortunately, cannot doubt as
to its object.

Adored one, fairest, and indeed only individual of
your sex, can you, could you doubt that if the world
still possessed its full complement of inhabitants,
823,060,413 according to the most recent estimate, I
should hesitate in selecting you from the 411,530,206½
females in existence previous to the late accident? Believe it not! Trust not the deceivers who — but I forget the late melancholy occurrence for the moment.

It is still damp in our — I beg your pardon — in my
neighborhood. I hope you are careful of your precious
health — so much depends upon it! The dodo is ex-
tinct — what if Man — but pardon me. Let me recom-
mend long india-rubber boots — they will excite no
remark, for reasons too obvious to mention.

May I hope for a favorable answer to my suit by the
bearer of this message, the carrier-goose, who was with

me during the rainy season in the top of the gigantic pine?

If any more favored suitor — What am I saying? If

*If any more favored suitor —
What am I saying? If any
recollection of the past is to come
between me and happiness, break
it gently to me, for my nerves
have been a good deal tried
by the loss of the human species
(with the exception of ourselves)
and there is something painful
in the thought of shedding tears in a
world so thoroughly saturated
with liquid*

*I am
(by the force of circumstances)*

Your Only lover and admirer

O.W.H. Fizit.   *Ultimus Smith*

Facsimile of the Conclusion of Ultimus Smith's Declaration

any recollection of the past is to come between me and happiness, break it gently to me, for my nerves have been a good deal tried by the loss of the human species (with the exception of ourselves) and there is something painful in the thought of shedding tears in a world so thoroughly saturated with liquid.

I am

(by the force of circumstances)

Your Only lover and admirer

Ultimus Smith

O. W. H. Fixit.

A few brief items of May of 1864 bring back a time of sadness for all the friends of Nathaniel Hawthorne.

May 11, 1864. — J. T. F. went to see Dr. Holmes about Hawthorne's health. The latter came to town looking very very ill. O. W. H. thinks the shark's tooth is upon him, but would not have this known. Walked and talked with him; then carried him to "Metcalf's and treated him to simple medicine as we treat each other to ice cream."

O. W. H. picked up a New York pamphlet full of sneers against Boston "Mutual Admiration Society." "These whipper-snappers of New York will do well to take care," he says; "the noble race of men now so famous here is passing down the valley — then who will take their places! I am ashamed to know the names of these blackguards. There is ——, a stick of sugar-candy —— and ——, who is not even a gum-drop, and plenty like them."

Sunday, May 14. — Terrible days of war and change. . . .

May 19. — Hawthorne is dead.

Less than a year later came the record of another death — unique in that every survivor of the war-time seems to have remembered the very moment and circumstances of learning the overwhelming fact.

April 15, 1865. — Last night when I shut this book I wondered a little what event or person would come next, powerful enough to compel me to write a few words; and before I was dressed this morning the news of the assassination of the President became our only thought. The President, Seward, and his son!

Mrs. Andrew came in before nine o'clock to ask if we thought it would be expected of her to receive "the Club" on Monday. We decided "No," immediately, which chimed with her desire.

The city is weighed down by sadness. But Dr. Holmes expresses his philosophy for the consolation of all. "It will unite the North," he says. "It is more than likely that Lincoln was not the best man for the work of re-construction," etc. His faith keeps him from the shadows which surround many.

But it is a black day for us all. J. Wilkes Booth is in custody. Poor Edwin is in Boston.

April 22. — False report. Up to this date J. Wilkes Booth has not been taken. A reward of nearly $200,000 is set upon his head, but we believe him to have fled into Maryland or farther south, with some marauding party.

Henry Howard Brownell, the author of "War Lyrics," appears in the following extract, with Dr. Holmes, whose high opinion of this singer of naval battle was set forth in print of no uncertain tone. Of Forceythe Willson, a poet, not yet thirty years old, of whom great things were expected, Mrs. Fields wrote later in the same volume of the journal: "He affects me like a wild Tennyson. . . . He is an indigenous growth of our middle states. He was a pupil of Horace Mann, and appreciated him."

April 29, 1865. — Club dinner for J. T. F. Mr. Brownell was present, author of "The Bay Fight," as Dr. Holmes's guest. Dr. H. said privately to us, "Well, 't ain't much for some folks to do what I 'm doing for this man, but it 's a good deal for me. I don't like that kind of thing, you know. I find myself unawares in something the position of a lion-hunter, which is unpleasant !!!" He has lately discovered that Forceythe Willson, the author of a noble poem called the "Color Sergeant" ["The Old Sergeant"], has been living two years in Cambridge. He wrote to him and told him how much he liked his poem and said he would like to make his acquaintance. "I will be at home," the young poet replied to the elder, "at any time you may appoint to call upon me." This was a little strange to O. W. H., who rather expected, as the elder who was extending the right hand, to be called upon, I suppose, although he did not say so. He found a fortress of a man, "shy as Hawthorne," and "one who had not learned that the eagle's wings should sometimes be kept down, as we people who live in the world must," said the Professor to me afterward. "In State" by F. W. is a great poem.

More than a year later is found this characteristic glimpse of Dr. Holmes in the elation of finishing one of his books.

Wednesday, September 12, 1866. — After an hour J. went in to see Dr. Holmes. This was important. He had promised a week ago to hear him read his new romance, and he did not wish to show anything but the lively interest he really feels. . . .

Jamie returned in two hours perfectly enchanted. The novel exceeded his hopes. No diminishing of power is to be seen; on the contrary it seems the perfect fruit of a life. It is to be called "The Guardian Angel." Four parts are already completed and large books of notes stand ready for use and reference. Mrs. Holmes came in to tell Mr. Fields she wished Wendell would not publish anything more. He would only call down newspaper criticism, and where was the use. "Well, Amelia, I have written something now which the critics won't complain of. You see it's better than anything I have ever done." "Oh, that's what you always say, Wendell, but I wish you'd let it alone!" "But don't you see, Amelia, I shall make money by it, and that won't come amiss." "No indeed, Mr. Fields, not in these times with our family, you know." "But there's one thing," said the little Professor, suddenly looking up to Mr. Fields; "if anything should happen to me before I get the story done, you would n't come down upon the widder for the money, would you now?" Then they had a grand laugh all round. He is very nervous indeed about his work and read it with great reluctance, yet desired to do so. He had read it to no one as yet until Mr. Fields should hear it.

Wendell, his son, had just returned from England, bringing a young English Captain of Artillery home with him for the night, the hotels being crowded. The captain's luggage was in the entry. The Professor drew J. aside to show him how the straps of the luggage were arranged in order to slip in the address-card. "D' ye see that — good, ain't it? I 've made a drawing of that and am going to have some made like it."

Near the end of 1866, Mrs. Fields, after a few words of realization that something lies beyond the age of thirty, pictures "the Autocrat" at her own breakfast-table, with General John Meredith Read, afterwards minister to Greece, and already, before that age of thirty which the diarist was just completing, an important figure in the military and political life of New York. A few sentences from the following passage are found in Mrs. Fields's article on Dr. Holmes, which appeared first in the "Century Magazine," and then in "Authors and Friends."

It comes over me to put down here and now the fact that this year for the first time others perceived, as well as myself, that I have passed the freshness and lustre of youth — but I do not feel the change as I once thought I must — life is even sweeter than ever and richer though I can still remember the time when thirty years seemed the desirable limit of life — now it opens before me full of uncompleted labor, full of riches and plans — the wealth of love, the plans of eternity.

Friday morning. — Professor Holmes and Adjutant General Read of New York (a young man despite his title) breakfasted here at eight o'clock. They were both here punctually at quarter past eight, which was early for the season, especially as the General was late out, at a ball, last night. He was only too glad of the chance, however, to meet Dr. Holmes, and would have made a far greater effort to accomplish it. The talk at one time turned upon Dickens. Dr. Holmes said he thought him a greater genius than Thackeray and was never satisfied with admiring his wondrous powers of observation and fertility of reproduction; his queer knack at making scenes, too, was noticeable, but especially the power of beginning from the smallest externals and describing a man to the life though he might get no farther than the shirt-button, for he always failed in profound analysis. Hawthorne, beginning from within, was his contrast and counterpart. But the two qualities which Dickens possesses and which the world seems to take small account of, but which mark his peculiar greatness, are the minuteness of his observations and

MRS. FIELDS
From a crayon portrait made by Rowse in 1863

his endless variety. Thackeray had sharp corners in
him, something which led you to see he could turn
round short upon you some day, although sadness was
an impressive element in his character — perhaps a
sadness belonging to genius. Hawthorne's sadness was
a part of his genius — tenderness and sadness.

On Monday, February 25, 1867, Mrs. Fields made
note of the Saturday Club dinner of two days before, at
which the guests were George William Curtis, "Petro-
leum V. Nasby," and Dr. Hayes of Arctic fame, of
whom Mrs. Fields had written a few days before: "He
wears a corrugated face, and his slender spirited figure
shows him the man for such resolves and expeditions.
We were carried away like the hearers of an Arabian
tale with his vivid pictures of Arctic life." But apparently he was not the chief talker at the Saturday Club
meeting, for Mrs. Fields wrote of it: "Dr. Holmes was
in great mood for talk, but Lowell was critical and interrupted him frequently. 'Now, James, let me talk
and don't interrupt me,' he once said, a little ruffled
by the continual strictures on his conversation." But
by the time that Longfellow's sixtieth birthday came
round on the following Wednesday, Dr. Holmes was
ready for it with the verses, "In gentle bosoms tried and
true," recorded in Longfellow's diary, and for another
encounter with Lowell, who also celebrated the day
with a poem, beginning "I need not praise the sweetness of his song." Mrs. Fields's diary records her husband's account of the evening: —

February 28, 1867. — Thursday morning. Jamie had a most brilliant evening at Longfellow's. A note came in from O. W. H. towards night, saying he was full of business and full of his story, but he *must* go to L.'s. Lowell's poem in the morning had helped to stir him. J. reached his door punctually at eight. There stood the little wonder with hat and coat on and door ajar, his wife beside him. "I would n't let him go with anybody else," she said. "Mr. Fields, he ought not to go out tonight; hear him, how he wheezes with the asthma. Now, Wendell, *when* will you get home?" "Oh," said he, "I don't know. I put myself into Mr. Fields's hands." "Well, Mr. Fields, how early can you get him home?" "About twelve," was the answer. "Now that's pretty well," said the Doctor. "Amelia, go in and shut the door. Mr. Fields will take care of me." So between fun and anxiety they chatted away until they were fairly into the street and in the car. "I 've been doing too much lately between my lectures and my story, and the fine dinners I have been to, and I ought not to go out tonight. Why, it 's one of the greatest compliments one man ever paid another, my going out to Longfellow's tonight. By the way, Mr. Fields, do you appreciate the position you hold in our time? There never was anything like it. Why, I was nothing but a roaring kangaroo when you took me in hand, and I thought it was the right thing to stand up on my hind legs, but you combed me down and put me in proper shape. Now I want you to promise me one thing. We 're all growing old, I 'm near sixty myself; by and by the

FIELDS, THE MAN OF BOOKS AND FRIENDSHIPS

brain will begin to soften. Now you must tell me when the egg begins to look addled. People don't know of themselves."

He had been to two large dinners lately, one at G. W. Wales's, which he said was the finest dinner he had ever seen, the most perfect in all its appointments, decorated with the largest profusion of flowers, in as perfect taste as he had ever seen. "Why, even the chair you sat in was so delicately padded as to give pleasure to that weak spot in the back which we all inherit from the fall of Adam." The other was at Mrs. Charles Dorr's, where there were sixteen at table and the room "for heat was like the black hole at Calcutta," but the company was very brilliant. Mr. and Mrs. Winthrop, Mrs. Parkman, Dr. Hayes, etc. He sat next Mrs. ——; says she is a thorough-bred woman of society, the daughter of a politician, the wife, first of a millionaire and now of a man of society. "I like such a woman now and then; she never makes a mistake." Mrs. —— was thoroughly canvassed at the table, "picked clean as any duck for the spit and then roasted over a slow fire," as O. W. H. afterward remarked to Mrs. Parkman, who is a very just woman and who weighed her well in the balances.

When they arrived at L.'s, my basket of flowers stood surrounded by other gifts, and Longfellow himself sat crowned with all the natural loveliness of his rare nature. The day must have been a happy one for him. . . . O. W. H. had three perfect verses of a little poem in his hand which he read, and then Lowell talked, and they had great merriment and delight together.

The two following passages from the diary for 1868 seem to indicate that Dr. Holmes made a double use of his poem, "Bill and Joe," written in this year, included in his "Poems of the Class of '29," and according to the entry of July 17, read at the Harvard Phi Beta Kappa dinner of 1868 : —

January 16, 1868. — We had just finished dinner when Professor Holmes came in with his poem, one of the annual he contributes to the class-supper of the "Boys of '29." He read it through to us with feeling, his voice growing tremulous and husky at times. It was pleasant to see how he enjoyed our pleasure in it. The talk turned naturally after a little upon the question of Chief Justice, when he took occasion to run over in his mind the character and qualifications of some of our chief barristers. "As for Bigelow [1] (who has just gone out of office and it is his successor over whom they are struggling), as for Bigelow, it is astonishing to see how every bit of that man's talent has been brought into use; all he has is made the most of. Why, he 's like some cooks, give 'em a horse and they will use every part of him except the shoes."

Friday, July 17, 1868. — Last evening Dr. Holmes came in fresh from the Phi Beta dinner at Cambridge. [2]

---

[1] George Tyler Bigelow, of the Harvard Class of 1829.

[2] Harvard festivals were frequently noted. After the great day on which Lowell gave his *Commemoration Ode*, Mrs. Fields wrote (July 22, 1865): "What an ever-memorable day, the one at Harvard! The prayer of Phillips Brooks, the ode of Lowell, the address of Dr. Putnam and the Governor, and the heartfelt verses of Holmes, and the lovely music and the hymns. But

He said, "I can't stop and I only came to read you my verses I read at the dinner, they made such a queer impression. I did n't mean to go, but James Lowell was to preside and sent me word that I really must be there, so I just wrote these off, and here they are — I don't know that I should have brought them in to read to you, but Hoar declares they are the best I have ever done." At length, in the exquisite orange of sunset, he read those delightful verses, full, full of feeling, "Bill and Joe." We did not wonder the Phi Beta boys liked them. I shall be surprised if every boy, especially those who find the almond blossoms in the hair, as W. says, does not like them, and if they do *not* win for him a more universal reputation than he has yet won. . . .

I was impressed last night with the nervous energy of O. W. H. His leg by a slight quiver kept time to the reading of his verses, and his talk fell before and after like swift rain. He does not go away from town but sways between Boston and Cambridge all these perfect summer days; receiving yesterday, the hottest day of this or many years, Motley at dinner, and going perpetually, and writing verses and letters not a few. His activity is wonderful; think of writing letters these warm delicious evenings by gaslight in a small front study on the street! It hurts him less than his wife, partly because the intellectual vivacity and excitement

Lowell's Ode!! How it overtops the whole of what is preserved on paper beside! Charles G. Loring presided. 'Awkwardly enough done,' said O. W. H.; 'It is a delicate thing to introduce a poet, he should be delivered to the table as a falconer delivers the falcon into the air, but Mr. Loring puts you down hard on the table — ca-chunk.'"

keeps him up, partly because he is physically fitted to
bear almost everything but cold. How fortunate for the
world that while he lives he should continue his work so
faithfully. He will have no successor, at least for many
a long year, after we have all gone to sleep under our
green counterpanes and Nature has tucked us up well
in yearly violets.

Earlier in the year Dr. Holmes and Mrs. Stowe met
in Charles Street.

Wednesday morning, January 29, 1868. — Last night
Professor Holmes, Mrs. Stowe, her daughter Georgie,
and the Howellses, took tea here. The Professor came
early and was in good talking trim — presently in came
Mrs. Stowe, and they fell shortly into talk upon Home-
opathy and Allopathy. He grew very warm, declared
that cases cited of cures proved nothing, and we were all
"incompetent" to judge! We could not but be amused
at his heat, for we were more or less believers in Home-
opathy against his one argument for Allopathy. In vain
Mrs. Stowe and I tried to turn and stem the fiery tide:
Georgie or Mrs. Howells would be sure to sweep us back
into it again. However, there were many brilliant things
said, and sweet and good and interesting things too.
The Professor told us one curious fact, that chemists had
in vain analyzed the poison of rattlesnakes and could
not discover the elements of destruction it undoubtedly
possesses. Also that, when Indians poison their arrows
with it, they hang up the liver of a white wolf and make

one snake after another bite it until the liver is entirely impregnated; they then leave it to dry until disintegrated, when they moisten and apply round the necks of the arrows — *not on the point.* He had a long quiet chat with Mrs. Stowe before the evening ended. They compared their early Calvinistic education and the effect produced upon their characters by such training.

Tuesday, April 13, 1869. — Dr. Holmes and his wife and Mr. Whittier dined here. The talk was free, totally free from all feeling of constraint, as it could not have been had another person been present. Whittier says he is afraid of strangers, and Dr. Holmes is never more delightful than under just such auspices. Dr. Holmes asked Whittier's undisguised opinion of Longfellow's "New England Tragedies" — "honest opinion now," said he. "Well, I liked them," said Whittier, half reluctantly — evidently he had found much that was beautiful and in keeping with the spirit of the times of which Longfellow wrote, and their passionless character did not trouble him as it had O. W. H.   Presently, he added that he was surprised to find how he had preserved almost literally the old text of the old books he had lent Longfellow twelve years ago, and had measured it off into verse. "Ah," said O. W. H., "you have said the severest thing after all — 'measured off'; that's just what he has done. It is one of the easiest, the very commonest tricks of the rhymster to be able to do this. I am surprised to see the ease with which I can do it myself." They spoke then of "Evangeline," which both agreed in awarding unqualified praise.

"Only," said Whittier, "I always wondered there was no terrible outburst of indignation over the outrage done to that poor colony. The tide of the story runs as smoothly as if nothing had occurred. I long thought of working up that story myself, but I am glad I did not, only I can't understand its being so calm." They talked on religious questions of course, the Professor holding that sin being finite, and of such a nature that we could both outgrow it and root it up, Whittier still returning to the ground that sin was a "very real thing."

It is impossible to represent the clearness and swiftness of Dr. Holmes's talk. The purity of heart and strength of endeavor evident in the two poets makes their atmosphere a very elevating one and they evidently naturally rejoiced in each other's society.

Mrs. Holmes had not been out to dine before this winter. Jamie sent us a pot of strawberries growing, which delighted everybody.

Before the following passage was written, in 1871, Dr. Holmes had moved from Charles Street to Beacon Street; Mr. Fields, in impaired health, had retired from active business as a publisher and was devoting himself chiefly to writing and lecturing; and Mrs. Fields, already interested in the establishment of Coffee Houses for the poor in the North End and elsewhere, had begun the notable work in public charities to which her energies were so largely given for the remaining forty-four years of her life. In the Coöperative Workrooms, still rendering their beneficent services, and in the larger organization of the Associated Charities, embodying a principle now widely adopted throughout the land, the labors of this generous spirit, never content to give all it had to the gracious life within its own four walls, have borne enduring fruits.

1871. — Thursday afternoon last (June 22) went to Cambridge for a few visits, and coming home stopped at Dr. Holmes's, at his new house on Beacon St. Found them both at home, sitting lonely in the oriel window looking out upon a glorious sunset. They were thinking of the children who have flown out of their nest. Dr. Holmes was very friendly and sweet. He talked most affectionately with J., told him he no longer felt a spur to write since he had gone out of business; he needed just the little touch of praise and encouragement he used to administer to make him do it; now he did not think he should ever write any more worth mentioning. He had been in to see the Coffee House and entertained us much by saying he met President Eliot near the door one day just as he was going in, but he was ashamed of doing so until they had parted company. There was something so childlike in this confession that we all laughed heartily over it. However he got in at last, and "tears as big as onions stood in my eyes when I saw what had been accomplished." "You must be a very happy woman," he went on to say. I told him of the new one in Eliot Street about to be opened this coming week.

At the end of the summer of 1871, when Mr. and Mrs. Fields were beginning to learn the charms of the North Shore town of Manchester, where they established the "Gambrel Cottage" on "Thunderbolt Hill" which gave a summer synonym to the hospitality of Charles Street, they journeyed one day to Nahant for a mid-day dinner with Longfellow. Here Mrs. Fields's sister, Louisa, Mrs. James H. Beal, was a neighbor of the poet. Another neighbor was the late George Abbot James, and in Longfellow's diary for September 4, 1871, is the entry: "Call on Dr. Holmes at Mr. James's. Sumner still there. We discuss the new poets." Mrs. Fields reports a continuation of the talk with the same friends.

Wednesday, September 6, 1871. — Dined with Mr. Longfellow at Nahant. The day was warm with a soft south wind blowing, and as we crossed the beach white waves were curling up the sands. . . . The dear poet saw us coming from afar and walked to his little gate to meet us with such a sweet cordial welcome that it was worth going many a mile to have that alone. The three little ladies, his daughters, and Ernest's wife, were within, but they came warmly forward to give us greeting; also Mr. Sam. Longfellow was of the party. A few moments' chat in the little parlor, when Longfellow saw Holmes coming in the distance (he had an opera-glass, being short-sighted, and was sitting on the piazza with J.). "Hullo!" said he, "here comes Holmes, and all dressed up too, with flowers in his button-hole." Sure enough, here was *the* Professor to have dinner with us also. He was full of talk as ever and looking remark-ably well. Longfellow asked with much interest about Balaustion and Joaquin Miller, neither of which he had read. Holmes criticized as if unbearable and beyond the pale of decency Browning's cutting of words, "Flower o' the pine," and such characteristic passages. Longfellow spoke of a volume of poems he had received of late from England in which "saw" was made to rhyme with "more." Holmes said Keats often did that. "Not ex-actly, I think," said L., "'dawn' and 'forlorn,' per-haps." "Well," said H., "when I was in college" (I think he said college, certainly while at Cambridge) "and my first volume was about to appear, Mrs. Fol-som saw the sheets and fortunately at the very last moment for correction discovered I had made 'for-lorn' rhyme with 'gone,' and out of her own head and without having time to consult with me she substituted 'sad and wan.'" [1] The Professor went on to say that he must confess to a tender feeling of regret for his "so forlorn" to this very day, but he supposed every writer of poems must have his keen regrets for the numerous verses he could recall where he had wrestled with the English language and had lost something of his thought in his struggle with the necessities of art. We shortly after went to dinner, where the talk still continued to turn on art and artists, chiefly musical, the divorcement of music and thought; a thinker or man of intellect in listening to music comes to a comprehension of it,

[1] This anecdote of the revision of *The Last Leaf*, written in 1831, is told a little differently in the annotations of Holmes's Complete Works.

Holmes said, mediately, but a musician feels it directly through some gift of which the thinker knows nothing. Longfellow always recalls with intense delight hearing Gounod sing his own music in Rome — his voice was hardly to be mentioned among the fine voices of the world, indeed it was small, but his rendering was exquisite. Canvassing T. B. Read's poems and speaking of "Sheridan's Ride," which has been so highly praised, "Yes," said Holmes, "but there are very poor lines in it, but how often, to use Scripture phrase, there is a fly in the ointment." The talk went bowling off to Père Hyacinthe. "He was very pleasant," said Holmes, "it was most agreeable to meet him, but you could only go a short distance. His desire was to be a good Catholic, and ours is of course quite different. It was like speaking through a knot-hole after all."

The dumb waiter bounced up. "We cannot call that a *dumb* waiter," said L., "but I had an odd dream the other night. I thought Greene (G. W.) came bouncing up on the waiter in that manner and stepped off in a most dignified fashion with a crushed white hat on his head. He said he had just been to drive with a Spanish lady !"

Sumner (Charles) came up to the piazza. He had dined elsewhere and came over as soon as possible for a little talk. Holmes talked on, although we all said, "Mr. Sumner — here is Mr. Sumner," without perceiving that the noble Senator was sitting just outside the cottage window waiting for us to rise, and began to converse about him. Longfellow grew nervous and rose to speak with Sumner — still Holmes did not perceive, and went on until Jamie relieved us from a tendency to convulsions by voting that we should join the Senator. Then Sumner related the substance of an amusing letter of Cicero's he had just been reading in which Cicero gives an account to his friend of a visit he had just received from the Emperor Julius Cæsar. He had invited Julius to pass a few days with him, but he came quite unexpectedly with a thousand men! Cicero, seeing them from afar, debated with another friend what he should do with them, but at length managed to encamp them. To feed them was a less easy matter. The emperor took everything quite easily, however, and was very pleasant, "but," adds Cicero, "he is not the man to whom I should say a second time, 'if you are passing this way, give me a call.'"

Again, in 1873, Longfellow, Holmes, and Sumner are found together at the dinner-table with Mrs. Fields, this time in Charles Street. When she made use of her diary at this point, for her article on Dr. Holmes which appeared first in the "Century Magazine" (1895), it was with many omissions. The passage is now given almost entire. It should be said that the Misses Towne, mentioned at the beginning of it, were friends and summer neighbors at Manchester.

Saturday, October 11, 1873. — Helen and Alice Towne have come to pass Sunday with us. Charles Sumner, Longfellow, Greene, Dr. Holmes came to dine. Mr. Sumner seemed less strong than of late and I fancied he

suffered somewhat while at table during the evening,
but he told me he was working at his desk or reading
during fourteen consecutive hours not infrequently at
present, as he was in the habit of doing when uninterrupted by friendly visits. He said he was very fond of
the passive exercise of reading; the active exercise of
composition was of course agreeable in certain moods,
but reading was a never-ending delight. He spoke of
Lord Brougham, and Mrs. Norton and her two beautiful sisters. Both he and Mr. Longfellow recalled them
in their youthful loveliness, but Mr. Sumner said when
he was in England the last time he saw the Duchess of
Somerset, who was a most poetic looking creature in her
youth and (I believe) the youngest of the three sisters,
so changed he should never have guessed who it might
be. She was grown a huge red-faced woman. (Longfellow laughed, referring to her second marriage and
said, "Yes, she had turned a Somerset!") Dr. Holmes
sparkled and coruscated as I have seldom heard him
before. We are more than ever convinced that no one
since Sydney Smith was ever so brilliant, so witty,
spontaneous, naïf, and unfailing as Dr. Holmes. He
talked much about his class in College: "There never
was such vigor in any class before, it seems to me —
almost every member turns out sooner or later distinguished for something. We have had every grade of
moral status from a criminal to a Chief Justice, and we
never let any one of them drop. We keep hold of their
hands year after year and lift up the weak and failing
ones till they are at last redeemed. Ah, there was one

exception — years ago we voted to cast a man out who had been a defaulter or who had committed some offense of that nature. The poor fellow sank down, and before the next year, when we repented of this decision, he had gone too far down and presently died. But we have kept all the rest. Every fourth man in our class is a poet. Sam. Smith belongs to our class, who wrote 'My Country, 't is of Thee.' Sam. Smith will live when Longfellow, Whittier, and all the rest of us have gone into oblivion — and yet what is there in those verses to make them live? Do you remember the line 'Like *that* above'? I asked Sam. what 'that' referred to — he said 'that rapture'!! — (The expression of the rapid talker's face of contempt as he said this was one of the most amusing possible.) — Even the odds and ends of our class have turned out something. . . . Longfellow, I wish I could make you talk about yourself." — "But I never do," said L. quietly. "I know you never do, but you confessed to me once." — "No, I don't think I ever did," said L. laughing.

Greene was for the most part utterly speechless. He attended with great assiduity to his dinner, which was a good one, and Longfellow was watchful and kind enough to send him little choice things to eat which he thought he would enjoy.

Holmes was abstemious and never ceased talking — "Most men write too much. I would rather risk my future fame upon one lyric than upon ten volumes. But I have said Boston is the hub of the universe. I will rest upon that."

All this report is singularly dry compared with the wit and humor which radiated about the table. We laughed till the tears ran down our cheeks. Longfellow was intensely amused. I have not seen him laugh so much for many a long day. We ladies sat at the table long after coffee and cigars in order to hear the talk. . . .

Sumner said he had been much displeased by a remark Professor Henry Hunt made to him a few days ago. He said Mr. Agassiz was an *impediment* in the path of science. What did such men as Hunt and John Fiske mean by underrating a man who has given such books to the world as Agassiz has done, not to speak of his untiring efforts in the other avenues of influence! "It means just this," said Holmes: "Agassiz will not listen to the Darwinian theory; his whole effort is on the other side. Now Agassiz is no longer young, and I was reading the other day in a book on the Sandwich Islands of an old Fejee man who had been carried away among strangers, but who prayed he might be carried home, that his brains might be beaten out in peace by his son according to the custom of those lands. It flashed over me then that our sons beat out our brains in the same way. They do not walk in our ruts of thoughts or begin exactly where we leave off, but they have a new standpoint of their own. At present the Darwinian theory can be nothing but an hypothesis; the important links of proof are missing and cannot be supplied; but in the myriad ages there may be new developments."

I thought the young ladies looked a little tired sitting, so about nine o'clock we left the table — still the

LOUIS AGASSIZ

talk went on for about four hours when they broke up.

With two letters from Dr. Holmes this rambling chronicle of his friendship with Mr. and Mrs. Fields must end. The first of the communications is a mere fragment of his everyday humor:

Beverly-Farms-by-the-Depot
July 18*th*, 1878

Dear Mr. Fields: —

The Corner sends me a book directed to me here, but on opening the outside wrapper I read "James T. Fields, Esq., Jamaica Plain, Boston, Mass." The book, which is sealed up (or stuck up, like many authors), measures 7 x 5, nearly, and is presumably idiotic, like most books which are sent us without being ordered.

Perhaps you have received a similar package which on opening you found directed to O. W. Holmes, Esq., Peak of Teneriffe, Boston. If so, when the weather grows cool again and we can make up our minds to face the title page of the dreaded volume, we will make an exchange.

Always truly yours,

O. W. Holmes

The second letter, written ten years after Dr. Holmes, in moving from Charles to Beacon Street, had made the last of his "justifiable domicides," strikes a more serious note, revealing that quality of true sympathy so closely joined in abundant natures with true humor. Mr. Fields had died in April of 1881, and Mrs. Fields had

applied herself at once to the preparation of her volume,
"James T. Fields: Biographical Notes and Personal
Sketches," drawing freely upon the diaries from which
many of the foregoing pages, then passed over, are now
taken. The performance of this loving labor must have
done much towards the first filling of a life so grievously
emptied. Already the intimate and beloved companionship of Miss Jewett had come into it.

294 Beacon St., November 16, 1881

My dear Mrs. Fields: —

I feel sure there will be but one voice with regard to
your beautiful memorial volume. If I had any misgivings that you might find the delicate task too difficult — that you might be discouraged between the
wish to draw a life-like picture and the fear of saying
more than the public had a right to, these misgivings
have all vanished, and I am sure your finished task
leaves nothing to be regretted. As he was in life,
he is in your loving but not overwrought story. I do
not see how a life so full of wholesome activity and
genuine human feeling could have been better pictured
than it is in your pages. Long before I had finished
reading your memoir in the proofs I had learned to
trust you entirely as to the whole management of the
work on which you had entered. All I feared was
that your feelings might be overtasked, and that the
dread of coming before the public when your whole
heart was in the pages opened to its calm judgment
might be more than you could bear.

And now, my dear Mrs. Fields, there must come a period of depression, almost of collapse, after the labor and the solace of this tender, tearful, yet blessed occupation.   I think you need the kind thoughts and soothing words — if words have any virtue in them — of those who love you more than while each day had its busy hours in which the memory of so much that was delightful to recall kept the ever-returning pangs of grief a little while in abeyance.   It must be so.   But before long, quietly, almost imperceptibly, there will, I hope and trust, return to you the quieting sense of all that you have done and all that you have been for that life which for so many happy years you were privileged to share.   How few women have so perfectly fulfilled, not only every duty, but every ideal that a husband could think of as going to make a happy home!   This must be and will be an ever-growing source of consolation.

Forgive me for saying what many others must have said to you, but none more sincerely than myself.

I do not know how to express to you the feeling with which Mrs. Holmes looks upon you in your bereavement.   I should do it injustice if I attempted to give it expression, for she lives so largely in her sympathies and her endeavors to help others that she could not but sorrow deeply with you in your affliction and wish there were any word of consolation she could add to the love she sends you.

Believe me, dear Mrs. Fields,

Affectionately yours,

O. W. Holmes

For thirteen years longer, till his death in 1894 at the age of eighty-five, Dr. Holmes was a prolific writer of notes, more often than letters, to Mrs. Fields. The sympathy of tried and ripened friendship runs through them all. In the Charles Street house the younger friends might see from time to time this oldest friend of their hostess. When he came no more, it was well for those of a later day that his memory was so securely held in the retrospect and the record of Mrs. Fields.

IV

CONCORD AND CAMBRIDGE VISITORS

THE volumes in which Mrs. Fields brought to light many passages from her journals stand as red and black buoys marking the channel through which the navigator of these pages must steer his course if he is to avoid the rocks and shoals of the previously published. In her books it was but natural that she should deal most freely with those august figures in American letters who so towered above their contemporaries as to attach the longer and more portentous adjective "Augustan" to the circle formed by the joining of their hands. If it has become the fashion to look back upon the American Augustans and the English Victorians with similarly mingled feelings, in which tolerance stands in a growing proportion to the admiration and respect which formerly ruled supreme, it is the unaltered fact that the figures of the American group dominated both the local and the national scene of letters in their day, and that their historic significance is undiminished. But it is rather as human beings than as literary figures that they reveal themselves in the sympathetic records of Mrs. Fields — human beings who typified and embodied a state of thought and society so remote in its characteristic qualities from the prevailing conditions of this later day as to be approaching steadily that "equal date with Andes and with Ararat" of which one of them wrote in words quite unmistakably his own.

Perhaps no single member of the group is represented in Mrs. Fields's journals so often as Dr. Holmes by illuminating pages which she herself left unprinted. For this reason, and because Concord and Cambridge visitors to Charles Street were in fact so much a "group," it has seemed wise to assemble in this place passages that relate to one after another of the "Augustan" friends in turn. Sometimes they appear as separate subjects of record, sometimes in company with their fellows. That majestic figure, Nathaniel Hawthorne, whose death in 1864 made the earliest gap in the circle of figures most memorable, shall be first to step forth, like one of his own personages of the Province House, from the shadows in which indeed he lived.

The long chapter on Hawthorne in "Yesterdays with Authors," and that small volume about him which Mrs. Fields contributed in 1899 to the "Beacon Biographies," constitute the more finished portraits of the man as his host and hostess in Charles Street saw him. His letters to Fields are quoted at length in "Yesterdays with Authors," and contribute an autobiographic element of much importance to any study of Hawthorne. But there are illuminating passages that were left unpublished. In one of them, for example, Hawthorne, in a letter of September 21, 1860, after lamenting the state of his daughter's health, exclaimed: "I am continually re-

HAWTHORNE IN 1857

minded, nowadays, of a response which I once heard
a drunken sailor make to a pious gentleman who asked
him how he felt: 'Pretty d——d miserable, thank
God!' It very well expresses my thorough discomfort
and forced acquiescence." In another, of July 14,
1861, after the calamity that befell Longfellow in the
tragic death of his wife through burning, Hawthorne
wrote to Fields: —

"How does Longfellow bear this terrible misfortune? How are his own injuries? Do write and tell
me all about him. I cannot at all reconcile this calamity
to my sense of fitness. One would think that there
ought to have been no deep sorrow in the life of a man
like him; and now comes this blackest of shadows,
which no sunshine hereafter can ever penetrate! I
shall be afraid ever to meet him again; he cannot again
be the man that I have known."

In the words, "I shall be afraid ever to meet him
again," the very accent of Hawthorne is clearly heard.
Still another manuscript letter, preserved in the Charles
Street cabinet, should now be printed to round out the
story of Hawthorne's reluctant omission from his
"Atlantic" article — "Chiefly about War Matters" —
that personal description of Abraham Lincoln which
Fields was unwilling to publish in his magazine in
1862, but afterwards included in his "Yesterdays with
Authors." [1] In that place, however, he used but a few
words from the following letter.

[1] See *Yesterdays with Authors*, p. 98, and *The Atlantic Monthly and Its
Makers*, p. 46.

CONCORD, *May* 23, '62

DEAR FIELDS: —

I have looked over the article under the influence of a cigar and through the medium (but don't whisper it) of a glass of arrack and water; and though I think you are wrong, I am going to comply with your request. I am the most good-natured man, and the most amenable to good advice (or bad advice either, for that matter) that you ever knew — so have it your own way. The whole description of the interview with Uncle Abe and his personal appearance must be omitted, since I do not find it possible to alter them, and in so doing, I really think you omit the only part of the article really worth publishing. Upon my honor, it seemed to me to have a historical value — but let it go. I have altered and transferred one of the notes so as to indicate to the unfortunate public that it here loses something very nice. You must mark the omission with dashes, so — x x x x x x x.

I have likewise modified the other passage you allude to; and I cannot now conceive of any objection to it.

What a terrible thing it is to try to get off a little bit of truth into this miserable humbug of a world! If I had sent you the article as I first conceived it, I should not so much have wondered.

I want you to send me a proof sheet of the article in its present state before making any alterations; for if ever I collect these sketches into a volume, I shall insert it in all its original beauty.

With the best regards to Mrs. Fields,

Truly yours,

Nath[L] Hawthorne

P. S.   I shall probably come to Boston next week, to the Saturday Club.

If these unpublished letters add something to the more formal portraits of Hawthorne drawn by Fields and his wife, still other lines may be added by means of the unconscious, fragmentary sketches on which the portraits were based. In Mrs. Fields's diaries the following glimpses of Hawthorne in the final months of his life are found.

December 4, 1863. — Hawthorne and Mr. and Mrs. Alden passed the night with us; he came to town to attend the funeral of Mrs. Franklin Pierce. He seemed ill and more nervous than usual. He brought the first part of a story which he says he shall never finish.[1] J. T. F. says it is very fine, yet sad. Hawthorne says in it, "pleasure is only pain greatly exaggerated," which is queer to say the least, if not untrue. I think it must be differently stated from this. He was as courteous and as grand as ever, and as true. He does not lose that all-saddening smile, either.

Sunday, December 6, 1863. — Mr. Hawthorne returned to us. He had found General Pierce overwhelmed with sadness at the death of his wife and greatly needing his companionship, therefore he accompanied him the

---

[1] *The Dolliver Romance.*

whole distance to Concord, N. H. He said he could not generally look at such things, but he was obliged to look at the body of Mrs. Pierce. It was like a carven image laid in its richly embossed enclosure and there was a remote expression about it as if it had nothing to do with things present. Harriet Prescott was there. He had some talk with her and liked her. He was more deeply impressed than ever with the exquisite courtesy of his friend. Even at the grave, while overwhelmed with grief, Pierce drew up the collar of Hawthorne's coat to keep him from the cold.[1]

We went to walk in the morning and left Mr. Hawthorne to read in the library. He found a book called "Dealings with the Dead," which he liked — indeed he said he liked no house to stay in better than this. He thought the old edition of Boccaccio which belonged to Leigh Hunt a poor translation. He has already written the first chapter of a new romance, but he thought so little of the work himself as to make it impossible for him to continue until Mr. Fields had read it and expressed his sincere admiration for the work. This has given him better heart to go on with it. He talked of the magazine with Mr. F.; told him he thought it was the most ably edited magazine in the world, and was bound to be a success, with this exception: he said, "I fear its politics — beware! What will you do when in a year or two the politics of the country change?" "I will quietly wait for that time to come," said J. T. F.; "then I can tell you."

[1] Fields drew upon this paragraph for one in *Yesterdays with Authors*, p. 112.

As the sunset deepened Mr. Hawthorne talked of his early life. His grandfather bought a township in Maine and at the early age of eleven years he accompanied his mother and sister down there to live upon the land. From that moment the happiest period of his life began and lasted until he was thirteen, when he was sent to school in Salem. While in Maine he lived like a bird of the air, so perfect was the freedom he enjoyed. During the moonlight nights of winter he would skate until midnight alone upon the icy face of Sebago Lake, with all its ineffable beauty stretched before him and the deep shadows of the hills on either hand. When he was weary he could take refuge sometimes in a log cabin (there were several in this region), where half a tree would be burning on the broad hearth and he could sit by that and see the stars up through the chimney. All the long summer days he roamed at will, gun in hand, through the woods, and there he learned a nearness to Nature and a love for free life which has never left him and made all other existence in a measure insupportable. His suffering began with that Salem school and his knowledge of his relatives who were all distasteful to him. He said, "How sad middle life looks to people of erratic temperaments. Everything is beautiful in youth — all things are allowed to it." We gave him "Pet Marjorie" to read in the evening — a little story by John Brown. He thought it so beautiful that he read it carefully twice until every word was grasped by his powerful memory. . . .

Talking of England, Hawthorne said she was not a

powerful empire. The extent over which her dominions extended led her to fancy herself powerful. She is much like a squash vine which runs over a whole garden, but once cut at the root and it is gone at once.

We talked and laughed about Boswell, whom he thinks one of the most remarkable men who ever lived, and J. T. F. recalled that story of Johnson who, upon being told of a man who had committed some misdemeanor and was upon the verge of committing suicide in consequence, said, "Why does not the man go somewhere where he is not known, instead of to the devil where he is known?"

Hawthorne was in the same class at college with Longfellow, whom he says he could not appreciate at that time. He was always finely dressed and was a tremendous student. Hawthorne was careless in dress and no student, but always reading desultorily right and left. Now they are deeply appreciative of each other.[1]

Hawthorne says he wants the North to beat now; 't is the only way to save the country from destruction. He has been strangely inert and remote upon the subject of the war; partly from his deep hatred of everything sad. He seemed to feel as if he could not live and face it.

He was intensely witty, but his wit is of so ethereal a texture that the fine essence has vanished and I can remember nothing now of his witty things!

[1] Only a month after making this entry, Mrs. Fields wrote in her journal: "A note came from Longfellow saying he had received a sad note from Hawthorne. 'I wish we could have a little dinner for him,' he says, 'of two sad authors and two jolly publishers — nobody else.'"

It would be a pity to truncate the following passage by confining the record of Fields's day in Concord to his glimpse of Hawthorne, already recorded, with emendations, in the "Biographical Notes."

Saturday, January 9, 1864. — J. T. F. passed yesterday in Concord. He went first to see Hawthorne, who was sitting alone gazing into the fire, his grey dressing-

From a letter of Hawthorne's after a visit to Charles Street

gown, which became him like a Roman toga, wrapped around his figure. He said he had done nothing for three weeks. Yet we feel his romance must be maturing in his mind. General Barlow and Mrs. Howe had sent word they were coming to call, so Mrs. Hawthorne had gone out to walk (been thrown out on picket-duty, Mrs. Stowe said) and had left word at home that Mr. Hawthorne was ill and could see no one. After his visit there, full of affectionate kindness, J. T. F. proceeded to dinner with the Emersons. Here too the reception was most hearty, but he fancied there were no servants to speak of at either house. Mrs. E. looked deadly pale, but her wit coruscated marvellously; even Mr. Emerson grew silent to listen. She said a committee of three, of which she was one, had been formed to pronounce upon certain essays (unpublished) of Mr. Emerson, which they thought should be printed now. She thought some of them finer than any of his published essays. He laughed a great deal at the fun she *poked* at the earlier efforts.

From there J. T. F. proceeded to see the Thoreaus. The mother and sister live well, but lonely it should seem, there without Henry. They produced 32 volumes of journal and a few letters. The idea was to print the letters. We hope it may be done. Their house was like a conservatory, it was so filled with plants in beautiful condition. Henry liked to have the doors thrown open that he might look at these during his illness. He was an excellent son, and even when living in his retirement at Walden Pond, would come home every day. He supported himself too from a very early age.

Here follows a passage also used by Fields in "Yesterdays with Authors," but in a rendering so moderated that the original entry in the journal is quite another thing.

Monday, March 28. — Mr. Hawthorne came down to take this as his first station on his journey for health. He shocked us by his invalid appearance. He has become quite deaf, too. His limbs are shrunken but his great eyes still burn with their lambent fire. He said, "Why does Nature treat us so like children! I think we could bear it if we knew our fate. At least I think it would not make much difference to me now what became of me." He talked with something of his old wit at times; said, "Why has the good old custom of coming together to get drunk gone out? Think of the delight of drinking in pleasant company and then lying down to sleep a deep strong sleep." Poor man! He sleeps very little. We heard him walking in his room during a long portion of the night, heavily moving, moving as if indeed waiting, watching for his fate. At breakfast he gave us a most singular account of an interview with Mr. Alcott. He said: "Alcott was one of the most excellent of men. He could never quarrel with anyone." But the other day he came to make Mr. H. a call, to ask him if there was any difficulty or misunderstanding between the two families. Mr. Hawthorne said no, that would be impossible; "but I proceeded," he continued, "to tell him it was not possible to live upon amicable terms with Mrs. Alcott. . . . The old man acknowledged the truth of all that I said (indeed who should know it better), but I comforted him by saying in time of illness or necessity I did not doubt we should be the best of helpers to each other. I clothed all this in velvet phrases, that it might not seem too hard for him to bear, but he took it all like a saint."

April, 1864. — When Mr. Hawthorne returned after watching at the death-bed of Mr. Ticknor, his mind was in a healthier condition, we thought, than when he left, but the experience had been a terrible one. I can never forget the look of pallid exhaustion he wore the night he returned to us. He said he had scarcely eaten or slept since he left. "Mr. Childs watched me so closely after poor Ticknor died, as if I had lost my protector and friend, and so I had! But he stuck by as if he were afraid to leave me alone. He stayed past the dinner hour, and when I began to wonder if he never ate himself, he departed and sent another man to watch me till he should return!" Nevertheless he liked Mr. Childs and spoke repeatedly of his unwearying kindness. "I never saw anything like it," he said; yet when he was abstractedly wondering where his slippers were, I overheard him say to himself, "Oh! I remember, that cursed Childs watched me so I forgot everything."

He spoke of the coldness of somebody and said, "Well, I think he would have felt something if he had been there!" He said he did not think death would be so terrible if it were not for the undertakers. It was dreadful to think of being handled by those men.

He was often wholly overcome by the ludicrous view of something presented to him in the midst of his grief. There was a black servant sleeping in the room that last night, whose name was Peter. Once he snored loudly, when the dying man raised himself with an appreciation of fun still living in him and said, "Well done, Peter!"

In every account of the last week of Hawthorne's life, the shock he received through the illness and death of his friend and traveling companion, Ticknor, in Philadelphia, is an item of sombre moment. The two men had left Boston together late in March — Hawthorne, sick and broken, writing but once, in a tremulous hand, to his wife during the ill-starred journey; Ticknor, giving himself unstintingly to the restoration of Hawthorne's health, and stricken unto death before a fortnight was gone. The circumstances are suggested in the entry that has just been quoted from Mrs. Fields's journal. They stand still more clearly revealed in the last letter written by Hawthorne to Fields, who refers to it in "Yesterdays with Authors," and adds that the news of Ticknor's death reached Boston on the very day after this letter was written, all too evidently with a feeble hold upon the pen.

PHILADELPHIA, CONTINENTAL HOTEL
Saturday morning

DEAR FIELDS : —

I am sorry to say that our friend Ticknor is suffering under a severe billious attack since yesterday morning. He had previously seemed uncomfortable, but not to an alarming degree. He sent for a physician during the night, and fell into the hands of an allopathist, who, of course, belabored with pills and powders of various kinds, and then proceeded to cup, and poultice, and blister, according to the ancient rule of that tribe of savages. The consequence is that poor Ticknor is already very much reduced, while the disorder flourishes as luxuriantly as if that were the doctor's sole object. He calls

it a billious colic (or bilious, I know not which) and says
it is one of the severest cases he ever knew. I think him
a man of skill and intelligence, in his way, and doubt
not that he will do everything that his views of scientific
medicine will permit.

Since I began writing the above, Mr. Bennett of Boston tells me the Doctor, after this morning's visit, requested the proprietor of the Continental to telegraph
to Boston the state of the case. I am glad of it, because
it relieves me of the responsibility of either disclosing
bad intelligence or withholding it. I will only add that
Ticknor, under the influence of a blister and some powders, seems more comfortable than at any time since his
attack, and that Mr. Bennett (who is an apothecary, and
therefore conversant with these accursed matters) says
that he is in a good state. But I can see that it will be
not a very few days that will set him upon his legs again.
As regards nursing, he shall have the best that can be
obtained; and my own room is next to his, so that I can
step in at any moment; but that will be of almost as
much service as if a hippopotamus were to do him the
same kindness. Nevertheless, I have blistered, and pow-
dered, and pilled him and made my observation on
medical science and the sad and comic aspects of human
misery.

Excuse this illegible scrawl, for I am writing almost
in the dark. Remember me to Mrs. Fields. As regards
myself, I almost forgot to say that I am perfectly well.
If you could find time to write Mrs. Hawthorne and
tell her so, it would be doing me a great favor, for I

doubt whether I can find an opportunity just now to do it myself. You would be surprised to see how stalwart I have become in this little time.

Your friend,

N. H.

Barely more than a month later, Hawthorne, traveling with another friend, Franklin Pierce, died in New Hampshire. Through the years that followed, the friendship of the Fieldses with his widow and children afforded many occasions for brief affectionate record in the chronicles of Charles Street.[1]

The two entries that follow touch, respectively, upon glimpses of Hawthorne's immediate family at Concord, in the summer of 1865, and of his surviving sister in the summer of 1866.

Sunday, July 9, 1865. — Passed Friday in Concord. Called at the Emersons, but were disappointed to find them all in town, Jamie particularly, who wished to tell him that his new essay on Character is not suited to the magazine. Ordinary readers would not understand him and would consider it blasphemous. He thinks it would do more good if delivered simply to his own disciples first, in a volume of new essays uniform with the others.

Dined with Sophia Hawthorne and the children, the first real visit since that glorious presence has departed.

[1] In Rose Hawthorne Lathrop's *Memories of Hawthorne* the relation between the two households is indicated in a sentence containing the nicknames of Mr. and Mrs. Fields: "My father also tasted the piquant flavors of merriment and luxury in this exquisite domicile of Heart's-Ease and Mrs. Meadows."

What an altered household! She feels very lonely and is like a reed. I fear the children find small restraint from her. Poor child! How tired she is! Will God spare her further trial, I wonder, and take her to his rest? . . . Went to call on Sophia Thoreau.[1] . . . We saw a letter from Froude, the historian, to H. T., as warmly appreciative as it was possible for a letter to be; also "long good histories," as his sister said, from his admirer Cholmondely. His journal is in thirty-two volumes and when J. T. F. spoke of wishing for an editor to condense these, she said there was no hurry and she thought the man would come. We spoke of Sanborn. She said, "He knows a great deal, but I never associate him with my brother."

She is a woman borne down with ill health. She seemed to possess, as we saw her, something of the self-sustaining power of her brother, the same repose and confidence in her fate, as being always good. Dear S. H. says she has **this** when she thinks of her brother, but often loses it when the surface of her life becomes irritated and she is disabled for work. Her aged mother, learning we were there, got up and dressed herself and came down, to her daughter's great surprise. She has an immense care in that old lady evidently.

July 24, 1866. — We left just before eleven for Amesbury, to see Mr. Whittier, driving over to Beverly in an open wagon. It was one of the perfect days. As Keats said once, the sky sat "upon our senses like a sapphire crown." We turned away after a time from the

---

[1] Thoreau's younger sister.

high road into a wood path, picking our way somewhat slowly to avoid the overhanging bushes and the rainy pools left in the ruts. We soon found ourselves near a place called Mt. Serat where we knew Miss Hawthorne lived, the only surviving sister of Nathaniel, and Mr. Fields determined at once to call upon her. To my surprise, in spite of the fine weather and her woodland life habitually, she was at home, and came down immediately as if she were sincerely glad to see us. She is a small woman, with small fine features, round full face, fresh-looking in spite of years, brilliant eyes, nervous brow, which twists as she speaks, and very nervous fingers. In one respect she differed from her brother — she was exquisitely neat (nor do I mean to convey the idea by this that he was unneat, but he always gave you a sense of disregarded trifles about his person and we frequently recall his reply to me when I offered to brush his coat one morning, "No, no, I never brush my coat, it wears it out !"), and gave you a sense of being particular in little things. I seemed to see in her another difference — a deterioration because of too great solitude —powers rusted—a decaying beauty—while with Hawthorne solitude fed his genius, solitude and the pressure of necessity. Utter solitude lames the native power of a woman even more than that of a man, for her natural growth is through her sympathies. She is a woman of no common mould, however. Lucy Larcom calls her a hamadryad, and says she belongs in the woods and should be seen there. I wish to see her again upon her own ground. She asked us almost immediately if we

would not come with her to the woods, but our time
was too short. From thence we held our way, and soon
came by train to Newburyport and Amesbury. Whittier
was at home, ready with an enthusiastic welcome.

To these memorials of Hawthorne must be added
yet another, copied from a pencilled sheet preserved by
Mrs. Fields in an envelope endorsed in her handwriting,
" The original of a precious and extraordinary letter
written by Mrs. Nathaniel Hawthorne while her husband
lay dead." Printed now, I believe for the first time,
nearly sixty years after it was written, it rings with a devotion and exaltation which time is powerless to touch :

I wish to speak to you, Annie.

A person of a more uniform majesty never wore
mortal form.

In the most retired privacy it was the same as in
the presence of men.

The sacred veil of his eyelids he scarcely lifted to
himself — such an unviolated sanctuary as was his
nature, I, his inmost wife, never conceived nor knew.

So absolute a modesty was not before joined to so
lofty a self-respect.

But what must have been that self-respect that he
never in the smallest particular dishonored!

A conscience more void of offense never bore witness
to GOD within.

It was the innocence of a baby and the grand comprehension of a sage.

To me — himself — even to me who was himself in unity — he was to the last the holy of holies behind the cherubim.

So unerring a judgment that a word from him would settle with me a chaos of doubts and questions that seemed perplexing to ordinary apprehension.

So equal a justice that I often wondered if he were human in this — for this seemed to partake of omniscience both of love and insight.

An impartiality of regard that solved all men and subjects in one alembick.

Truth and right alone he deigned to regard.   Far below him was every other consideration.

A tenderness so infinite — so embracing — that GOD'S alone could surpass it.   It folded the loathsome leper in as soft a caress as the child of his home affections — was not that divine!

Was it not Christianity in one action!   What a bequest to his children — what a new revelation of Christ to the world was that!   And for him — whom the sight and touch of unseemliness and uncleanness caused to shudder as an Eolian string shudders in the tempest.

Annie! to the last action in this house he was as lofty, as majestic, as imperial and as gentle — as in the strength of his prime, as on the day he rose upon my eye and soul a King among men by divine right!

When he awoke that early dawn and found himself unawares standing among the "Shining Ones" do you think they did not suppose he had been always with them — one of themselves?   Oh, blessed be GOD for

so soft a translation — as an infant wakes on its
mother's breast so he woke on the bosom of GOD and
can never be weary any more, nor see nor touch an
unclean thing. A demand for beauty and perfection
that was inexorable. Yet though a flaw or a crack
gave him so fine agony, no one, no one was ever so
tolerant as he!

Hawthorne's allusion to Alcott brings the figure of that
Concord personage on the scene. The picture of him in
Charles Street is so sharpened in outline by certain
remarks upon him by the elder Henry James, a somewhat more frequent visitor, that the passages relating
to the two men are here joined together. The first
recorded glimpses of James occurred in the course of a
visit to Newport.

September 23, 1863. — Received a visit at Newport
from Henry James. His son was badly wounded in two
places at Gettysburg. He spoke of the reviews of his
work among other topics. "Who wrote the review in the
Examiner?" asked Mr. F. "Oh! that was *merely*
Freeman Clarke," he replied; "he is a smuggler in theol-
ogy and feels towards me much as a contraband towards
an exciseman?" Speaking of fashion, he said, "there was
good in it," although it appears to be a drawback to the
residents here while it lasts. He anticipates a change in
European affairs; the age of ignorance is to pass away
and strong democratic tendencies will soon pervade

Europe. The march of civilization will work its revenge against aristocratic England, he believes.

Mr. James considers that people make a mistake to expect reason from Carlyle. "He is an artist, a wilful artist, and no reasoner. He has only genius."

October 16, 1863. — Mr. Alcott breakfasted with us. He said all vivid new life was well described by his daughter Louisa. She was happier now that she had made a success. "She was formerly not content to wait, but so soon as she became content, then good fortune came, as she always does." I told him we enjoyed deeply reading his MSS. of "The Rhapsodist" (Emerson) last night. He said he thought it was finally brought into presentable shape! "When in a more imperfect condition," he continued, "I read it to Mr. Emerson. The modest man could only keep silent at such a time, but he conveyed to me the idea that he should prefer the paper should not be printed in the 'Commonwealth.' Later I again read it, when he said, 'If I were dead.' I have reason to believe that in its present shape he would not object to its presentation."[1] He talked of his own valuable library and asked what he should do with it by and by. J. T. F. suggested it should go to the Union Club, which pleased him much. "That is the place," said he. "If it were known this was my intention, might I not also be entitled to consideration at the Club?"

[1] In 1865 Alcott printed privately and anonymously the essay, *Emerson*, which appeared later in his acknowledged volume, *Ralph Waldo Emerson, an Estimate of his Character and Genius* (Boston, 1882). This was evidently *The Rhapsodist.*

Among his books is a copy of Milton's "World of Words," owned by Sir Ferdinand Gorges, who early colonized the state of Maine.

He talked of Thoreau. "There will be seven or eight volumes of his works. Next should come the letters, with the commendatory poems prefixed. Come up to Concord and we will talk it over. If you go to see Miss Thoreau, arrange to talk with her in the absence of the mother, who would interrupt and speak again of the whole matter. Make Helen[1] feel that Henry will receive as much for his books as if he had made his own bargain, for he was good at a bargain and they are a little hard — that is, they do not understand all the bearings of many subjects."

The good old man has come to Boston, being asked to perform funeral ceremonies over the bodies of two children. He asked for my Vaughan. "A beautiful poem which is not known is much at such a time," he observed inquiringly. To which I heartily responded.

Mr. Emerson came in to see Mr. Fields today. "I shall reconsider my reluctance to have Mr. Alcott's article published provided he will obtain consideration by it," was his generous speech. He said he had begun to prepare a new volume of poems, "but I must go down the harbor before I can finish a little poem about the islands. I took steamboat yesterday and went down, but a mist came up and my visit was to no purpose."

February 19, 1864. — This morning early called upon Mrs. Mott of Pennsylvania. Found Mr. James with

---

[1] Thoreau's older sister.

her. He observed that circumstances had placed him above want, and inheritance had given him a position in the world which precluded his having any knowledge of the temptations which beset many men. His virtues were the result of his position rather than of character — an affair of temperament. He said society was to blame for much of the crime in it, and as for that poor young man who committed the murder at Malden, it was a mere fact of temperament or inheritance. He soon broke off his talk, saying it was "pretty well to be caught in the middle of such weighty topics in the presence of two ladies at 10 o'clock in the morning." Then we talked of houses. He wishes a furnished house for a year in Boston until his departure.

July 28. — Still hot, with a russet sun. Mr. and Mrs. Henry James called in the evening. He talked of "Sterling." "He was not stereotyped, but living, his eye burned; he was very vivacious, although he saw Death approaching. He was one of the choicest of friends." Afterward he talked of Alcott's visit to Carlyle. Carlyle told Mr. James he found him a terrible old bore. It was almost impossible to be rid of him, and impossible also to keep him, for he would not eat what was set before him. Carlyle had potatoes for breakfast and sent for strawberries for Mr. Alcott, who, when they arrived, took them with the potatoes upon the same plate, where the two juices ran together and fraternized. This shocked Carlyle, who would eat nothing himself, but stormed up and down the room instead. "Mrs. Carlyle is a naughty woman," said Mr. J., "she wishes to make a sensation and does not mind sometimes following and imitating her husband's way." Mr. J. said Alcott once made him a visit in New York and when he found he could not go to Brooklyn to attend Mr. A.'s "conversation," the latter said, "Very well; he would talk over the heads with him then before it was time to go." They got into a great battle about the premises, during which Mr. Alcott talked of the Divine paternity as relating to himself, when Mr. James broke in with, "My dear sir, you have not found your *maternity* yet. You are an egg half hatched. The shells are yet sticking about your head." To this Mr. A. replied, "Mr. James, you are *damaged goods* and will come up *damaged goods in eternity*."

We laughed much before they left at a story about a man who called to ask money of John Jacob Astor. The gentleman was ushered into a twilight library, where he fancied himself alone until he heard a grunt from a deep chair, the high back of which was turned towards him; then the gentleman advanced, found Mr. Astor there and saluted him. He opened the business of the subscription to him, and was about to unfold the paper when Mr. Astor suddenly cried out, "Oo—oo—oo—ooooooo!" "What is the matter, my dear sir," said he, "are you ill? [growing alarmed] Where is the bell? Let me ring the bell." Then running to the door, he shouted, "Madame, madame." Then to Mr. Astor, "Pray, sir, what is the matter?" "Oo—oo—oo." "Have you a pain in your side!!" In a moment the household came running thither, and as the housekeeper bent over him, he cried, "Oo — oo — these horrid wretches sending to me for money!!" As may be believed, our friend of the subscription paper beat a hasty retreat and here ended also our evening.

A few days later there was an evening with Sumner and others, who talked of affairs in Washington. Mr. and Mrs. James were of the company. "These men," wrote Mrs. Fields, "despond with regard to the civil government. They have more faith that our military affairs are doing well. Chiefly they look to Sherman as the great man. Mr. James was silent; he believes in Lincoln." And there is the final note: "We must not forget Mr. James's youth, who was 'aninted with isle of Patmos.'"

July 10, 1866. — Forceythe Willson came and talked purely, lovingly, and like the pure character he aspires to be. He said Mr. Alcott talked with him of temperaments lately, with much wisdom. He said the blonde was nearest to perfection, that was the heavenly type. "You are not a blonde," said the seer calmly, and, said Willson to me, "I was much amused and pleased too; for when I regarded the old man more closely I discovered *he* himself was a blonde."

October 6, 1867. — Mr. Henry James and his daughter came to call. We chanced to ask him about Dr. G—— of New York, a physician of wide reputation in the diagnosis of disease. He is an old man now, but with so large a practice that he will see no new patients. Mr.

James says, however, that he is a humbug, that is, as I understood. He is a man of discernment which he turns to the best account, but not a man of deep insight or unwonted development. Suddenly J. remembered that there was once a Dr. —— of New York who was also famous. The moment his name was mentioned Mr. James became quite a new man. His enthusiasm flamed. Dr. —— died at the early age of 38, and, according to the saying of the world, insane. "Yet he was no more insane than I am at this moment as far as the action of his mind was concerned, which was always perfectly clear. Several years before his death he was pursued by spirits which often kept him awake all night. His wife was a heavenly woman and a Swedenborgian. The spirits did not come to her, but she was persuaded that they did come to him. They so disturbed his life that he used to say he was ready to die, in order to pursue his tormentors and ferret out the occasion of his trouble. At one time they told him that in every age a man had been selected to do the bidding of the Lord God, to be the Lord Christ of the time, and he must fit himself to be that man. They prescribed for him therefore certain fasts and austerities which he religiously fulfilled, only asking in return an interview in which some sign should be given him. They promised faithfully, but when the time arrived it was postponed; and this occurred repeatedly, until he felt sure of the deceit of the parties concerned."

Through the medium of these spirits Dr. —— became at length estranged from his wife. He went West to obtain a divorce, and while on this strange errand occurred a breach between himself and Mr. James. The latter wrote him a letter urging him away from the dead, which the doctor took as interference. The poor man returned to New York and at length shot himself. His wife never harbored the least animosity against him for his undeserved treatment. (Mr. J. looked like an invalid, but was full of spirit and kindness. He not infrequently speaks severely of men and things. Analysis is his second nature.)

March 5, 1869. — Jamie had an unusually turbulent and exciting day, and was thoroughly weary when night came. Henry James came first, and had gone so far as to abuse Emerson pretty well when the latter came in. "How do you do, Emer-son," he said, with his peculiar intonation and voice, as if he had expected him on the heels of what had gone before. Mr. James calls his new book, "The Secret of Swedenborg." Jamie thinks his article on Carlyle too abusive, especially as he stayed in his house, or was there long and familiarly. But his love of country was bitterly stung by Carlyle in "Shooting Niagara and After."

Saturday, March 13, 1869. — Mr. Emerson read in the afternoon. The subject was Wordsworth in chief, but the time was far too short to do justice to the notes he had made. In the evening we went to Cambridge to hear Mr. James read his paper on "Woman." We took tea first with the family and afterward listened to the lecture. He took the highest, the most natural, and the most religious point of view from which I have heard the subject discussed. He dealt metaphysically with it, after his own fashion, showing the subtle inherent counterparts of man to woman, showing to what extremes either would be led without the other. He spoke with unmingled disgust of the idea of woman, except for union in behalf of some charity for the time, forsaking the sanctity and privacy of her home to battle and unsex herself in the hot and dusty arena of the world.

(The members of the Woman's Club asked him to write this lecture for them. He did not wish to spare the time, but promised to do so if they would invite him afterward to deliver it in public. They disliked the lecture so much that, although they *did* send him a public invitation, there were but twenty people present.)

Nothing could be holier or more inspiring than his ideal of womanhood. She is the embodied social idea, the genius of home, the light of life — "ever desiring novelty her life without man would be a long chase from one field to another, accompanied by *soft gospel truth.*"

He did n't fail to whip the "pusillanimous" clergy, and as the room was overstocked with them, it was odd to watch the effect. Mr. James is perfectly brave, almost inapprehensive, of the storm of opinion he raises, and he is quite right. Nothing could be more clearly his own and inherent, than his views in this lecture, nothing which the times need more. He helps to lay that dreadful phantom of yourself which appears now and then conjured up by the right people, haranguing the crowd and endeavoring to be something for which you were clearly never intended by Heaven. I think I shall never forget a pretty little niece of Mrs. Dale Owen, who was with her at the first Club meeting in New York. Her face was full of softness and Madonna-like beauty, but she was learning to contract her brow over ideas and become "strong" in her manner of expressing them. It was a kind of nightmare.

Summer, 1871. — Mr. Alcott, Mr. Howison, Mr. Harris, the latter two lovers of philosophy, have been here this week. Channing is still writing poems in Concord, says Alcott. The latter smiles blandly at his own former absurdities, but he does not eat meat, and continues his ancient manner of living among books. The old gentleman gave me this wild rose as he went away. He quoted Vaughan, talked of a book of selections he would wish to see made, "a honey-pot into which one might dip at leisure," also an almanac suitable for a lady, of the choicest things among the ancient writers. He was full of good sayings and most witty and attractive. He is somewhat deaf, but he bears this infirmity as he has borne all the ills of life with a mild sweet heroism most marked and worthy of love and to be copied.

Sunday, April 20, 1873. — Last night Mr. and Mrs. Henry James, Alice, and Mr. DeNormandie dined here. Mr. James looked very venerable, but was at heart very young and amused us much. He gave a description of Mr. George Bradford being run over by the horse-car, because of his own inadvertence in part, and of the

good-natured crowd who insisted upon his having resti-
tution for what he considered, in part, at least, his own
fault. "Ain't you dead?" said one. "267 Highland
Ave. is the number, don't forget," said another; "you
can prosecute." "Where's my hat?" he asked meekly.
"Better ask if ye're not dead, and not be looking for
your hat," said another.

He also told us of a visit of Elizabeth Peabody to the
Alcotts. He said: "In Mr. A. the moral sense was wholly
dead, and the æsthetic sense had never yet been born!"

It may well have been after a visit to the Fieldses at
the seashore town of Manchester that Henry James
wrote this undated characteristic note which embodies
the feeling of many another guest: —

MY DEAR FIELDS: —
Pride ever goes before a fall. I scorned my wife's solic-
itude about her umbrella as unworthy of an immortal
mind, and now I am reduced to pleading with you to
preserve my lost implement in that line, and when you
next come to town to bring it with you and leave it for
me at Williams' book store, corner of School Street,
where I will reclaim it.

Alas! The difference between now and then! Such
an atmosphere as we are having this morning! And yet
we did not need the contrast to impress us with a lively
sense of the lovely house, the lovely scenes, and the
lovely people we had left. We came home fragrant
with the sweetest memories, and the way we have been

making the house resound with the fame of our enjoyment would amuse you. Alice and her aunt came home
just after us, and we have done nothing but talk since
we arrived.   Good bye; give my love to that angelic
woman, whom I shall remember in my last visions,
and believe me, faithfully,

Yours also,

H. J.

Henry James's letters to Mr. and Mrs. Fields, of which
a number are preserved by the present generation of
the James family, abound in characteristic felicities. In
one of them — they are nearly all undated — he regrets
his inability to read a lecture of his own at Mrs. Fields's
invitation, on the ground that his unpublished writings
are "all too grave and serious, not for you individually
indeed, but for those 'slumberers in Zion' who are apt,
you know, to constitute the bulk of a parlour audience."
In another he is evidently declining an invitation to hear
a reading of Emerson's in Charles Street : —

SWAMPSCOTT, May 11

MY DEAR MRS. FIELDS : —

My wife — who has just received your kind note in
rapid route to the Dedham Profane Asylum, or something of that sort —begs leave to say, through me as a
willing and sensitive medium, that you are one of those
arva beata, renowned in poetry, which, visit them never
so often, one is always glad to revisit, which are attractive in all seasons by their own absolute light, and with-

out any Emersonian pansies and buttercups to make them so. This enthusiastic Dedhamite says further, in effect, that while one is deeply grateful for your courteous offer of a seat upon your sofa to hear the Concord sage, she yet prefers the material banquet you summon us to in your dining-room, since there we should be out of the mist and able to discern between nature and cookery, between what eats and what is eaten at all events, and feel a thankful mind that we were in solid comfortable Charles Street, instead of the vague, wide, weltering galaxy, and should be sure to deem Annie and Jamie (*I* am sure of Annie, I think my wife feels equally sure of Jamie) lovelier fireflies than ever sparkled in the cold empyrean. But alas, who shall control his destiny? Not my wife, whom multitudinous cares enthrall; nor yet myself, whom a couple of months' enforced illness now constrains to a preternatural activity, lest the world fail of salvation. . . .

P. S. Who *did* contrive the comical title for his lecture — "Philosophy of the People"? I suspect it was a joke of J. T. F. It would be no less absurd for Emerson himself to think of philosophizing than it would be for the rose to think of botanizing. Emerson is the Divinely pompous rose of the philosophic garden, gorgeous with colour and fragrance. What a sad lookout there would be for tulip and violet and lily and the humble grape, if the rose should turn out philosophic gardener as well! Philosophy *of the people*, too! But that was Fields, or else it was only R. W. E. after dining with F. at the Union Club and becoming demoralized.

The final paragraph of a single other note suggests in sum the relation between James and his Charles Street friends : —

Speaking of Mr. Fields always reminds me of various things so richly endowed in the creature in all good gifts; but the dominant consideration in my mind associated with him is his beautiful home and there chiefly that atmosphere and faultless womanly worth and dignity which fills it with light and warmth and makes it a real blessing to one's heart every time he falls within its precincts. Please felicitate the wretch for me, and believe me, my dear Mrs. Fields,

Your true friend and servant,

July 8.   H. J.

Though not related either to Alcott or to Henry James, the following entry, on October 16, 1863, should be preserved — and as well in this place as in another. It refers to the second of the three Josiah Quincys who were mayors of Boston in the course of the nineteenth century.

Mr. Josiah Quincy dropped in to see J. T. F. He had lately been traveling in the West, he said. People complimented him upon his youthful appearance and his last letter to the President. "I am glad you liked the letter," he said, "but my father wrote it." At the next town people pressed his hand and thanked him for his staunch adherence to the Anti-slavery cause as expressed in the "Liberator." "Oh," his reply was, "that was my brother Edmund Quincy"; a little farther on a friend complimented his brilliant story in the last "Atlantic" magazine. "That was by my son J. P. Quincy," he was obliged to answer. Finally, when his exploits in the late wars at the head of the 20th Regiment were recounted, he grew impatient, said it was his son Colonel Quincy, but he thought it high time he came home, instead of travelling about to receive the compliments of others.

In giving the title, "Glimpses of Emerson," to one of the chapters in her "Authors and Friends," Mrs. Fields described accurately the use she made of her records and remembrances of that serene Olympian who glided in and out of Boston to the awe and delight of those with whom he came into personal contact. "Olympian" must be the word, since "Augustan" connotes something quite too mundane to suggest the effect produced by Emerson upon his sympathetic contemporaries. Did they realize, I wonder, how fitting it was that this prophet of the harmonies of life should live in a place the name of which is spoken by all but New Englanders as if it signified not a despairing *Væ victis*, but the very bond of peace? All the adjectives of benignity have been bestowed upon Emerson. Mrs. Fields's "Glimpses" of him suggest that atmosphere, as of mountain solitudes, in which he moved; that air of the heights which those who moved beside

EMERSON

From the marble statue by Daniel Chester French in the Concord Public Library

him were fain to breathe.   His "Conversations" in public and private places, a form of intellectual refresh-
ment suggested by Mrs. Fields and conducted, to
Emerson's large material advantage, by her husband,
appear to-day as highly characteristic of their time, —
the sixties and seventies, — and the light thrown upon
them by her journal illuminates not only him and her,
but the whole society of "superior persons" in which
Emerson was so dominating a figure. By no means all
of that light escaped from her manuscript journals to
the printed page of "Authors and Friends." In the
hitherto unprinted passages now given there are further shafts of it, sometimes slender in themselves, but
joining to show the very Emerson that came and went
in Charles Street.

There was a furtive humor in Emerson, which expressed itself more accurately in his own words than in
anything written about him. A pleasant trace of it is
found in a note to Fields addressed, "My dear Editor,"
dated "Concord, October 5, 1866," and containing these
words: "I have the more delight in your marked overestimate of my poem, that I had been vexed with a
belief that what skill I had in whistling was nearly or
quite gone, and that I must henceforth content myself
with guttural consonants or dissonants, and not attempt
warbling."

There is a clear application of the Emersonian philosophy to domestic matters in a letter written by Mrs.
Emerson to Mrs. Fields, a week after the fire which
drove the poet's family from his house at Concord, in

the summer of 1872. Mrs. Fields—as if in fulfillment of Emerson's words on the proffer of some previous hospitality: "Indeed we think that your house should have that name inscribed upon it — 'Hospitality'" — had invited the dislodged Emersons to take refuge under her roof. Mrs. Emerson, replying, wrote:—

We are most happily settled in the "Old Manse," where our cousin, Miss Ripley, assures us we can be accommodated — to her satisfaction as well as our own — until our house is rebuilt. Only the upper half is destroyed and we shall, I trust, so well restore it that you will not know — when we shall have the pleasure of welcoming you there — except for its fresh appearance, that anything has happened. I should not use such a word as "calamity," for truly the whole event is a blessing rather than a misfortune. We have received such warm expressions of kindness from our friends, and have witnessed such disinterested action and brave daring in our town's people, that we feel — in addition to our happiness in the sympathy of friends in other places — as if Concord was a large family of personal friends and well-wishers. They command not only our gratitude but our deep respect, for their loving and personal self-forgetfulness.

Mr. Emerson and Ellen join me in affectionate and grateful acknowledgments to yourself and to Mr. Fields.

Ever your friend,

LILIAN EMERSON

CONCORD, *July* 31, 1872.

It is in the atmosphere of the mutual relation revealed in many letters from Emerson and his household to Mr. and Mrs. Fields that the following reports of encounters with him — a few out of many similar passages in her journals — should be read.

December 3, 1863. — Last Tuesday Mr. Emerson lectured in town. Mrs. E. and Edith came to tea. She was troubled because she was a little late. She is a woman of proud integrity and real sweetness. She has an awe of words. They mean so much to her that her lips do not unlock save for truth or kindliness or beauty or wisdom. The lecture was for today — there was much of Carlyle, chastisement, and soul. After the lecture they came home with us and about 20 friends. Wendell Phillips was in his sweetest mood. He spoke of Beecher and Luther and of the vigorous, healthy hearts of these men who swayed this world. He said Hallam speaks disparagingly of Luther. I could not but think of Sydney Smith's friend who spoke "disparagingly of the Equator." Alden too came in wearied after his lecture. Senator Boutwell spoke in praise of life in Washington, the first man. Sunshiny Edith passed the night with us.

January 5, 1864. — Mr. Emerson came today to see J. T. F. He says Mr. Blake, who holds the letters of Thoreau in his hands, is a terribly conscientious man, "a man who would even return a borrowed umbrella." He became acquainted with Blake when he was connected with theological matters, "and he believed wholly in me at that time, but one day he met Thoreau and he never came to my house afterwards. His conscientiousness is equalled perhaps by that of George Bradford, who accompanied us once to hear Mr. Webster speak. There was an immense crowd, Mr. Bradford became separated from the party, and was swept into a capital place within the lines. When he found himself well ensconced in front of the speaker, he turned about and saw us, and with a look of great concern said: 'I have no ticket for this place and I can't stay.' We besought him not to be so foolish as to give up the place, but nothing would tempt him to keep it."

He was in fine mood.

Wednesday, September 6. — Mr. Emerson went to see Mr. Fields. "There are fine lines in Lowell's Ode," he said. "Yes," answered J. T. F., "it is a fine poem." "I have found fine lines in it," replied the seer. "I told Lowell once," he continued, "that his humorous poems gave me great pleasure; they were worth all his serious poetry. He did not take it very well, but muttered, 'The Washers of the Shroud,' and walked away."

J. T. F. found Emerson sitting by the window in his new office, highly delighted with it.

September 30, 1865. — Jamie went to dine with the Saturday Club. Professor Nichol was his guest. Sam. Ward (Julia's brother) was Longfellow's. Lowell, Holmes, Hoar, Emerson and a few others only were present. Judge Hoar related an amusing anecdote of having sent a beautiful basket of pears to the Concord exhibition this year. He said Mr. Emerson was one of the judges, and he thought he would be pleased with the pears because a few years ago he was in the garden one day and, observing that very tree, which was not then very flourishing, had told Judge Hoar that more iron and more animal matter were needed in the soil. "Forthwith," said the Judge, "I planted all my old iron kettles and a cat and a dog at the foot of the tree and these pears were the result. I have kept two favorite terriers ready to plant if necessary beside, but the fruit for the present seems well enough without them."

Judge Hoar said also that he knew a man once with a prodigious memory; before dinner he could recall General Washington, after dinner he remembered Christopher Columbus!

Saturday, October 7, 1865. — Tuesday, 3, Edith Emerson was married to William Forbes. The old house threw wide its hospitable doors and the stairway and rooms were covered with leaves and flowers and the whole place was as beautiful as earthly radiance and joy can make a home. Poor Mrs. Hawthorne, laden with her many sorrows, threw off her black robe for that day that she might rejoice with others. Edith made her own marriage wreath, and even Mr. Emerson wore white gloves. Old Mrs. Ripley and many aged and many beautiful persons were there.

In 1866 Emerson, long exiled from the good graces of his Alma Mater, was restored to them by the bestowal of an honorary degree. In 1867 the restoration was completed by his election as an Overseer of Harvard College and his appearance, after an interval of thirty years, as the Phi Beta Kappa orator. In this capacity he read his address on the "Progress of Culture" on July 18, 1867. Of the manner in which he did it, and of the effect he produced on his hearers, Lowell wrote immediately to Norton, in a letter often quoted, "He boggled, he lost his place, he had to put on his glasses; but it was as if a creature from some fairer world had lost his way in our fogs, and it was *our* fault, not his." "Phi Beta Day" was still a local festival of much brilliance, which was thus reflected in 1867 on the pages of Mrs. Fields's journal.

Thursday, July 18, 1867. — Arose at five and worked in my garden until breakfast. Then it was time to dress for Phi Beta at Cambridge. We drove out, leaving home at nine o'clock. We expected Professor Andrew D. White to go with us, but he called still earlier to say he had been summoned to a business meeting by President Hill. The day was soft and pleasant with a clouded sky. We were among the first on the ground, but we had the pleasure of waiting a few moments to see our friends arrive before we were admitted to the church. Only ladies went in. I went with Mrs. Quincy, the poet's [1] wife (poet for the day, for he is apt to disclaim this title usually), and we found good places in the gallery; by and by, however, Mrs. Dana beckoned to me to come and sit with them, so I changed my seat to a place on the lower floor. It was an impressive sight to see those

[1] Josiah Phillips Quincy.

men come in (though they kept us waiting until twelve
o'clock)—Lowell, Emerson, Dana, Hale, and all the
good brave men we have with few exceptions. First
came Quincy's poem, then Mr. Emerson's address —
both excellent after the manner of the men. Poor Mr.
E.'s MSS. was in inextricable confusion, and in spite of
the chivalry of E. E. Hale, who hunted up a cushion that
he might see better, the whole matter seemed at first
out of joint in the reader's eyes. However that may have
been, it was far from out of joint in our eyes, being noble
in aim and influence, magnetic, imaginative. I felt
grateful that I had lived till that moment and as if I
might come home to live and work better. Thank
Heaven for such a master! He was evidently put out
and angry with himself for his disorder and, taking Mr.
Fields's arm as he came from the assembly, had to be
somewhat reassured that it was not an utter failure.

Mrs. Dana tried to carry me to lunch, most kindly.
I could not make up my mind to go anywhere after
what I had heard, but for a moment to see if the good
Jameses were well, and thence homeward. It seemed,
if I could ever work, it must be then.

At half-past six Jamie returned from the dinner,
where J. R. Lowell presided in the most elegant and brilliant manner. In calling out Agassiz he told the story
of the sailor who was swallowed by a whale and finding
time rather heavy on his hands thought he would in-
scribe his name on the bridge of bone above his head;
but looking for a place, jack-knife in hand, he found
that Jonah was before him — so he said Agassiz, etc.

And of Holmes he said that the Professor and himself were like two buckets in a well: when one of them presided at a dinner, the other made it a point to bring a poem; when one bucket came up full, the other went down empty. And so on through all. Phillips Brooks, the distinguished preacher of Philadelphia, was there, and many other men of note.

Out of the many notes relating to Emerson's lectures, a few passages may be taken as typical. Perhaps the best unpublished pages are those on which the philosopher is seen, with his wife and daughter, against the social background of the time and place.

October 19, 1868. — The weeks spin away so fast I have no time for records, and yet last Sunday and Monday we had two pleasant parties, especially Monday, after Mr. Emerson's first lecture. We were 14 at supper. Mrs. Putnam and Miss Oakey among the guests, but the Emersons, who are always pleased and always full of kindliness, enjoyment, and Christianity, I believe give more pleasure than they receive wherever they are entertained. Edward is full of his grape-culture in Milton, Ellen full of good works, Mrs. Emerson very hot against her brother's opponents, Morton and those who take sides with him now that Morton himself is in the earth-mould first.[1] Mr. Emerson, alive and alert on all topics, talked openly of the untruthfulness of the

---

[1] An allusion to the controversy over the claims of Dr. Jackson and Dr. Morton to the discovery of ether.

Peabodys, of the beauty of "Charles Auchester," of Mr. Alcott's school, of Dana's politics as superior perhaps to Butler and yet not altogether sound and worthy, conservatism being so deep in his blood.

Thursday we drove our friends to Milton Blue Hill after the Emersons had gone, returned to dine and Selwyn's theatre in the evening. Herman Merivale was of the party — son of Thackeray's friend. The Stephens went on Wednesday. Thursday we dined in Milton with Mrs. Silsbee; it was a wet nasty day. Friday, Saturday and Sunday we were quietly enough here, Jamie with a fearful cold. Surely all this is unimportant enough as regards ourselves; but I like to remember when Mr. Emerson came and what he said and how he looked, for it is a pure benediction to see him and I honor and love him.

February 20, 1869. — Heard Emerson again, and Laura was with me; we drank up every word eagerly. He read Donne, Daniel, and especially Herbert; also *vers de société;* the facility of these old divines giving them a power akin to what has produced these familiar rhymes.

He said Herbert was full of holy quips; fond of using a kind of irony towards God, and quoted appropriately. Beautiful things of Herrick, too, he read, but treated Vaughan rather unjustly, we thought.

Lowell sat just behind; I could imagine his running commentary on many of Mr. Emerson's remarks, which were often more Emersonian than universal, or true. The facility of the old poets seemed to impress him with almost undue reverence. He is extremely natural and easy in manner and speech during these readings. He bent his brows and shut his eyes, endeavoring to recall a passage from Ben Jonson as if we were at his own dinner-table, and at last when he gave it up said, "It is all the more provoking as I do not doubt many a friend here might help me out with it."

His respect for literature, often in these degenerate days smiled upon from some imaginary hills by surrounding multitudes, is absolute and regnant. It is religion and life, and he reiterating them in every form.

The first and second of the "Conversations" arranged for Emerson by Fields are duly described in the journal. In the evening that followed the second, Emerson and his daughter dined at Charles Street, in company with Longfellow and his daughter Alice, William Morris Hunt and his wife, Dr. Holmes, and the Fieldses. The scene and talk were recorded by the hostess.

. . . Coming home, Ellen's trunk had not arrived, so she came, like a good child, most difficult in a woman grown, to dinner in her travelling dress. Alice Longfellow looked very pretty in a polonaise of lovely olive brown over black; a little feather of the same color in her hair. Rooshue [Mrs. Hunt] and her husband came in their everydays too. I wore a lilac polonaise with a yellow rose — I speak of the latter because it seemed to please W. M. Hunt to see the dash of color. . . .

Hunt convulsed us with a story of seeing a man run
through by an iron bolt, when a distinguished physician is called in; the physician asks if he can sleep
well, and a thousand and one questions of like rele-
vancy, to all of which the patient only replies by gasps
of agony. Hunt acted the whole scene famously. The
sunset too delighted him as it gilded the old sheds back
of the house and made them "like Solomon's temple."
Longfellow has written to Miss Rossetti, the author of
the "Shadow of Dante," to thank her for her pleasant
book. He asks her the difficult question why Dante
puts Venus nearest the sun. Also he points out her
fault of saying the spirits of the blest inhabited the
planets, whereas Dante clearly states that they all
lived in one heaven but visited the planets.

The truth of Hawthorne's tale of the minister with
the black veil was hunted up. His name was Moody
and he was one of the Emerson family. It seems the
poor man in his youth shot a boy by accident, and as
he grew older a morbid temper settled upon him and he
did not think himself fit to preach; so he withdrew
from the ministry but taught a small school, always
wore a black veil, literally a handkerchief. Ellen said
her aunt was taught by him and she appeared anxious
to set the matter right. Rose Hawthorne and her husband have been to see Mr. Emerson, and he likes them
both well; thinks Rose looks happy and the young man
promising, which is much. There is hope of Una's
recovery and return.

After dinner, we ladies looked over manuscripts for

a time until Longfellow went — when Mrs. Hunt went
to the piano and played and sang. Finally he came, and
they sang their little duets together and afterward she
sang a song with words by Channing about a pine tree,
set to a scrap of a sonata by Helen Bell, and after that a
touching German song with English words — then she
read Celia's [Mrs. Thaxter's] new poem to Mr. Emerson,
called "The Tryst." She read it only pretty well, which
disgusted her; and she said it reminded her of William's
reading, which was the worst she ever knew; he could
literally stop in the middle of a sentence because it
happened to be the bottom of a page, and ask her what
it meant. At that he took Celia's poem and read it
through word for word like a school-boy, looking up at
her to see if he was right and should go on. She laughed
immoderately, and as for Mr. Emerson, J. said his eyes
left their wonted sockets and went to laugh far back in
his brain.

Putting down his book, Hunt launched off into his
own life as a painter. His lonely position here without
anyone to look up to in his art — his idea of art being
entirely misunderstood, his determination *not* to *paint*
cloth and cheeks, but to paint the glory of age and the
light of truth. He became almost too excited to find
words, but when he did grasp a phrase, it was such a
fine one that it went a great way. His wife sat by making running comments, but when he said, "If any man
who was talking could not be heard, he would naturally
try to talk so that he could be heard," we tried to urge
him to stand firm and to assure him that his efforts were

A CORNER OF THE CHARLES STREET LIBRARY

neither lost nor in vain. "If the books you wrote were left all dusty and untouched upon the shelves, don't you think you would try to write so that people should want them? I am sure you would." His wife tried to say he must stand in the way he knew was right — as did we all — but he seemed to think it too hard, too Sisyphus-like a labor. The portrait of little Paul is still unsold. After keeping the carriage waiting one hour and a half, they went — a most interesting pair.

Tuesday, April 23. — Shakespeare's birthday. Emerson and his daughter passed the night with us and Edith Davidson, Ellen's "daughter," came to breakfast. We talked over again the pleasure of the night before. Emerson had never heard Hunt talk before and had seldom found Longfellow so expansive. Holmes met J. in the course of the day, and told him he had a real good time, though he did have a thumping headache — he was much pleased with Alice Longfellow.

Tuesday, May 21. — Call from Mr. Emerson, Mrs. E. and Ellen. They came in a body to thank me, which Mrs. Emerson did in a little set speech after her own fashion, at which we all laughed heartily — especially at the "profit" clause. Indeed we had a very merry time altogether. Mr. Emerson gave "Queenie" permission to look all about the room, "for indeed there was not such another in all Boston — no indeed [half soliloquizing], not such another." Then he looked about and told them the wrong names of the painters, and would have been entirely satisfied if he had not referred to me, when I was obliged to tell the truth and so from that time he made me speaker. He said he should do his very best for the university class for women for next December to make up for having served them so badly this winter. He said I had *very gently* reminded him of

How do you suppose that unskilful scholars are to live, if Fields should one day die? *Serus in coelum redeat!*

Affectionately yours &c.

R. W. Emerson

Mrs Annie Fields.

From a note of Emerson's to Mrs. Fields

his entire forgetfulness to fulfil an engagement or half-engagement to come to speak to them this winter. "Queenie" told me she was one of the few persons who had read Miss Mitford's poems, "Blanche" and all the rest, and liked them very much. So the various portraits of the old lady interested her much.

They came down to Boston, Mrs. E. said, on purpose to make this call. I had just returned home from a long drive about town on business, so it was the best possible moment for me.

Our first thought this morning (J's. and mine) was, how could Mr. Emerson finish his course of "Conversations," which had been so brilliant until the last, in so unsatisfactory a manner. His matter was for the most part old, and he finished with reading well-known hymns of Dr. Watts and Mrs. Barbauld. I fear we were all disappointed. Some of the lectures (especially the one on "Love") have been so fine that we were bitterly disappointed.

A later reference to Emerson shows him in Philadelphia, and through the eyes of a qualified observer there. The passage was written at Manchester-by-the-Sea, to which Mr. and Mrs. Fields had begun to pay summer visits even before 1872, and where they soon acquired that cottage of their own on "Thunderbolt Hill," which belied its name in serving as the most peaceful of retreats for Mrs. Fields and the friends she was constantly summoning to her side through all the remainder of her life.

Tuesday, August 25, 1872. — Miss A. Whitney came Saturday and remained until Monday morning. Sunday evening we passed at Mrs. Towne's. Mrs. Annis Wister [1] of Pennsylvania had just arrived, a dramatic

[1] Daughter of the Rev. William Henry Furness, of Philadelphia, and translator of German novels.

creature, who tells and tells again at request, with as much amiability as talent, her wonderful story of Father Donne, the Irish priest, who performed the marriage ceremony for one of her servants. Mrs. Wister, in spite of a lisp, has a thoroughly clear enunciation. She never leaves a sentence unfinished nor suffers the imagination to complete any corner of her picture. She is exceedingly lively and witty, and Miss Whitney, whose mind is quite different and altogether introverted, busied over her artistic. conceptions, could not help a feeling of envy. The gift of narration, so rare in this country, has been carefully cultivated by Mrs. Wister, and poor Miss Whitney could only wonder and admire. I could see her fine large eyes glow with pleasure and desire as she listened to her. Mrs. Wister told me an odd thing, which shows her as an individual. She asked me how the testimonial to Mr. Emerson was progressing, as her father was much interested and thought nothing he possessed too good to be given at once to Mr. Emerson, nor indeed worthy of his acceptance, and she would like to write him. I told her I believed the sum had reached $10,000, and had already been presented. This led her to say the friendship of her father for Mr. Emerson, and indeed their mutual friendship, as she then believed it to be, dated back to their youth, when Mr. Emerson was first writing his poems and delighting over the illustrations her father would make for them. As she grew up, she became dissatisfied at the relation between them. She thought Mr. Furness, her father, gave much more to Mr. Emerson in the way of friendship than Mr. Emerson ever appreciated. This went on until she became about eighteen years of age, when Mr. Emerson chanced to be visiting them in Pennsylvania. One day she was standing upon the stairs near the front door, and Mr. Emerson was ready to go out and waiting there for her father, who had withdrawn for a moment. Her heart was full, and suddenly she turned upon Mr. Emerson, and said, "Mr. Emerson, I think you cannot know what a treasure you have in this friendship of my father. He loves you dearly and I fear you cannot appreciate what it is to have the love of such a man as my father." She says to this day she grows "pank," as the Scotchman said, all over at such presumption, but she could not help it.

I asked what Mr. Emerson replied. He looked surprised, she said, and cast his eyes down, and then said earnestly that he knew and felt deeply how unworthy he was to enjoy the riches of such a friendship.

This incident presented Mrs. Wister as well as Mr. Emerson under a keen light. They could never understand each other.

From October, 1872, until the following May, Emerson and his daughter Ellen were traveling abroad. On their return Mrs. Fields wrote in her journal : —

Thursday, May 27, 1873. — The Nortons came home with the Emersons day before yesterday. Emerson came to pass an hour with J. T. F. before going to Concord. His son Edward had come down to meet him and

was full of excitement over the reception his father was
to receive and of which he was altogether ignorant. He
was overjoyed to be on the old ground again and comes
back to value the old friends even more than ever. He
must have been much pleased by the joy testified in
Concord, but we have only the newspaper account of
that. He has been fêted more than ever in England, and
Ellen was rather worn out by the ovations; but her
general health is much improved. The Nortons, who
returned in the same steamer, tell me Miss Emerson
was fêted for her own sake and was his rival! Her
"American manners" became all the rage in that world
of novelty. One night a gentleman sitting next her at
dinner introduced the word "æsthetic." She said she
did not understand what he meant by that word!

On the voyage Emerson was devoted to his daughter
and full of fun in all his talk with her. He would tuck
her up in blanket shawls and go up and down, hither
and yon, to make her comfortable — then he would
laugh at her for being such an exacting young lady and
would be very ironical about the manner in which she
would allow him to wait on her. "And yet," he said,
turning to the Nortons, "Ellen is the torch of religion
at home."

Throughout the journals Mrs. Fields's references to
meetings of the Saturday Club, and the records of conversations reported by her husband after these lively
gatherings, are frequent. In one brief entry Parkman,
Lowell, and Emerson appear in a conjunction that could

hardly have been happy at the moment, but the con-
cluding words of the passage may well stand, for their
appreciation of Emerson, at the end of these pages concerned chiefly with him.

August 26, 1874. — . . . Parkman said to Lowell,
and a more strange evidence of lapse of tact could hardly
be discovered, "Lowell, what did you mean by 'the land
of broken promise'?" Emerson, catching at this last,
said, "What is this about the land of broken promise?"
clearly showing he had never read Lowell's Ode upon the
death of Agassiz — whereat Lowell answered not at all,
but dropped his eyes and silence succeeded, although
Parkman made some kind of futile attempt to struggle
out of it. Emerson said, "We have met two great losses
in our Club since you were last here — Agassiz and
Sumner." "Yes," said Lowell, "but a greater than
either was that of a man I could never make you believe
in as I did — Hawthorne." This ungracious speech
silenced even Emerson, whose warm hospitality to the
thought and speech of others is usually unending.

In "Authors and Friends" Mrs. Fields concerned
herself with Longfellow and Whittier at even greater
length than with Holmes and Emerson. The Whittier paper, besides, was printed as a small separate volume; and in Samuel T. Pickard's "Life of Whittier,"
as in Samuel Longfellow's biography of his brother,
the letters from Whittier, as from Longfellow, to Mrs.
Fields, and to her husband, bear witness to valued

intimacies. Neither to Whittier nor to Longfellow, therefore, does it seem desirable to devote a special section of these papers; nor yet to Lowell, who never became the subject of published reminiscences by Mrs. Fields, perhaps for the very reason that he figures

This is my picter'
Improved on by Rowse,
The sole one my victor
Allows in her house;
I don't give 'em others,
  But Fields is a friend,
So, when he calls, it follers
  My best I should send;
Straighten the hair now,
  Gray the beard, — well,
The likeness is fair now
  Of yours
                        J. R. L.

Elmwood: 30th Decr 1863.

Facsimile of autograph inscription on a photograph of Rowse's crayon portrait of Lowell given to Fields

somewhat less frequently than the others in her journal. Yet there are many allusions to him, and in addition to the letters to Fields which Norton selected for his "Letters of James Russell Lowell," and Scudder

JAMES RUSSELL LOWELL
From the crayon portrait by Rowse in the Harvard College Library

for his biography of Lowell, a surprising number of unprinted, characteristic communications, both to Fields and to his wife, testify to their friendship. The remainder of this chapter cannot be more profitably employed than by drawing from Mrs. Fields's journal passages relating to these and other local guests of the Charles Street house, and supplementing the diary especially with a few of Lowell's sprightly letters to his successor in the editorship of the "Atlantic Monthly." It may be remarked, as fairly indicative of the relations between Lowell and the Fieldses through many years, that when they visited England in 1869 their traveling companion was Lowell's daughter Mabel.

Here, to begin with, is a note written to accompany one of Lowell's most familiar poems, "After the Burial," when he sent the manuscript to the editor of the "Atlantic." Lowell's practice of shunning capitals at the beginning of his letters, except for the first personal pronoun, is observed in the quotations that follow: —

ELMWOOD, *8th March,* 1868

MY DEAR FIELDS : —

when I am in a financial crisis, which is on an average once in six weeks, I look first to my portfolio and then to you. The verses I send you are most of them more than of age, but Professors don't write poems, and I even begin to doubt if poets do — always. But I suppose you will pay me for my name as you do others, and so I send the verses hoping you may also find something in *them* that is worth praise if not coin. Consolation and commonplace are twin sisters and I doubt not one sat at each ear of Eve after Cain's misunderstanding with his brother. In some folks they cause resentment, and this little burst relieved mine under some desperate solacings after the death of our first child, twenty-one years ago. I trust there is nothing too immediately personal to myself in the poem to make the publishing of it a breach of that confidence which a man should keep sacred with himself.

With kind regards to Mrs. Fields, I remain always yours,

J. R. LOWELL

Another typical letter, dated "Elmwood, 12th July, 1868, ¼ to 9 AM wind W. by N. Therm 88°," begins : —

MY DEAR FIELDS : —

as I swelter here, it is some consolation for me that you are roasting in that Yankee-baker which we call the W^{te} M^{ts}. That repercussion of the sun's heat from so many angles at once (the focus being the tourist) always struck me as one of the sublimest examples of the unvarying operation of natural laws. I wish you and Mrs. Fields might be made exceptions, but it can hardly be hoped.

Before the end of the month Fields had escaped the

perils of New Hampshire heat, and paid a visit to Elmwood, thus chronicled by Mrs. Fields: —

July 25, 1868. — J. went out to see Lowell last night.
As he passed Longfellow's door, "Trap," the dog, was
half-asleep apparently on the lawn, but hearing a foot-
step he leaped up and, seeing who it was, became overjoyed, leaped upon him and covered his hands with
caresses. He stayed some time playing with him. Lowell was alone in his library, looking into an empty fire-
place and smoking a pipe. He has been in Newport for
a week, but was delighted to return to find his "own
sponge hanging on its nail" and to his books. He had
become quite morbid because, while J. was away, a
smaller sum than usual was sent him for his last poem.
He thought it a delicate way of saying they wished to
drop him. He was annoyed at the thought of having
left out of his article on Dryden one of the finest points,
he thought, that was making Dryden to appear the
"Rubens" of literature, which he appears to him to be.
Lowell is a man deeply pervaded with fine discontents.
I do not believe the most favorable circumstances would
improve him. Success, of which he has a very small
share considering his deserts (for his books have a nar-
row circulation), would make him gayer and happier;
whether so wise a man, I cannot but doubt.
He wears a chivalric, tender manner to his wife.

In the following autumn, Bayard Taylor and his
wife were paying a visit in Charles Street, and Lowell

appears in Mrs. Fields's journal as one of the friends summoned in their honor.

Thursday morning, November 19, 1868. — Mr. Parton came to breakfast and Dr. Holmes came in before we had quite done. O. W. H. was delighted to see Mr. P., because of his papers on "Smoking and Drinking." He believes smoking paralyzes the will. Taylor, on the contrary, feels himself better for smoking; it subdues his physical energy so he can write; otherwise he is nervous to be up and away and his mind will not work.

At dinner we had Lowell, Parton, Mr. and Mrs. Taylor, Mr. and Mrs. Scott-Siddons and, later, Aldrich. Lowell talked most interestingly, head and shoulders beyond everybody else. The Siddonses left early, the gentlemen all smitten by her beauty and loveliness. A kind of childish grace pervaded her and she was beautiful as a picture. I could not wonder at their delight. Lowell's talk after their departure was of literature, of course. He has been reading Calderon for the last six months, in the original. He finds him inexhaustible almost. Speaking of novels, he said Fielding was the master, although he considers there are but two perfect creations of individual character in all literature; these are Falstaff and Don Quixote; all the rest fell infinitely below — are imperfect and unworthy to stand by their side. Tom Jones he thought might come in, in the second rank, with many others, but far below. He said he could not tell his boys at Cambridge to read Tom Jones, for it might do them harm; but Fielding painted his own experience and the result was unrivalled. Thackeray and the rest were pleasant reading, very pleasant, and yet how could he tell his class that he read Tom Jones once a year![1] He scouted the idea of Pickwick or anybody else approaching his two great characters. They stood alone for all time. Rip Van Winkle was suggested, but he said in the first place that was not original. Few persons knew the story perhaps in the old Latin (he gave the name, but unhappily I have forgotten it) but it was only a remade dish after all.

Friday. — Bayard Taylor and his wife left for New York. Mr. Parton dined out and we had a quiet evening at home and went to bed early. (Parton thinks it would be possible to make the "Atlantic Monthly" far more popular. He suggests a writer named Mark Twain be engaged, and more articles connected with life than with literature.)

It is easy to believe that Lowell's talk must have sounded much like his letters, which so often sound like talk. Witness the following sentences from a letter of December 21, 1868, in reply, apparently, to an appeal for a new essay for the "Atlantic": —

[1] One of Lowell's reminiscences at the Saturday Club, recorded two years earlier by Mrs. Fields, suggests his essential youthfulness of spirit. Apropos of a story told by Dr. Holmes, "Lowell said that reminded him of experiments the boys at his school used to make on flies, to see how much weight they could carry. One day he attached a thread, which he pulled out of his silk handkerchief, to a fly's leg, and to the other end a bit of paper with 'the master is a fool' written on it in small distinct letters. The fly flew away and lighted on the master's nose; but he, regardless of all but the lessons, brushed him off, and the fly rose with his burden to the ceiling."

Well, well, I am always astonished at the good nature of folks, and how much boring they will stand from authors. As I told Howells once, the day will come when a wiser generation will drive all its literary men into a corner and make a *battue* of the whole lot. However, "after me, the deluge," as Nero said, and I suppose they'll stand another essay or two yet, if I can divine, or rather if I have absorbed enough of the general feeling about something to put a point on it.

It's a mercy I'm not conceited! I should like to be, and try to be, and have fizzes of it now and then, but they soon go out and leave a *fogo* behind them I don't like. But if I only were for a continuance I should be as grand a bore as ever lived — as grand as Wordsworth, by Jove! I would come into town once a week to read you over one of my old poems (selecting the longest, of course), and point out its beauties to you. You would flee to *Tierra del Fuego* (ominous name!) to escape me. You would give up publishing. You would write an epic and read a book just to *me* every time I came. But no, it is too bright a dream. Let me [be] satisfied with my class, who have to hear me once a week, and with just enough conceit to read my lectures as if I had not stolen 'em, as I am apt to do now. Look out for an essay that shall [make] Montaigne and Bacon cross as the devil — when they come to read it! It will come ere you think.

Yours ever,

Fabius C. Lowell

A few weeks later Lowell was writing again to Fields,

on January 12, 1869, about a fiftieth birthday party at Elmwood : —

I am going to celebrate my golden wedding with Life, on the 22nd of next month, by a dinner or a supper or something of the kind, and I want you to *jine*. I shall get together a dozen or so of old friends, and it will be a great satisfaction for you and me to see how *much grayer* the rest of 'em are than we. I shall fit my invitations to this end, and the bald and hoary will have the chance of the lame, the halt, and the blind in the parable. If it should be a dinner, it won't matter, but if a supper, be sure and forget your night-key and then you won't have any anxiety, nor Mrs. Fields either. Of course, I shall have an account of the affair in the papers with a list of the gifts (especially in money) and the names of all who *donate*. You will understand by what I have said that it is to be one of those delightful things they call a "surprise party," and I expect to live on it for a year — one friend for every month.

A week later, in the course of a letter accepting the invitation of Mr. and Mrs. Fields for Lowell's daughter to accompany them to Europe, he wrote : "Do you see that —— is to commence his autobiography in 'Putnam's Magazine'? At least, I take it for granted from the title — The Ass in Life and Literature? If sincerely done, it will be interesting."

For all the transcendentalism of the circle to which Mrs. Fields bore so intimate a relation, there emanated from Lowell and others an atmosphere of sincerity which helped to preserve the equilibrium of the more easily swayed. Mrs. Fields herself was not immune to the appeal of some of the "isms" of the time and place, but an entry in her journal for January 18, 1870, shows her in no great peril of being swept away by them: —

Attended yesterday a meeting of what is called the Radical Club. Mr. Channing spoke, Mr. Higginson, Wendell Phillips, Mrs. Howe, Mrs. Lucy Stone, Mr. Bartol, Wasson, J. F. Clarke, Edna Cheney. Mr. Whittier was present and a room full of "come-outers." Mr. Channing and Mr. Phillips were reverent, though I think Mr. Phillips more definite, and perhaps consequently more conservative, in what he said. Certainly Mr. Phillips's speech was highly satisfactory. On the whole there was much vague talk and restless expression of self without any high end being furthered. I thought much of Mr. Higginson's talk and Mr. Wasson's irreverent answer were untrue. Perhaps I am wrong in saying no good end is attained by such a meeting. Perhaps a closer understanding of what we do believe is the result. But there is much unpleasant in the unnatural and excited view of the inside ring.[1]

There was, moreover, a constant corrective at hand in the persons of the local wits, among whom Long-

[1] After an evening of high discussion at Mrs. Howe's in an earlier year, Mrs. Fields wrote in her journal (October 4, 1863) : "The talk grew deep, and after it was over, she [Mrs. Howe] recalled the saying of Mrs. Bell, after a like evening, when she called for 'a fat idiot.'"

fellow's brother-in-law, Thomas Gold ("Tom") Appleton, was of the most clear-sighted. His definition of
Nahant as "cold roast Boston," and his prescription
for tempering the gales on a particularly windy Boston
corner by tethering a shorn lamb there, have secured
him something more than a local survival. He frequently left his mark on the pages of Mrs. Fields's
diary — once venturing seriously into prophecy on
the spiritual future of Boston, in terms which will seem,
at least, *in partibus infidelium*, to have received a certain confirmation at the hands of time. In the diary
the following entry is found: —

Sunday, November 6, 1870. — Appleton (Tom, as the
world calls him) came in soon after breakfast Sunday
morning. He talked very wisely and brilliantly upon
Art, its value and purpose to the state, the necessity
for the Museum. He said our people were far more literary than artistic. The sensuous side of their nature
was undeveloped. The richness of color, the glory of
form, was less to them than something which could set
the sharp edge of their intellect in motion. "Besides,
what is Boston going to do," he said, "when these fellows die who give it its honor now, Longfellow, Holmes,
and the rest? They can't live forever, and with them
its glory will depart without it is sustained by a founda-
tion for art in other directions. Harvard University will
do something to keep it up, but not much, and unless a
distinct effort be made now, Boston will lose its place
and go behind." He became much excited by the lack

of appreciation for William Story in Boston, and the abuse of the Everett statue, which he considers good in its way and as marking the highest point in Everett's oratorical fame, that is, when he lifted his hand to indicate the stars in his address at Albany, and set his fame some points nearer the luminaries which inspired him, by his fine eloquence.

He said a merchant told him one day that he did n't like Story's portrait statues, but his ideal work he was delighted with. "You lie!" I said to him. "The beautiful Shepherd-Boy which I helped to buy and bring to Boston you know nothing of — you can't tell me now in which corner of the Public Library it is hidden away. I tell you, you lie!"

He spoke of the Saturday Club, and said that, although he sometimes smiled at Holmes's enthusiasm over it, he believed in the main he was quite right, and it would be remembered in future as Johnson's Club has been, and recorded and talked of in the same way.

Unfortunately I don't see their Boswell. I wish I could believe there was a single chiel amang them takin' notes.[1]

On December 14, 1870, the diary recorded a dinner at which Longfellow, Osgood, Aldrich, Holmes, Dana, Howells, Lowell, and Bayard Taylor were the guests. It celebrated the completion of Taylor's translation of "Faust." Of the talk of Lowell and Longfellow, Mrs. Fields wrote : —

[1] If Mrs. Fields had lived to see *The Early Years of the Saturday Club* (Boston, 1918), she would have found that I drew from the notes in her own diary a large portion of the memoir of James T. Fields which it contains.

Before dinner I found opportunity for a short talk with Lowell upon literature. He thinks the chief value of Bret Harte is his local color and it would be a fatal mistake for him to come East, in spite of Taylor's representation of the aridity of intellectual life now in California. Taylor finds the same reason for leaving his native place. He regrets his large house, and frankly says he is tired of living there, tired of living alone, there being really no one in the vicinity with whom he can associate as on equal grounds. There is no culture, not even a love for it, in the neighborhood.

But I have not said half enough of Longfellow. He scintillated all the evening, was filled with the spirit of the time and the scene, sweetly reprimanded Taylor for not having time to give him a visit also, darted his *jeux d'esprit* rapidly right and left, often setting the table in a roar, a most unusual thing with him. Holmes at the other end was talking about the natural philosophers who "invented facts." Lowell took exception, said it was an impossible juxtaposition of ideas and words. Holmes defended himself by quoting (I think the name was Carius; whoever it was, Lowell said at once and rather warningly, he is a very distinguished name) a series of created facts by which he said a woman was not articulated or not as a man is (perhaps I have not his exact ideas); whereat Longfellow at once held up the *inarticulate* woman to the amusement of the table. Then they began to talk of the singular persons this world contains, "quite as strange as Dickens," as they always say; and Taylor, who introduced the

subject, proceeded to relate an incident which happened
to him in a cheap coffee house in New York. It was
near a railway station, so he dropped in, finding it convenient so to do, at an hour not usually popular with
the frequenters of such establishments. It was empty
save for an extraordinary figure with long arms, short
legs and misshapen body, who, hearing a glass of ale
ordered, came forward and said if he pleased he would
like to have *his* ale at the same table for the sake of
company. There was nothing to do but to comply,
which Taylor of course did, whereupon the strange
creature, never asking who Taylor was, went on to
relate that *he* was the great man-monkey of the world
who could hang from a tree and eat nuts and make the
true noise in the throat better than any other; he had
no competitor except one of the Ravel brothers, but
he (Ravel) was not the real thing; he himself alone
could make the noise perfectly. . . .

They all drank the exquisite Ehrbacher Rhine wine
from tall green German glasses of antique form, which
delighted them greatly. Jamie was much entertained by
Holmes's finding them "good conversational aperient,
but ugly. I should always have them on the table, but
they are not handsome." Longfellow was delighted with
my Venetian lace bodice; it seemed to have a flavor of
Venice about it in his eyes. It was a real pleasure to
me to see his appreciation of a thing Jamie and I really
enjoy so much.

I have not reported all, by any means, but time fails
me now. A thought of Dickens was continually present,

as it must be forever at a company dinner-table. How many beautiful feasts have I enjoyed by his side! There is none like him, none.

Taylor wrote a friendly German inscription in his book and presented me after dinner.

There were amusing traits of Elizabeth Peabody given. Longfellow remembered that the first time he met her was in a carriage. She was taken up in the dark. Hearing his name mentioned, she leaned forward and said, "Mr. Longfellow, can you tell me which is the best Chinese Grammar?"

A midsummer entry of the same year suggests the part that an editor's wife may play in the successful conduct of a magazine, if only through sharing the enthusiasm that attends the first reading of a manuscript of distinguished merit.

Saturday, July 16, 1870. — A perfect summer day. Jamie did not go to town, but with a bag full of letters and MSS. concluded to remain here. He fell first upon a MS. by Henry James, Jr., a short story called "Compagnons de Voyage," and after tasting of it in our room and finding the quality good (though the handwriting was execrable), I invited my dear boy to a favorite nook in the pasture where we could hear the sea and catch a distant gleam of its blue face while we were still in shadow and fanned by oak leaves. It was one of those delicious seasons which summer can bring to the dullest heart, I believe and hope. We lay down with

our feet plunged into the cool delicious grass, while I
read the pleasant tale of Italy to the close. I do not
know why success in work should affect us so power-
fully, but I could have wept as I finished reading, not
from the sweet low pathos of the tale, which was not
tearful, but from the knowledge of the writer's success.
It is so difficult to do anything well in this mysterious
world.

On the very next day Lowell wrote Fields a letter
which must have been read with delight by such friends
of Dickens as the Fieldses. The decorated sonnet which
filled its third sheet is reproduced herewith in facsimile:
the plainness of Lowell's script renders type superflu-
ous. The mere fact that the death of Dickens could
have called forth clerical expressions provoking Lowell
to such scorn is in itself a measure of the distance we
have travelled since 1870. The verses are not included
in Lowell's "Poetical Works," nor are they listed in the
"Bibliography of James Russell Lowell," compiled by
George Willis Cooke. With two slight changes they
may be found, however, over Lowell's signature, in
"Every Saturday," for August 6, 1870.

ELMWOOD, 17th July, 1870

MY DEAR FIELDS : —

I can stand it no longer ! If Dickens is to be banned,
the rest of us might as well fling up our hands. This
hot weather, too, gives a foretaste that raises well-
founded apprehension. It is a good primary school for

On some recent Sermons.

"His death eclipsed the gaiety of nations, & impoverished
the public stock of harmless pleasure": Johnson on Garrick
=

A man of genius, simple, warm, sincere,
He left a world grown kindlier that he came,
His hand the hungry knew but not his name;
Dumb creatures snuffed a friend when he drew near,
And the strange dog pricked one suspicious ear,
Then couched his head secure. Safe be this fame
From critics' measured praise or close-picked blame,—
He loved God's gentler face & made it dear.
Was then Stylites' post the better way
Than mingling with his kind, a man with men,
Like Him that was & was not such as they?
I judge ye not, but, to my simple ken,
If on your guideboards the right names be kept,
Some foe hath changed their places while ye slept.

Bulldog

Terrier

I think name will do instead of names, which
befogged the theis in the next verse.

Facsimile of Lowell's "Bulldog and Terrier" sonnet

the Institution of which the Rev'ds Fulton and Dunn seem to be ushers. Instead of going to Church today, where I might have heard something not wholly to my advantage, as the advertisements for *lost* people say, I have written a sermon. It is not a proper sonnet, but a cross between that and epigram — a kind of bull-terrier, in short, with the size of the one and the prick-ears and docked tail of the other, nor without his special talent for rats. Is there any grip in his jaw or no? He is good-natured and scarce shows his teeth.

The thing is an improvisation and the weather awfully hot!

Sweltered your servant sits and sweats and swears: (for alliteration only) but if you would like it for the "Atlantic," why here it is on the next leaf. Or, if too late, why not "Every Saturday"? I could not even think of it sooner, for I have been wrestling with a bad head and an article on Chaucer, and I fear they have thrown me. I want rest, and a bath of poetry, but where may the wicked hope for either? My sonnet (if Leigh Hunt would let me call it so) hit me like a stray shot from nowhere that I could divine, and five minutes saw it finished. So why may it not be good? It came, anyhow, as a poem comes — though it isn't just that. But my dog isn't bad? He is from the life at any rate.

I shall make use of my first leisure to get into Boston. But I have got bedevilled with the text of Chaucer and am working on it with my usual phrenzy — thirteen hours, for example, yesterday, collating texts and writing into margins. I comfort myself that my Chaucer will bring a handsome price at my *vandoo!* I shall be easier in my coffin if it run up handsomely for Fanny and Mabel.

Do you want an essay for your "Almanac" if one should come, which is doubtful? I need one or two more to make a little volume, and I need a little volume for nameless reasons. O, if I could sell my land! I would transmute that gold into poetry. Or if only poems would come when you whistle for 'em!

Give my kindest regards to Mrs Fields.

Yours always,

J. R. L.

From my study, this first day for three weeks without a drowsy pain in my knowledge box, I really feel a little lively, and wonder at myself. But don't be alarmed — it won't last, any more than money does, or principle in a politician, or hair, or popular favor — or paper.

Lowell and Longfellow continue to make their appearances in Mrs. Fields's diary.

December 7, 1871. — Last Sunday Charlotte Cushman dined here. Our guests asked to meet her were Mr. and Mrs. Lowell and Mr. Longfellow; Miss Stebbins and Miss Chapman, her guests, also came. We had a lovely social time, Lowell making himself especially interesting, as he always does when he can once work himself up to the pitch of going out at all. He talked a while with me about poetry and his own topics after dinner. He said he was one of the few people who believed in absolute truth; that he always looked for certain qualities in writers, which if he could not discover, they no longer interested him and he did not care to read them. He discovered, for instance, in the writers who had survived the centuries the same kindred points, those points he studied until he discovered what the adamant was and where it was founded; then he would look into the writers of our own age to see if he could find the same stuff; there was little enough of it unfortunately. He does not like Reynolds's portrait of Johnson, thought it untrue, far too handsome, yet highly characteristic in the management of the hands, which portray the man as he was when talking better probably than anything ever did. Mrs. Lowell appeared to enjoy herself. J. says L. is always more himself if Mrs. L. is happy and talkative. They are thinking of Europe. Mabel is to be married in April, and afterward they probably go at once to Europe.

A small party of friends assembled in the evening. Longfellow was the beloved and observed and worshipped among all.

April 11, 1872. — Last night Jamie dined with Longfellow. John Field of Pennsylvania and Lowell were the two other guests. J. was there twenty minutes before the rest arrived, and Longfellow gave him an account of the wedding of a school-mate of mine, —— ——, an excellent generous-hearted, generously built woman, with a little limping old clergyman who has already had three wives and whose first name is——. Longfellow said, in memory of what had gone before, the organist,

HENRY WADSWORTH LONGFELLOW
From a photograph taken in middle life

as if driven by some evil spirit, played "Auld Lang Syne," as the wedding procession came in, consisting of the bride and her brother, two very well-made large persons and the elderly bridegroom limping on behind all alone. The organist suddenly stopped at this point, breaking off with a queer little quirk and shiver as if he only then discovered what he was doing. Indeed the whole wedding appeared to have points to affect the risibles of the poet. He could hardly speak of it without laughter. He said, moreover, that it was, he thought, disgusting and outrageous for old men to get married.

Tuesday, September 23, 1872. — Longfellow came to town to see Jamie, in one of his loveliest moods. The day was so warm and fine, such a day of dreams, that he proposed to him every kind of excursion. "Come," he said, "let us go to the tea stores and smell the tea; the warm atmosphere will bring out all the odors and we can get samples!" And again, "Come, let us go to the wharves and see the vessels just in from Italy or Spain. It will be a lovely sight in this soft sky, and we can hear the men speak in their native tongues." Unhappily all these seductions were in vain, for Jamie was busy and was to lecture in Grantville in the evening. L. said: "At half-past eight I shall think of you doing thus and thus" (sawing the air with his arms). L. continued: "You know I have very strange people come to me — a man came a day or two ago by the name of Hyers, who has just published a book describing his own career. He believes that he is fed by the Lord! 'How do you mean?' asked I, with the knowledge that we were all fed in the same way. 'Why,' said H., 'He leaves *pies and peanuts on the sidewalks for me.*'" Longfellow could hardly contain himself — but "after all," he said, "that is very like Greene : when Greene comes to me, he always takes his money to come and go, just like my own sons and without so much as a thank you. But I like to have Greene come because he enjoys it so much and it is so strange. He amuses me. Then Appleton too, with his odd fancies, it would be hard to find a stranger man than he. He amused me immensely the other day by fancying an Indian, 'Great Fire,' or 'Hole in the Wall,' or some such fellow, coming to Boston for the first time. Passing a perruquier's, he sees the window filled with masses of false hair; taking them to be scalps and the window to be an exhibition of these tokens of prowess, he rushes in, embraces the little perruquier behind the counter, treats him like a brother, and almost frightens the small hairdresser out of his senses!!"

L. likes Joaquin [Miller] much. Of course, he said, there are some things about him not altogether agreeable, such as flinging a quid of tobacco out of his mouth under the table; "but I don't mind those things; perhaps," he added, "perhaps I might have done the same as a youth of 20!!!"

Thursday, June 12, 1873. — Dined last night with the Aldriches and Mr. Bugbee at Mr. Lowell's beautiful old Elmwood.[1] It was a perfect night, cool, fresh, moon-

---

[1] This was in the midst of Aldrich's occupancy of Elmwood, during Lowell's two years' absence in Europe.

lighted, after a muggy day of heat. After dinner I went into the fine old study with Aldrich, where he showed me two or three little poems he has lately written. He was all ready to talk on literary topics and much in earnest about his own satisfaction over "Miss Mehitable's Son" (which is indeed a very good story), and was full of disgust over the "Nation's" cool dismissal of it. It was too bad; but that Dennet of the "Nation" is beneath contempt because of the slights he throws upon good literary work. Aldrich says he found "Asphodel" all worn to pieces, read and reread in the upstairs study. He finds Mr. Lowell's library in curious disorder with respect to modern books. He is an easy lender and an easy borrower. The result is, everything is at loose ends. Only two volumes of Hawthorne can be found, for instance. . . .

Such wonderful colors overspread our bay this evening, the wide heavens, and all that lay between, it seemed an unreal and magic glory, and I recall dimly Hawthorne's disgust when he endeavored to describe a landscape. The Lord, he says, expressed himself in this glory; how shall we therefore interpret into language when he himself has taken this form of speech as the only adequate expression to convey his meaning to us? Who does not feel this in looking at the glories of Nature in this perfect season?

And here is a final glimpse of Longfellow, at Manchester-by-the-Sea, shortly after Don Pedro of Brazil had visited him in Cambridge: —

Thursday, July 6, 1876. — A fine rushing wind — no rain, but a wind that seemed to tear everything up by the roots. I dared not venture out in the morning. To our surprise and delight Mr. Longfellow came to dine. He was pleased to find Anna here, and fell to talking of Heidelberg in German with her and quoting the poets most delightfully. We sat in the front hall and rejoiced over his presence as he talked, for he was in a fine talking mood. He told us of the Emperor's visit and of his soldierly though most simple bearing; how he came to call upon him after his dinner, and when, as he rose to go, Longfellow said, "Your Majesty, I thank you for the honor you have done me." He said, "Ah! no, Longfellow, none of your nonsense, let us be friends together. I hope you will write to me. I will write you first and you must promise to answer." As they walked down the garden path together, Longfellow raised his hat and stepped one side as he was about to get into his carriage. "No, no," he said laughingly, "there you are at it again." In short, he has left a pleasant memory behind.

Longfellow told us his maids broke everything he possessed; at last they had broken a very beautiful Japanese vase or bowl which Charley brought home — so he had made a Latin epitaph for the maid. Unhappily I recall only the last line: —

Nihil tetigit quod non fregit.

He described Blumenbach very amusingly, whose lectures on Natural History he attended as a youth in

Heidelberg. He descended from his desk one day and came and rested his hand on the rail just before which L. was seated. He had been speaking of Platonic love. "Und die Platonische Liebe ist nach Amerika gegangen," he said, looking at Longfellow. The whole student audience roared and applauded.

He was in the loveliest spirits and manners. His friendly ways to my three friendless girls were not only such as to excite them profoundly, but there was sincere feeling in his invitation to them to call upon him and in his questions in their behalf.

The wind subsided as we sat together; the two young Bigelows sang "Maid of Athens" and one or two other songs, and then he departed. How sorry we were as we watched his retreating figure, as he and dear J. wound down the hill in the little phaeton.

Mrs. Fields's gallery of friends would be incomplete without a single sketch of Whittier's familiar outline. Out of many which the diaries contain, one may best be taken, for it shows him in company with that other friend, Celia Thaxter, whom also Mrs. Fields counted among the few to whose memory she devoted special chapters in her "Authors and Friends"; and it brings the three together at Mrs. Thaxter's native Isles of Shoals, so long a mecca of the "like-minded."

July 12, 1873. — I shall not soon forget our talk one afternoon in the parlor at "The Shoals." Whittier, as if inspired by that spirit residing in us which is the very ground-work of the Quaker belief, began to speak of Emerson's faith and of the pain it gave him to see the name of Jesus placed in his writings as but one among many. When he discoursed with Emerson of these things, he could have no satisfaction. Celia, on the other

From a note of "Dear Whittier" to Mrs. Fields

hand, said she did not understand these things; she never prayed. "I am sure thee does without knowing it," said W.; "else what do thy poems mean? Thee has not set prayer perhaps, but some kind of a prayer thee must have. No human being can exist without it. But what troubles me also in Emerson is that I can find no real faith in immortality." Here I took up the question. I had heard Mr. Emerson at Thoreau's grave, afterward speaking expressly on immortality, and in both discourses I felt deeply his faith in our future progress and enduring life. Whittier was inclined to think me mistaken. I think too that his use of Jesus' name is to prevent the worship of him instead of the One God. Whittier asked Celia to read a discourse of Emerson's, which she did aloud; and again he spoke of the beauty of childlike worship, the necessity for it in our natures, and quoted some lovely hymns. His whole heart was alive and poured out toward us as if he longed tenderly like the prophet of old to breathe a new life into us. I could seem to see that he reproached himself that so many days had passed without his trying to speak more seriously. He was not perfectly well after this — a headache overtook him before our talk was over and did not leave him until he found himself in Amesbury again. I trust it did so there. . . .

Whittier said one day, when we were talking of the "Life of Charlotte Brontë" by Mrs. Gaskell, and I was saying how sad it was she should have made the old man, her father, suffer unto death, as she did, by telling the tale of his bad son's life, and "still worse," I said, "she came out in the Athenæum and declared that her story was false, when she knew it was true, hoping to comfort the old man," — "I don't know," said Whittier; "I am inclined to think that was the best part of it, if her lie would have done the old man any good!"

After we had our long afternoon session of talk over Emerson and future existence and the unknowable, Celia stood up and stretched herself and said, "How good it has been with the little song-sparrow putting in his oar above it all!"

And what of Mrs. Fields herself, a woman of nearly forty when this last passage was written? For the most part the diary reveals her but indirectly. Yet in the midst of all her pictures of her friends, a fragment of self-portraiture is occasionally found; and to one of them the reader of these pages is entitled.

Proposed Dedication of Whittier's "Among the Hills" to Mrs. Fields. In a letter to Mrs. Fields, Whittier wrote: "I would like thy judgment about it. Would this do?" In altered form it appears in the book.

December 18, 1873. — Have been looking over "Wilhelm Meister"! I struck upon that marvellous passage, "I reverence the individual who understands distinctly what he wishes; who unweariedly advances; who knows the means conducive to his object, and can seize and use them. How far his object may be great or little is the next consideration with me"; and much more quite as good to the same end. It prompts me to say what I wish to do in life.

Aristotle writes: "Virtue is concerned with action, art with production." The problem of life is how to harmonize the two—either career must become *prominent* according to the nature of the individual. I discern in myself: 1st, the desire to serve others unselfishly according to the example of our dear Lord; 2nd, the desire to cultivate my powers in order to achieve the highest life possible to me as an individual existence by stimulating thought to its finest issues through reflection, observation, and by profound and ceaseless study of the written thoughts of the wisest in every age and every clime.

To fulfil these aims we must be able to answer the simple question promptly to ourselves: "What then shall I do tomorrow and today?" Then, the decision being made, the thing alone must have all the earnestness put into it of a creature who knows that the next moment he may be called to his account.

As a woman and a wife my first duty lies at home; to make that beautiful; to stimulate the lives of others by exchange of ideas, and the repose of domestic life; to educate children and servants.

2nd, To be conversant with the very poor; to visit their homes; to be keenly alive to their sufferings; never allowing the thought of their necessities to sleep in our hearts.

3rd, By day and night, morning and evening, in all times and seasons when strength is left to us, to study, study, study.

Because I have put this last, it does not stand last in importance; but to put it first and write out the plan for study which my mind naturally selects would be to ignore that example of perfect life in which I humbly believe, and to return to the lives of the ancients, so fine in their results to the few, so costly to the many. But in the removed periods of existence, when solitude may be our blessed portion, what a joy to fly to communion with the sages and live and love with them!

I have written this out for the pleasure of seeing if "I distinctly understand what I wish." It is a wide plan, too wide, I fear, for much performance, but therefore perhaps more conducive to a constant faith.

V

WITH DICKENS IN AMERICA[1]

WHEN Mrs. Fields wrote the "Personal Recollections" of Oliver Wendell Holmes which appear in her "Authors and Friends," she quoted, with a few changes prompted by modesty, this passage from a letter received from him at Christmas, 1881 : "Except a few of my immediate family connections, no friends have seen me so often as a guest as did you and your husband. Under your roof I have met more visitors to be remembered than under any other. But for your hospitality I should never have had the privilege of personal acquaintance with famous writers and artists whom I can now recall as I saw them, talked with them, heard them in that pleasant library, that most lively and agreeable dining-room. How could it be otherwise with such guests as he entertained with his own unflagging vivacity and his admirable social gifts?"

One of the visitors thus encountered by Dr. Holmes was Charles Dickens. Here was a guest after the host's own heart — and the hostess's. The host stood alone among publishers as a friend of the authors with whom it was his business to deal. Out of them all there was none with whom he came to stand on terms of closer sympathy and friendship than with Dickens. They had

[1] The greater part of this chapter appeared in *Harper's Magazine* for May and June, 1922.

first met when Dickens came to America in 1842, and Fields was by no means the conspicuous figure he was to become. When he visited Europe in 1859–60, with his young wife, whose personality was to contribute its own beauty and charm to the hospitality of 148 Charles Street for many years to come, they dined with Dickens in London, visited him at Gad's Hill, and had much discussion of a plan, which Fields had been urging upon him in correspondence, for Dickens to come to America for a course of readings. As early as in one of the letters of this time, Dickens wrote to Fields: "Here I forever renounce 'Mr.' as having anything whatever to do with our communication, and as being a mere preposterous interloper." From such beginnings grew the intimacy which caused Dickens, when he drew up the humorous terms of a walking-match between Dolby, his manager, and Osgood, Fields's partner, while the Boston readings of 1868 were in progress, to define Fields as "Massachusetts Jemmy" and himself as the "Gad's Hill Gasper" by virtue of his "surprising performances (without the least variation) on that true national instrument, the American catarrh."

The visits of Dickens to America, first in 1842, then in the winter of 1867–68, have been the subject of abundant chronicle. For the first of them there is the direct record of his "American Notes," besides those indirect reflections in "Martin Chuzzlewit," which wrought an effect described by Carlyle in the characteristic saying that "all Yankee-doodledom blazed up like one universal soda bottle." Many memorials of the second

CHARLES DICKENS

From a portrait by Francis Alexander, for many years in the Fields house, and now in the Boston Museum of Fine Arts

visit are preserved in Fields's "Yesterdays with
Authors," and in John Forster's "Life" both visits are
of course recorded.

There is, besides, one source of intimate record of
Dickens in America which hitherto has remained almost
untouched.[1] This is found in the diaries of Mrs. Fields,
filled, as the preceding pages have shown, not merely
with her own sympathetic observations, but with many
things reported to her by her husband. To him it was
largely due that Dickens crossed the Atlantic near the
end of 1867. Landing in Boston, and soon beginning
his extraordinarily popular readings, he found in the
Charles Street house of the Fieldses a second home.
"Steadily refusing all invitations to go out during the
weeks he was reading," wrote Fields in his "Yesterdays
with Authors," "he went only into one other house besides the Parker, habitually, during his stay in Boston."
In that house Mrs. Fields wrote the diaries from which
the following passages are taken. There Dickens was
not merely a warmly welcomed friend and guest at
dinner, but for a time an inmate. Henry James, summoning after Mrs. Fields's death his remembrances of
her and of her abode, found in it "certain fine vibra-
tions and dying echoes" of all the episode of Dickens's
second visit. "I liked to think of the house," he wrote,
"I could n't do without thinking of it, as the great
man's safest harborage through the tremendous gale

[1] A few passages from it, relating to Dickens, are included in *James T.
Fields: Biographical Notes and Personal Sketches.* When they are occasionally repeated here, it is in their original form, and not as Mrs. Fields
edited them for publication.

of those even more leave-taking appearances, as fate was to appoint, than we then understood."

In Dickens's state of physical health while the Fieldses were thus seeing him, lay the only token of an end not far off. All else was gayety and delight. The uncontrollable laughter — where does one hear quite parallel notes to-day? — the simplicities of game and anecdote, the enthusiastic yielding of complete admiration, the glimpses of august figures of an earlier time — all these serve equally to take one back over more than half a century, into a state of society about which an element of myth begins to form, and to bring out of that past the living, human figure of Dickens himself.

For the most part these extracts from the diaries call for no explanations.

Several months before the great visitor's arrival his coming was heralded by his business agent, of whom Mrs. Fields wrote : —

August 14, 1867. — Mr. Dolby arrived today from England (Mr. Dickens's agent), a good, healthy, kindly natured man of whom Dickens seems really fond, having followed him to the steamer in Liverpool from London to see that all things were comfortably arranged for him. He says Dickens has lamed one of his feet with too much walking of late. He is here to arrange for 100 nights, for which he hears he may receive $200,000 ; the readings to begin the first of December and to be chiefly given in New York City.

August 15, 1867. — Our day was quiet enough, but

when J. came down, he held us quite spellbound and magnetized all the evening with his account of Dickens, which Mr. Dolby had given him. He says Dolby himself is a queer creature when he talks. He has a stutter which leads him to become suddenly stately in the middle of a homely phrase and to give a queer intonation to his voice, so that he did not dare look at Osgood (who was a listener also) lest they should both explode with laughter.

Dickens now has five dogs; for these the cook prepares daily five plates of dinner. One day the plates were all ready when a small pup stole in and polished off the five plates. He fainted away immediately, and in this condition was discovered by the cook, who put him under the pump and revived him; but he had been going about looking like the figure 8 ever since.

Dickens is a warm friend of Fechter. One day, returning from a reading tour, his man met him at the station saying, "The fifty-eight boxes have come, sir." "What?" said Mr. Dickens. "The fifty-eight boxes have come, sir." "I know nothing of fifty-eight boxes," said the other. "Well, sir," said the man, "they are all piled up outside the gate and we shall soon see, sir." They proved to be a Swiss chalet complete, handles, blinds, not a bit wanting, which Fechter had sent him. It is put up in a grove near the house, where it presents a very picturesque effect.

Dickens allows nothing to escape his attention and gives "one small corner of the white of one eye" to his household concerns, though he seems not to observe.

His daughter Mary has the governance of the servants, Miss Hogarth of the cellar and provisions. There is a system in everything with which he has to do. When he gives a reading, he is present in the hall at half-past six, although the reading does not begin until eight; for Dickens cannot go about as other people do, he must go when the people do not press upon him. On reaching the private room, his servant brings his evening dress, reading desk, screen, lamps, when he arranges the hall, examines the copper gas-tubes to see if in order, dresses himself and is ready to begin. In Liverpool the other night he had advertised to read "Sergeant Buzfuz," instead of which by accident he read "Bleak House." Mr. Dolby spoke to him as soon as he had finished, telling him the mistake he had made. He at once returned to the desk, and said, "My friends, it is half-past ten o'clock and you see how tired I am, but I will still read Sergeant Buzfuz's speech if you expect it." "No, no," the crowd shouted; "you're tired. No, no, this ought to do for tonight." One tall man raised himself up in the gallery and said, "Look here, we came to hear Pickwick and we ought to hef it." "Very well, my friend," replied Dickens, immediately, "I will read Sergeant Buzfuz for your accommodation solely"; and thereat he did read it to a breathless and delighted audience.

At length came Dickens himself, and the diary takes up the tale: —

November 18, 1867. — Today the steamer is tele-

"THE TWO CHARLES'S" (CHARLES DICKENS AND CHARLES FECHTER).

From a Humorous Drawing by Alfred Bryan, 1879.

DICKENS AND FECHTER

graphed with Dickens on board, and the tickets for his readings have been sold. Such a rush! A long queue of people have been standing all day in the street — a good-humored crowd, but a weary one.[1] The weather is clear but really cold, with winter's pinch in it.

November 19. — . . . Yesterday I adorned Mr. Dickens's room with flowers, which seemed to please him. He was in the best of good spirits with everything.

Thursday, November 21. — Mr. Dickens dined here. Agassiz, Emerson, Judge Hoar, Professor Holmes, Norton, Greene, dear Longfellow, last not least, came to welcome. Dickens sat on my right, Agassiz at my left. I never saw Agassiz so full of fun. . . .

Dickens bubbled over with fun, and I could not help fancying that Holmes bored him a little by talking at him. I was sorry for this, because Holmes is so simple and lovely, but Dickens is sensitive, very. He is fond of Carlyle, seems to love nobody better, and gave the most irresistible imitation of him. His queer turns of expression often convulsed us with laughter, and yet it is difficult to catch them, as when, in speaking of the writer of books, always putting himself, his real self, in, "which is always the case," he said; "but you must be careful of not taking him for his next-door neighbor."

[1] On this very day Lowell wrote in the course of a letter to Fields: "James tells me you had a tremendous *queue* this morning. Don't fail to get me tickets, and for the first night. I should like to see his reception. It will leave a picture on the brain. And why should I not be there to welcome him, as well as Tom, Dick, or Harry?"

He spoke of the fineness of his Parisian audience —
"the most delicately appreciative of all audiences."
He also gave a most ludicrous account of a seasick
curate trying to read the service on board ship last
Sunday. He tells us Browning is really about to marry
Miss Ingelow, and of Carlyle, that he is deeply saddened, irretrievably, by the death of his wife. Just as
we were in a tempest of laughter over some witticism
of his, he jumped up, seized me by the hand, and said
good-night. He neither smoked nor drank. "I never
do either from the time my readings 'set in,'" he said,
as if it were a rainy season. . . .

Among other interesting personal facts Dickens told
us that he had last year burned all his private letters.
An appeal from the daughter of Sydney Smith for some
of his letters set him thinking on the subject, and one
day when there was a big fire — [sentence unfinished].

Mr. Dickens left the table just as we were in a tempest of laughter. Dr. Holmes . . . was telling how inap-
preciative he had found some country audiences — one
he remembered in especial when his landlady accompanied him to the lecture and her face, he observed, was
the only one which relaxed its grimness! "Probably
because she saw money enough in the house to cover
your expenses," rejoined Dickens. That was enough;
the laughter was prodigious. . . .

Wednesday, November 27. — What a pity that these
days have flown while I have been unable to make any
record of them. J. has been to walk each day with
Dickens, and has come home full of wonderful things he

has said.[1] His variety is so inexhaustible that one can only listen in wonder.

Thursday, 28. — Thanksgiving Day. J. took Dickens to see the Aldriches' house. He was very much amused by what he saw there and has written out a full account to his daughter, Mrs. Collins. . . .

I have made no record of our supper party of Wednesday evening. We had Alfred to wait, and a pretty supper and more important by far (tho' the first a consequent of the last) a pretty company. There were Mr. Dickens and Mr. Dolby, Helen Bell and Mrs. Silsbee, Mr. and Mrs. Bigelow, Mr. Hillard and Louisa and Mr. Beal. Mrs. Bell sang a little before supper ("Douglas" for one) very gracefully with real feeling. At nine o'clock oysters and fun began; finally Mr. Dickens told several ghost stories, but none of them more interesting than a little bit of clairvoyance or what-you-will, which he let drop concerning himself. He said a story was sent to him for "All the Year Round," which he liked and accepted; just after the matter had been put in type, he received a letter from another person altogether from the one who had forwarded it in the first place, saying that *he* and not the first man was the author, and in proof of his position he supplied a date which was wanting in the first paper. Curiously enough, Mr. Dickens, seeing the story hinged upon a date and the date being

---

[1] Even after Dickens's return to England, his sayings found their way into Mrs. Fields's journal; as, for example: —

"*July* 4, 1868. — J. made me laugh this morning (it was far too hot to laugh) by telling me that Dickens said of Gray, the poet, 'No man ever walked down to posterity with so small a book under his arm!'"

but a blank in the MS., had supplied one, as it were by chance, and, behold! *it was the same date which the new man had sent.*

Sunday. — Dined with Mr. Dickens at six o'clock. Mr. and Mrs. Bigelow, Mr. Dolby and ourselves were the only guests.

After dinner we played two or three games which I will set down lest they should be forgotten.

Descriptions of "Buzz," "Russian Scandal," and another wholly innocent amusement may be omitted.

Monday night, December 2, 1867. — The first great reading! How we listened till we seemed turned into one eyeball! How we all loved him! How we longed to tell him all kinds of confidences! How Jamie and he did hug in the anteroom afterward! What a teacher he seemed to us of humanity as he read out his own words which have enchanted us from childhood! And what a house it was! Longfellow, Dana, Norton (Mrs. Dana, Jr., and the three little Andrews went with us), and a world of lovely faces and ardent admirers.

Tuesday came Miss Dodge and Mrs. Hawthorne, Julian, and Rose. The reading was quite as remarkable, tho' more quiet than that of the night before. As usual, we went to speak to him at his request after it was over. Found him in the best of spirits, but very tired. "You can't think," he said, "what resolution it requires to dress again after it is over!"

Monday, December 9. — Left home at 8 A.M. for

New York. The day was clear and cold, the journey somewhat long, but on the whole extremely agreeable. We only had each other to plague or amuse, as the case might be, and we had the new Christmas story of Dickens and Wilkie Collins (called "No Thoroughfare") to read, and so by sufficient attention to the peculiarities or follies or troubles of our neighbors and some forgetfulness of our own, we came to the Westminster Hotel at night, in capital spirits but *rather* frozen physically. We had scant time to dress and dine and to go to the Dickens reading. We accomplished it, nevertheless. Saw the rapturous enthusiasm, heard the "Carol" far better read than in Boston, because the applause was more ready and he felt stimulated by it. Afterward Mr. D. sent for us to come to his room. He was fatigued, of course, but we sat at table with him and after a while he began to feel warmer as vigor returned. He brought out his jewels for us to see — a pearl Count D'Orsay once wore, set with diamonds, etc. — laughed and talked about the way we dress and other bits of nonsense suggested by the time, all turned towards the fine light of Charles Dickens's lovely soul and returning with a fresh gleam of beauty. We left early lest we should overfatigue him.

Wednesday, December 11. — At four Dickens came to dinner in our room with Eythinge and Anthony, his American designer and engraver. Afterward we went to the "Black Crook" together, and then home to the hotel, where we sat talking until one o'clock. There is nothing I should like so much to do as to set down every word he said in that time, but much must go down to oblivion. . . .

He talked of actors and acting — said if a man's Hamlet was a sustained conception, it was not to be quarrelled with; the only question was, what a man of melancholy temperament would do under such circumstances. Talked of Charles Reade and the greatness of "Griffith Gaunt," and the pity of it that he did not stand on his own bottom instead of getting in with Dion Boucicault, etc., etc. But after dinner he unbent, and while we were in the box at the theatre showed how true his sympathies were with the actors, was especially careful to make no sound which could hurt their feelings by apparent want of attention. The play was very dull, so we sat and talked. He told me that no ballet dancer could have pretty feet, and one dreadful thing was they could never wash them, as water renders the feet tender and they must become horny. He asked about Longfellow's sorrow again and expressed the deepest sympathy, but said he was like a man purified by suffering.

We had punch in our room after the play, when he laughed till the tears ran down his cheeks over Bob Sawyer's party and the remembrance of the laughter he had seen depicted on the faces of people the night before. Jack Hopkins was such a favorite with J. that D. made up the face again and went over the necklace story until we roared aloud. At length he began to talk of Fechter and to describe the sensitive character of the man. He saw him first quite by accident in Paris, hav-

Cider Cups

Put into a large jug, 4 or 6 lumps of sugar (according to size) and the thin rind of a lemon. Pour in a very little boiling water, and thrust a napkin into the top of the jug so as to exclude the air. Leave it to stand, ten minutes, and then stir well. Add two wine-glasses of sherry, and one wine-glass of brandy. Stir again. Add one bottle of cider (poured in briskly), and one bottle of soda water. Stir again. Then fill up with ice. If there be any borage, put in a good handfull, as you would put a nosegay into water. Stir up well, before serving

Champagne cup.

Put into a large jug, 4 good lumps of sugar, and the thin rind of a lemon. Cover up and stir, as above. Add a bottle of champagne, and a good tumbler and a half of sherry. Stir well. Then fill up with ice. Borage as above. Stir up well, before serving.

Moselle cup

4 good lumps of sugar, and the thin rind of a lemon (as above). Cover up and stir, as above. Add a bottle of Schill Moselle, and a tumbler full of sherry. Then ice as before. A few sprigs of wild thyme, or of Jasmine, are better for this delicate cup than borage. Stir well, before serving.

Claret cup.

4 or 6 lumps of sugar as before; giving the preference to 6. The thin rind of a lemon as above. Cover up and stir, as above. Add a wine-glass of brandy, then a bottle of claret, then half a bottle of soda water. Then stir well and grate in nutmeg. Then add the ice. If Borage be used for this cup, half the Cider-Cup quantity will be found quite sufficient. Stir well, before serving.

* The best substitute for borage is a strip or two of the rind of a fresh cucumber. But it must not be left in the cup more than 10 minutes, or its flavour will be too strong. It is easily taken out with the spoon, as it will probably lie on the top of the ice. None of these cups should be made more than a quarter of an hour before serving. Never pour out of the jug, without first stirring.

Charles Dickens

His Mark

Reduced facsimile of Dickens's directions, preserved among the
Fields papers, for the brewing of pleasant beverages

ing strolled into a little theatre there one night. He was
making love to a woman, and so elevated her as well as
himself by the sentiment in which he enveloped her that
they trod into purer ether and in another sphere quite
lifted out of the present. "'By heavens!' I said, 'a man
who can do this can do anything!' I never saw two
people more purely and instantly elevated by the power
of love. The manner in which he presses the hem of the
dress of Lucy in the 'Bride of Lammermoor' is something surpassing speech and simply wonderful. The man
has a thread of genius in him which is unmistakable, yet
I should not call him a man of genius exactly, either."
Mr. Dickens described him as a man full of plans for
plays, one who had lost much money as a manager, too.
He was apt to come down to Gad's Hill with his head
full of plans about a play which he wished Mr. Dickens
to write out and which Fechter would act in the writing-
room, using Mr. Dickens's small pillow for a baby in a
manner to make the latter feel, if Fechter were but a
writer, how marvellous his powers of representation
would be. "I, who for so many years have been studying the best way of putting things, felt utterly amazed
and distanced by this man."

Before the end of our talk Mr. Dickens became penetrated by the memory of his friend and brought him
before us in all the warmth of ardent sympathy.
Fechter is sure to come to this country: we are sure to
have the happiness of knowing him (if we all live), and
in that event I shall consider last night as the beginning of a new friendship.

Sunday, December 22. — Another week has gone. We are again at home in our dear little nook by the Charles, and tonight the lover of Christmas comes to have dinner with us. We had a merry time last Sunday, and after we had separated the hotel must needs take fire — to be sure, I had been packing and was in my first sleep and knew nothing distinctly of it; but it was an escape all the same and Mr. Dickens rushed out to help, as he always seems to do. . . .

At night came Mr. Dickens and Mr. Dolby, Mr. Lowell and Mabel, Mr. and Mrs. Dorr, to dinner. It was really a beautiful Christmas festival, as we intended it should be for the love of this new apostle of Christmas. Mr. Dickens talked all the time, as he always will do, generously, when the moment comes that he sees it is expected, of Sir Sam. Baker, of Froude, of Fechter again, this time as if he did not know the man, but spoke critically as if he were a stranger, seeing Lowell's face when his name was mentioned, which inclined itself sneeringly.

We played games at table afterward, which turned out so queerly that we had storms of laughter.

What a shame it is to write down anything respecting one's contact with Charles Dickens and have it so slight as my accounts are; but the subtle turns of conversation are so difficult to render — the way in which he represents the woman who will not on any account be induced to look at him while he is reading, and at whom he looks steadily, endeavoring to compel the eyes to move — all these queer turns are too delicate to be set down. I thought I should have had a convulsion of laughter when Mrs. Dorr said Miss Laura Howe sat down in her (Mrs. D.'s) room and wrote out a charade in such an unparalleled and brilliant manner that nobody could have outshone her — not even the present company. "In the same given time, I trust?" said Dickens. "No, no," said the lady, persistently.

December 31. — The year goes out clear and cold. The moon was marvellously bright last night, and every time I woke there she was with her attendant star looking freshly in upon us sleeping mortals in her eternal, unwearied way. We received a letter from Charles Dickens yesterday, saying he was coming to stay with us when he returns. What a pleasure this will be to us! We anticipate his coming with continual delight! To have him as much as we can, at morning, noon, and night.

This letter, long preserved in an American copy of "A Christmas Carol" on the shelves of the Charles Street library, throws a light of its own on the physical handicaps with which Dickens was struggling through all this time.

WESTMINSTER HOTEL, NEW YORK
Sunday, Twenty-Ninth December, 1867

MY DEAR FIELDS :—

When I come to Boston for the two readings of the 6th and 7th I shall be alone, as Dolby must be selling elsewhere. If you and Mrs. Fields should have no other visitor, I shall be very glad indeed on this occasion to come to you. It is very likely that you may have some one with you. Of course you will tell me so if you have, and I will then reëmbellish the Parker House.

Since I left Boston last, I have been so miserable that I have been obliged to call in a Dr. — Dr. Fordyce Barker, a very agreeable fellow. He was strongly inclined to stop the Readings altogether for some few days, but I pointed out to him how we stood committed, and how I must go on if it could be done. My great terror was yesterday's Matinée, but it went off splendidly. (A very heavy cold indeed, an irritated condition of the uvula, and a restlessly low state of the nervous system, were your friend's maladies. If I had not avoided visiting, I think I should have been disabled for a week or so.)

I hear from London that the general question in society is, what will be blown up next by the Fenians.

With love to Mrs. Fields, Believe me,

Ever affectionately yours,

And hers,

CHARLES DICKENS

Saturday night, January 4. — All in readiness. Mr. Dickens arrived punctually with Mr. Osgood at half-past nine. Hot supper was soon in order and we put ourselves at it. The dear "chief" was in the best of good humor in spite of a cold which hangs about him and stuffs up head and throat, only leaving him for two hours at night when he reads. 'T is something to be in first-rate mood with such a cold. . . .

The Readings have been so successful in New York he cannot fail to be pleased, and he does not fail to show it. Kate Field, New Year's Eve, placed a basket of flowers on his table; he had seen her bright eyes and sensitive face, he said. I was glad for Kate, because he wrote her a little note, which pleased her, of course.

Wednesday, January 8, 12 A.M. — I take up the pen again, having bade our guest a most unwilling farewell. Last night he read "Copperfield" and the Trial from "Pickwick." It was an enormous house, packed in every extremity, receipts in gold about five hundred and ten pounds!! He was pleased, naturally, and read marvellously well even for him. He was somewhat excited and a good deal tired when he returned, and in spite of a light supper and stiff glass of punch, which usually contains soporific qualities, he could not sleep until near morning. He has been in the best of spirits during this visit — when he came downstairs last night to take a cup of coffee before leaving, he turned to J., saying, "The hour has almost come when I to sulphurous and tormenting gas must render up myself!" He has been afflicted with catarrh, which comes and goes and distracts him with a buzzing in his head. It usually leaves him for the two reading hours. This is convenient, but it probably returns with worse force.

Sunday night dinner went off brilliantly. Longfellow, Appleton, Mr. and Mrs. Thaxter came to meet "the chief" and ourselves. Unfortunately there was one empty seat which Rowse, the artist, had promised to fill, but was ill at the last and could not — curiously enough we had asked Osgood, Miss Putnam, and Mr. Gay besides, all kept away by accident when they would have given their eyes to come. In the course of the day he had been to see (with O. W. H.) the ground of the Parkman murder which has lately been so clearly described by Sir Emerson Tennent in "All the Year Round"; in the evening the talk turned naturally enough that way, when, after much surmise with regard to the previous life of the man, Mr. Longfellow looked up and with an assured, clear tone, said: "Now I have a story to tell! A year or two before this event took place Dr. Webster invited a party of gentlemen to a dinner at this house, I believe to meet some foreigner who was interested in science. The doctor himself was a chemist, and after dinner he had a large bowl placed in the centre of the table with some chemical mixture in it which he set on fire after turning the lamp low. A lurid light came from the bowl which caused a livid look upon the faces of those who sat round the table, and while all were observing the ghastly effect, Dr. Webster rose and, pulling a bit of rope from somewhere about his person, put it around his neck, reached his head over the bowl to heighten the effect, hung it on one side, and lolled his tongue out to give the appearance of a man who had been hanged ! ! ! The whole scene was terrible and ghastly in the extreme, and, remembered in the light of what followed, had a prescience frightful to contemplate." [1]

[1] See Forster's *Life*, III, 368, for the same story told by Dickens in a letter to Lord Lytton, without naming Longfellow as the narrator.

Appleton did not talk as much as usual, and we were rather glad; but Mrs. Thaxter's story took strong hold on Dickens's fancy, and he told me afterward that when he awaked in the night he thought of her. I have seldom sat at dinner with a gentleman more careful and fine in his choice and taste of food and drink than C. D. The idea of his ever passing the bounds of temperance is an absurdity not to be thought of for a moment. In this respect he is quite unlike Mr. Thackeray, who at times both ate and drank inordinately, and without doubt shortened his life by his carelessness in these particulars. John Forster, C. D.'s old friend, is quite ill with gout and some other ails, so C. D. writes him long letters full of his experiences. We breakfast at half-past nine punctually, he on a rasher of bacon and an egg and a cup of tea, always preferring this same thing. Afterward we talk or play with the sewing-machine or anything else new and odd to him. Then he sits down to write until one o'clock, when he likes a glass of wine and biscuit, and afterward goes to walk until nearly four, when we dine. After dinner, reading days, he will take a cup of strong coffee, a tiny glass of brandy, and a cigar, and likes to lie down for a short time to get his voice in order. His man then takes a portmanteau of clothes to the reading hall, where he dresses for the evening. Upon our return we always have supper and he brews a marvellous punch, which usually makes us all sleep like tops after the excitement. The perfect kindliness and sympathy which radiates from the man is, after all, the secret never to be told, but always to be studied and to thank God for. His rapid eyes, which nothing can escape, eyes which, when he first appears upon the stage, seem to interrogate the lamps and all things above and below (like exclamation points, Aldrich says), are unlike anything before in our experience. There are no living eyes like them, swift and kind, possessing none of the bliss of ignorance, but the different bliss of one who sees what the Lord has done and what, or something of what, he intends. Such charity! Poor man! He must have learned great need for that. . . . He is a man who has suffered, evidently. Georgina Hogarth he always speaks of in the most affectionate terms, such as "she has been a mother to my children," "she keeps the list of the wine cellar, and every few days examines to see what we are now in want of."

I hardly know anything more amusing than when he begs not to be "set a-going" on one of his readings by a quotation or otherwise, and [it is] odd enough to hear him go on, having been so touched off. He has been a great student of Shakespeare, which appears often in his talk. His love of the theatre is something which never pales, he says, and the people who go upon the stage, however poor their pay or hard their lot, love it, he thinks, too well ever to adopt another vocation of their free will. One of the oddest sights a green room presents, he says, is when they are collecting children for a pantomime. For this purpose the prompter calls together all the women in the ballet and begins giving out their names in order, while they press about him, eager for the chance of increasing their poor pay by the extra pittance their children will receive. "Mrs. Johnson, how many?" "Two, sir." "What years?" "Seven and ten." "Mrs. B."—and so on until the requisite number is made up. He says, where one member of a family obtains regular employment at the theatre, others are sure to come in after a time; the mother will be in the wardrobe, children in pantomime, elder sisters in the ballet, etc.

When we asked him to return to us, he said he must be loyal to "the show," and, having three or four men with him, ought to be at an hotel where he could attend properly to the business. He never forgets the needs of those who are dependent upon him, is liberal to his servants (and to ours also), and liberal in his heart to all sorts and conditions of men.

I have one deeply seated hope, that he will read for the Freed people before he leaves the country; and I cannot help thinking he will. . . .

For more than a month from the time of this entry Dickens was carrying the triumph of his readings into other cities than Boston. There he had left a faithful champion in the person of Mrs. Fields, who wrote in her diary on January 26, 1868: "It is odd how prejudiced people have allowed themselves to become about Dickens. I seldom make a call where his name is introduced that I do not feel the injustice done to him personally, as if mankind resented the fact that he had excited more love than most men." As his return to

Boston drew near, she wrote, February 18th: "We are anticipating and doorkeeping for the arrival of our friend. Whatever unpleasant is said of Charles Dickens I take almost as if said against myself. It is so hard to help this when you love a friend." On February 21st there is the entry: "We go to Providence tonight to hear 'Dr. Marigold.' I have been full of plans for next week, which is to be a busy season with us of company."

Saturday, February 22. — We have heard "Marigold"! To be sure, the audience was sadly stupid and unresponsive, but we were penetrated by it. . . . What a night we had in Providence! Our beds were comfortable enough, for which we were deeply thankful; but none of the party slept, I believe, except Mr. Dolby, and his rest was inevitably cut short in the morning by business. I believe I lay awake from pure pleasure after such a treat. Hearing "Marigold" and having supper afterward with the dear great man. We played a game at cards which was most curious — indeed, something more — so much more that I have forgotten to be afraid of him.

In writing the chapter, "Glimpses of Emerson," in "Authors and Friends," Mrs. Fields drew freely upon the entry that here follows in its fullness.

Tuesday morning, February 25. — Somewhat fatigued. The "Marigold" went off brilliantly. He never read better nor was more universally applauded. Mr.

Emerson came down to go, and passed the night here; of course we sat talking until late, he being much surprised at the artistic perfection of the performance. It was queer enough to sit by his side, for when his stoicism did at length break down, he laughed as if he must crumble to pieces at such unusual bodily agitation, and with a face on as if it hurt him dreadfully — to look at him was too much for me, already full of laughter myself. Afterward we all went in to shake hands for a moment.

When we came back home Mr. Emerson asked me a great many questions about C. D. and pondered much. Finally he said, "I am afraid he has too much talent for his genius; it is a fearful locomotive to which he is bound and can never be free from it nor set at rest. You see him quite wrong, evidently; and would persuade me that he is a genial creature, full of sweetness and amenities and superior to his talents, but I fear he is harnessed to them. He is too consummate an artist to have a thread of nature left. He daunts me! I have not the key."

When Mr. Fields came in he repeated, "Mrs. Fields would persuade me he is a man easy to communicate with, sympathetic and accessible to his friends; but her eyes do not see clearly in this matter, I am sure." "Look for yourself, dear Mr. Emerson," I answered, laughing, "and then report to me afterward."

While we were enjoying ourselves in this way, a great change has come to the country. The telegram arrived during the Reading bringing the news of the President's impeachment, 126 against 47. Since Johnson is to be thrust out, and since another revolution is upon us (Heaven help us that it be a peaceful one), we can only be thankful that the majority is so large. Mr. Dickens's account of the ability of Johnson, of his apparent integrity and of his present temperance, as contrasted with the present (reported) failures of Grant in this respect, have made me shudder, for I presume Grant is inevitably the next man. Mrs. Agassiz was evidently pleased with the appearance of General Grant and his wife. She liked their repose of manner and ease; but I think this rather a shallow judgment because poise and ease of manner belong to the coarsest natures and to the finest; in the latter it is conquest; and this is why these qualities have so high a place in the esteem of man; but it is likewise the gift of society people who neither feel nor understand the varied natures with whom they come in contact.

Longfellow is at work on a tragedy, of which no words are spoken at present. Today Mr. Dickens does not go out; he is writing letters home. Yesterday he and J. walked seven miles, which is about their average generally. . . .

February 27. — Longfellow's birthday. Last night Dickens went to a supper at Lowell's and J. passed the evening with Longfellow. L.'s tragedy comes on apace. He looks to Fechter to help him. Dickens has doubtless done much to quicken him to write. He has two nearly finished in blank verse, both begun since this month came in. J. returned at half-past eleven, bringing an unread newspaper in his pocket which L. had lent him, telling him to read something to me about Dickens and return. Ah me! We could have cried as we read! It was the saddest of sad letters, written at the time the separation from his wife took place. The gentleman to whom he wrote it has died and the letter has stolen into print. I only hope the poor man may never see it.

Tonight he reads "Carol" and "Boots" and sups here with Longfellow afterward.

An entry in Mrs. Fields's diary about two years later indicates with some clearness that she overestimated the sympathy between Longfellow and Dickens. After a visit from Longfellow, she wrote, May 24, 1870 : —

When Mr. L. talks so much and so pleasantly, I am curiously reminded of Dickens's saying to Forster, who lamented that he did not see Longfellow upon his return to London, "It was not a great loss this time, Forster; he had not a word to say for himself — he was the most embarrassing man in all England!" It is a difference of temperament which will never let those two men come together. They have no handle by which to take hold of each other. Longfellow told a gentleman at his table when J. was present that Dickens saved himself for his books, there was nothing to be learned in private — he never talked !!

To return to Dickens in Boston : —

Sunday, March 1. — What a week we have had! I feel utterly weary this morning, although I *did* start up with exceeding bravery and walked four miles just after breakfast, in order to see that the flowers were right at church and to ask some people to dinner today who could not, however, come. The air was very keen and exciting and I did not know I was tired until I came back and collapsed. Our supper came off Thursday, but *without* Dickens. His cold had increased upon him seriously and he was really ill after his long, difficult reading. But Longfellow was perfectly lovely, so easily pleased and so deeply pleased with my little efforts to make this day a festival time. Dickens and Whittier both sent affectionate and graceful notes when they found they really could not come. Our company stayed until two A.M., Emerson never more talkative and good. He is a noble purifier of the social atmosphere, always keeping the talk simple as possible but up to the highest pitch of thought and feeling.

Friday, the Dana girls, Sallie and Charlotte, passed the night with us and went to the reading and shook hands with Mr. Dickens afterward. They were perfectly happy when they went away yesterday. . . .

[The walking match between Dolby and Osgood to which the following paragraph refers has already been mentioned. The elaborately humorous conditions of the contest, drawn up by Dickens, are printed in "Yesterdays with Authors." "We have had such a funny paper from Dickens today," Mrs. Fields had written in her diary, on February 5th, "that it can only describe itself — Articles drawn up arranging for a walk and dinner upon his return here, as if it were some fierce legal document."]

I had barely time yesterday, after the girls left, to dress and prepare some flowers and some lunch and make my way in a carriage, first to the Parker House at Mr. Dickens's kind request, to see if all the table arrangements were perfect for the dinner. I found he had done everything he could think of to make the feast go off well and had really left nothing for me to suggest, so I turned about and drove over the mill-dam, following Messrs. Dickens, Dolby, Osgood, and Fields, who had left just an hour before on a walking match of six miles out and six in. This agreement was made and articles drawn up several weeks ago, signed and sealed in form by all the parties, to come off without regard to the weather. The wind was blowing strong from the northwest, very cold, and the snow blowing, too. They had turned and were coming back when I came up with them. Osgood was far ahead and, after saluting them all and giving a cheer for America, discovering too that they had refreshed on the way, I drove back to Mr. Osgood, keeping near him and administering brandy all the way in town. The walk was accomplished in precisely two hours forty-eight minutes. Of course Mr. Dickens stayed by his man, who was beaten out and out. They were all exhausted, for the snow made the walking extremely difficult, and they all jumped into carriages and drove home with great speed to bathe and sleep before dinner.

At six o'clock we were assembled, eighteen of us, for dinner, looking our very best (I hope) — at least we all tried for that, I am sure — and sat punctually down to our elegant dinner. I have never seen a dinner more beautiful. Two English crowns of violets were at the opposite ends of the table and flowers everywhere arranged in perfect taste. I sat at Mr. Dickens's right hand and next Mr. Lowell. Mrs. Norton sat the other side of our host, and he divided his attention loyally between us. He talked with me about Spiritualism as it is called, the humbug of which excites his deepest ire, although no one could believe more entirely than he in magnetism and the unfathomed ties between man and man. He told me many curious things about the traps which had been laid by well-meaning friends to bring him into "spiritual" circles. But he said, "If I go to a friend's house for the purpose of exposing a fraud in which she believes, I am doing a very disagreeable thing and not what she invited me for. Forster and I were invited to Lord Dufferin's to a little dinner with Home. I refused, but Forster went, saying beforehand to Lord Dufferin that Home would have no spirits about if he came. Lord Dufferin said, 'Nonsense,' and the dinner came off; but they were hardly seated at table when Home announced that there was an adverse influence present and the spirits would not appear. 'Ah,' said Forster, 'my spirits in this case were clearer than yours, for they told me before I came that there would be no manifestations tonight.'"

Speaking of dreams, he said he was convinced that no

man (judging from his own experience, which could not be altogether singular, but must be a type of the experience of others), he believed no writer, neither Shakespeare nor Scott nor any other who had ever invented a character, had ever been known to dream about the creature of his imagination. It would be like a man's dreaming of meeting himself, which was clearly an impossibility. Things exterior to oneself must always be the basis of our dreams. This talk about characters led him to say how mysterious and beautiful the action of the mind was around any given subject. "Suppose," he said, "this wine-glass were a character, fancy it a man, endue it with certain qualities, and soon fine filmy webs of thoughts almost impalpable coming from every direction, and yet we know not from where, spin and weave around it until it assumes form and beauty and becomes instinct with life. . . ."

Mr. Lowell asked him some question in a low voice about the country, when I heard him say presently that it was very much grown up, indeed he should not know oftentimes that he was not in England, things went on so much the same and with very few exceptions (hardly worth mentioning) he was let alone precisely as he would have been there.

He loves to talk of Gad's Hill and stopped joyfully from other talk to tell me how his daughter Mary arranged his table with flowers. He speaks continually of her great taste in combining flowers. "Sometimes she will have nothing but water-lilies," he said, as if the memory were a fragrance.

Some one has said, "We cannot love and be wise."
I will gladly give away the inconsistent wisdom, for
Jamie and I are truly penetrated with grateful love to
C. D.

Wednesday, March 3. — Mr. Dickens came over
last night with Messrs. Osgood and Dolby, to pass the
evening and have a little punch and supper and a merry
game with us. . . .

They left punctually before eleven, having promised
the driver they would not keep him waiting in the cold.
Jamie has every day long walks with him. He has told
him much regarding the forms and habits of his life.
He is fond of "Gad's Hill," and his "dear daughters"
and their aunt, Miss Hogarth, make his home circle.
What a dear one it is to him can be seen whenever his
thought turns that way; and if his letters do not come
punctually, he is in low spirits. He is a great actor and
artist, but above all a great and loving and well-beloved
man. (This I cling to in memory of Mr. Emerson's
dictum.)

I am deep in Carlyle's history and every little thing I
hear chimes in with that. After *the* dinner (at the
Parker) the other night, Mr. Dickens thought he would
take a warm bath; but, the water being drawn, he
began playing the clown in pantomime on the edge of
the bath (with his clothes on) for the amusement of
Dolby and Osgood; in a moment and before he knew
where he was, he had tumbled in head over heels, clothes
and all. A second and improved edition of "Les Noy-
ades," I thought. Surely this book is a marvel of thought

and labor.   Why, why have I left it unknown to myself
until now ? I fear, unlike Lowell, it is because I could
not read eighteen uninterrupted hours without apo-
plexy or some other 'exy, which would destroy what
power I have forever.

March 6. — Mr. Dickens dined here last night
without company except Messrs. Dolby and Osgood
and Howells. We had a very merry time. They had
been to visit the Cambridge Printing Office in the afternoon and had been shown so many things that "the
chief" said he began to think he should have a bitter
hatred against any mortal who undertook to show him
anything else in the world, and laughed immoderately
at J. T. F.'s proposition to show him the new fruit house
afterward. We all had a game of Nincomtwitch and
separated rather early because we were going to a party ;
and as C. D. shook me by the hand to say good-bye, he
said he hoped we would have a better time at this party
than *he* ever had at any party in all *his* life. A part of
the dinner-time was taken up by half guess and half
calculation of how far Mr. Dickens's manuscript would
extend in a single line. Mr. Osgood said 40 miles. J.
said 100,000 (! !). I believe they are really going to find
out. C. D. said *he* felt as if it would go farther than 40
miles, and was inclined to be "down" on Osgood until
he saw him doing figures in his head after a fearful
fashion. All this amusing talk served to give one a
strange, weird sensation of the value of words over time
and space ; these little marks of immeasurable value
covering so slight a portion of the rough earth ! Howells

talked a little of Venice, thought the Ligurians lived better than the Venetians. C. D. said they ate but little meat when *he* lived in Genoa; chiefly "pasta" with a good soup poured over it. . . .

He leaves Boston today, to return the first of April, so I will end this poor little surface record here, hoping always that the new sheet shall have something written down of a deeper, simpler, and more inseeing nature.

On the return of Dickens to Boston, Mrs. Fields dined with him at the Parker House, March 31, 1868, and, commenting on his lack of "talent" for sleeping, wrote in her diary : —

I remember Carlyle says, "When Dulness puts his head upon his mattresses, Dulness sleeps," referring to the apathetic people who went on their daily habits and avocations in Paris while men were guillotined by thousands in the next street. Mr. Dickens talked as usual, much and naturally — first of the various hotels of which he had late experience. The one in Portland was particularly bad, the dinner, poor as it was, being brought in small dishes, "as if Osgood and I should quarrel over it," everything being very bad and disgusting which the little dishes contained.

At last they came to the book, "Ecce Homo," in which Dickens can see nothing of value, any more than we. He thinks Jesus foresaw and guarded as well as he could against the misinterpreting of his teaching, that the four Gospels are all derived from some anterior written Scriptures — made up, perhaps, with additions and interpolations from the "Talmud," in which he expressed great interest and admiration. Among other things which prove how little the Gospels should be taken literally is the fact that *broad phylacteries* were not in use until some years after Jesus lived, so that the passage in which this reference occurs, at least, must only be taken as conveying the spirit and temper, not the actual form of speech, of our Lord. Mr. Dickens spoke reverently and earnestly, and said much more if I could recall it perfectly.

Then he came to "spiritualism" again, and asked if he had ever told us his interview with Colchester, the famous medium. He continued that, being at Knebworth one day, Lytton, having finished his dinner and retired to the comfort of his pipe, said : "Why don't you see some of these famous men ? What a pity Home has just gone." (Here Dickens imitated to the life Lytton's manner of speaking, so I could see the man.) "Well," said D., "he went on to say so much about it that I inquired of him who was the next best man. He said there was one Colchester, if possible better than Home. So I took Colchester's address, got Charley Collins, my son-in-law, to write to him asking an interview for five gentlemen and for any day he should designate, the hour being two o'clock. A day being fixed, I wrote to a young French conjuror, with whom I had no acquaintance but had observed his great cleverness at his business before the public, to ask him to accompany us. He acceded with alacrity. Therefore, with poor Chaun-

cey Townshend, just dead, and one other person whom
I do not at this moment recall, we waited upon Mr. Colchester. As we entered the room, I leading the way,
the man, recognizing me immediately, turned deadly
pale, especially when he saw me followed by the conjuror and Townshend, who, with his colored imperial
and beard and tight-fitting wig, looked like a member
of the detective police. He trembled visibly, became
livid to the eyes, all of which was visible in spite of
paint with which his face was covered to the eyes. He
withdrew for a few minutes, during which we heard
him in hot discussion with his accomplice, telling him
how he was cornered and trying to imagine some way
in which to get out of the trap, the other evidently urging him to go through with it now the best way he could.
He returned, therefore, and placed himself with his back
to the light, while it shone upon our faces. We sat
awhile in silence until he began, insolently turning to
me: 'Take up the alphabet and think of somebody who
is dead, pass your hands over the letters, and the spirit
will indicate the name.' I thought of Mary and took
the alphabet, and when I came to M, he rapped; but
I was sure that I had unconsciously signified by some
movement and determined to be more skilful the next
time.

For the next letter, therefore, he went on to H, and
then asked me if that was right. I told him I thought
the spirits ought to know. He then began with
some one else, but doing nothing he became hotter
and hotter, the perspiration pouring from his face, until

he got up, said the spirits were against him, and was about to withdraw. I then rose and told him that it was the most shameless imposition, that he had got us there with the intent to deceive and under false pretences, that he had done nothing and could do nothing. He offered to return our money — I said the fact of his taking the money at all was the point. At last the wretch said, turning to the Frenchman, 'I did tell you one name, Valentine.' 'Yes,' answered the young conjuror, with a sudden burst of English, 'Yes, but I showed it to you!' indicating with a swift movement of the hand how he had given him a chance." Then it was all up with Colchester, and more scathing words than those spoken by Dickens to him have been seldom spoken by mortal.

It was the righteous anger of one trying to avenge and help the world. Mr. Dickens always seems to me like one who, working earnestly with his eyes fixed on the immutable, nevertheless finds to his own surprise that his words place him among the prophets. He does not arrogate a place to himself there; indeed he is singularly humble (as it seems to us) in the moral position he takes; but for all that is led by the Divine Hand to see what a power he is and in an unsought-for manner finds himself among the teachers of the earth. He says nowhere is a man placed in such an unfair position as at church. If one could only be allowed to get up and state his objections, it would be very well, but under the circumstances he declines being preached to.

A few days later Mrs. Fields heard Dickens read the "Christmas Carol" for the last time in Boston.

Such a wonderful evening as it was!! We were on fire with enthusiasm and in spite of some people who went with us . . . looking, as C. D. said, as if they were sorry they had come, they were really filled with enthusiasm, and enjoying as fully as their critical and crossed natures would allow. He himself was full of fun and put in all manner of queer things for our amusement; but what he put in, involuntarily, when he turned on a man who was standing staring fixedly at him with an opera glass, was almost more than we could bear. The stolidity of the man, the fixed glass, the despairing, annihilating look of Dickens were too much for our equanimity.

Thursday. — Anniversary of C. D.'s marriage day and of John Forster's birthday. C. D. not at all well, coughing all the time and in low spirits. Mr. Dolby came in when J. was there in the morning to say there were two gentlemen from New Bedford (friends of Mr. Osgood's) who wished to see him. Would he allow them to come in? "No, I'll be damned if I will," he said, like a spoiled child, starting up from his chair! J. was equally amused and astonished at the outburst, but sleeplessness, narcotics, and the rest of the crew of disturbers have done their worst. My only fear is he may be ill. However, they had a walk together towards noon and he revived, but coughed badly in the evening. I think, too, only $1300 in the house was bad for his spirits!

April 7. — Dickens . . . told Jamie the other day in walking that he wrote "Nicholas Nickleby" and "Oliver Twist" at the same time for rival magazines from month to month. Once he was taken ill, with both magazines waiting for unwritten sheets. He immediately took steamer for Boulogne, took a room in an inn there, secure from interruption, and was able to return just in season for the monthly issues with his work completed. He sees now how the work of both would have been better done had he worked only upon one at a time.

After the exertion of last evening he looked pale and exhausted. Longfellow and Norton joined with us in trying to dissuade him from future Readings after these two. He does not recover his vitality after the effort of reading, and his spirits are naturally somewhat depressed by the use of soporifics, which at length became a necessity. . . . "Copperfield" was a tragedy last night — less vigor but great tragic power came out of it.

April 8. — In spite of a deluge of rain last night there was a large audience to hear Dickens, and Longfellow came as usual. He read with more vigor than the night before and seemed better. . . . The time approaches swiftly for our flight to New York. We dread to leave home and would only do it for *him*, besides, the pleasure must be much in the fact of trying to do something rather than in really doing anything, for I fear he will be too ill and utterly fatigued to care much about anything but rest.

Friday, April 10. — Left home at eight o'clock in the morning, found our dearly beloved friend C. D. already awaiting us, with two roses in his coat and looking as fresh as possible. It was my first ride in America in a compartment car. Mr. Dolby made the fourth in our little party and we had a table and a game of "Nincom" and "Casino" and talked and laughed and whiled away the time pleasantly until we arrived here at the Westminster Hotel in time for dinner at six. I was impressed all day long with the occasional languor which came over C. D. and always with the exquisite delicacy and quickness of his perception, something as fine as the finest woman possesses, which combined itself wondrously with the action of the massive brain and the rapid movement of those strong, strong hands. I felt how deeply we had learned to love him and how hard it would be for us to part.

At dinner he gave us a marvellous description of his life as a reporter. It seems he invented (in a measure) a system of stenography for himself; this is to say he altered Gurney's system to suit his own needs. He was a very young man, not yet 20, when at seven guineas a week he was engaged as reporter on the "Morning Chronicle," then a very large and powerful paper. At this period the present Lord Derby, then Mr. Stanley, was beginning his brilliant career, and O'Connell, Shiel, and others were at the height of their powers. Wherever these men spoke a corps of reporters was detailed to follow them and with the utmost expedition forward verbatim reports to the "Chronicle." Often and often he

has gone by post-chaise to Edinburgh, heard a speech
or a part of it (having instructions, whatever happened,
to leave the place again at a certain hour, the next reporter taking up his work where he must leave it), and
has driven all the way back to London, a bag of sovereigns on one side of his body and a bag of slips of paper
on the other, writing, writing desperately all the way
by the light of a small lamp. At each station a man on
horseback would stand ready to seize the sheets already
prepared and ride with them to London. Often and
often this work would make him deadly sick and he
would have to plunge his head out of the window to re-
lieve himself; still the writing went steadily forward on
very little slips of paper which he held before him, just
resting his body on the edge of the seat and his paper on
the front of the window underneath the lamp. As the
station was reached, a sudden plunge into the pocket of
sovereigns would pay the postboys, another behind him
would render up the completed pages, and a third into
the pocket on the other side would give him the fresh
paper to carry forward the inexorable, unremitting work.

At this period there was a large sheet started in which
all the speeches of Parliament were reported verbatim
in order to preserve them for future reference — a monstrous plan which fell through after a time. For this
paper it was especially desired to have a speech of Mr.
Stanley accurately reported upon the condition of Ireland, containing suggestions for the amelioration of the
people's suffering. It was a very long and eloquent
speech and took many hours in the delivery. There were

eight reporters upon the work, each to work three-quarters of an hour and then to retire to write out his portion and be succeeded by the next. It happened that the roll of reporters was exhausted before the speech came to an end and C. D. was called in to report the last portions, which were very eloquent. This was on Friday, and on Saturday the whole was given to the press and the young reporter ran down to the country for a Sunday's rest. Sunday morning had scarcely dawned "when my poor father, who was a man of immense energy, surprised me by making his appearance. The speech had come into Mr. Stanley's hands, who was most anxious to have it correctly given in order to have it largely circulated in Ireland, and he found it all bosh, hardly a word right, except at the beginning and the end. Sending immediately to the office, he had obtained my sheets, at the top of which, according to custom, the name of the reporter was written, and, finding the name of Dickens, had immediately sent in search of me. My father, thinking this would be the making of me, came immediately, and I followed him back to London. I remember perfectly the look of the room and of the two gentlemen in it as I entered — Mr. Stanley and his father. They were extremely courteous, but I could see their evident surprise at the appearance of so young a man. For a moment as we talked I had taken a seat extended to me in the middle of the room. Mr. Stanley told me he wished to go over the whole speech, and if I was ready he would begin. Where would I like to sit? I told him I was very well where I was and we would begin immediately. He tried to induce me to sit elsewhere or more comfortably, but at that time in the House of Commons there was nothing but one's knees to write upon and I had formed the habit of it. Without further pause then he began, and went on hour after hour to the end, often becoming very much excited, bringing down his hand with violence upon the desk near which he stood and rising at the end into great eloquence.

"In these later years we never meet without that scene returning vividly to my mind, as I have no doubt it does to his also, but I, of course, have never referred to it, leaving him to do so if he shall ever think fit.

"Shiel was a small man with a queer high voice and spoke very fast. O'Connell had a fine brogue which he cultivated, and a magnificent eye. He had written a speech about this time upon the wrongs of Ireland, and, though he repeated it many, many times during three months when I followed him about the country, I never heard him give it twice the same, nor ever without being himself deeply moved." [1]

Mr. Dickens's imitation of Bulwer Lytton is so vivid that I feel as if it were taking a glimpse at the man himself. His deaf manner of speaking he represents exactly. He says he is very brilliant and quick in conversation, and knows everything!! He is a conscientious and unremitting student and worker. "I have been surprised to see how well his books wear. Lately I have reread

[1] In *Yesterdays with Authors* (see pp. 230–31), Fields made use, with revisions and omissions, of this portion of his wife's diary.

'Pelham' and I assure you I found it admirable. His speech at the dinner given to me just before leaving was well written, full of good things, but delivered execrably. He lacks a kind of confidence in his own powers which is necessary in a good speaker."

Speaking of O'Connell, Mr. Dickens said there had been nobody since who could compare with him but John Bright, who is at present the finest speaker in England. Cobden was fond of reasoning, and hardly what would be called a brilliant speaker; but his noble truthfulness and devotion to the cause to which he had pledged himself made him one of the grandest of England's great men. I asked about Mrs. Cobden. He told me she had been made very comfortable and in a beautiful manner. After her husband's death, his affairs having become involved by some bad investment he had made, a committee of six gentlemen came together to consider what should be done to commemorate his great and unparalleled devotion to his country. The result was, instead of having a public subscription for Mrs. Cobden with the many unavoidable and disagreeable features of such a step, each of these gentlemen subscribed about £12,000, thus making £70,000, a sufficient sum to make her most comfortable for life. . . .

I have forgotten to say how in those long rides from Edinburgh the mud dashed up and into the opened windows of the post-chaise, nor how they would be obliged to fling it off from their faces and even from the papers on which they wrote. As Dickens told us, he flung the imaginary evil from him as he did the real in the days long gone, and we could see him with the old disgust returned. He said, by the way, that never since those old days when he left the House of Commons as a Reporter had he entered it again. His hatred of the falseness of talk, of bombastic eloquence, he had heard there made it impossible for him ever to go in again to hear anyone.

Sunday, April 12. — Last night we went to the circus together, C. D., J., and I. It is a pretty building. I was astonished at the knowledge C. D. showed of everything before him. He knew how the horses were stenciled, how tight the wire bridles were, etc. The monkey was, however, the chief attraction. He was rather drunk or tired last night and did not show to good advantage, but he knew how to do all the things quite as well as the men. When the young rope-dancer slipped (he was but an apprentice at the business, without wages, C. D. thought), he tried over and over again to accomplish a certain somersault until he achieved it. "That 's the law of the circus," said C. D.; "they are never allowed to give up, and it 's a capital rule for everything in life. Doubtless this idea has been handed down from the Greeks or Romans and these people know nothing about where it came from. But it 's well for all of us." . . .

At six o'clock Mr. Dickens and Mr. Dolby came in to dinner. He seemed much revived both in health and spirits, in spite of the weather. . . .

Dickens talked of Frédérick Lemaître; he is upwards of sixty years old now; but he has always lived a wretched life, a low, poor fellow; yet he will surprise the actors continually by the new points he will make. He will come in at rehearsal, go about the stage in an abject wretched manner, with clothes torn and soiled as he has just emerged from his vulgar, vicious haunts, and without giving sign or glimmer of his power. Presently he says to the prompter, who always has a tallow candle burning on his box, "Give me your candle"; then he will blow it out and with the snuff make a cross upon his book. "What are you going to do, Frédérick?" the actors say. "I don't know yet; you'll see by and by," he says, and day after day perhaps will pass, until one night when he will suddenly flash upon them some wonderful point. They, the actors, watching him, try to hold themselves prepared, and if he gives them the least hint will mould their parts to fit his. Sometimes he will ask for a chair. "What will you do with it, Frédérick?" He does not reply, but night after night the chair is placed there until he makes his point. He often comes hungry to the theatre, and the manager must give him a dinner and pay for it before he will go on. Fechter, from whom these particulars come, tells Dickens that there can be nothing more wonderful than his acting in the old scene of the miserable father who kills his own son at the inn. The son, coming in rich and handsome, and seeing this old sot about to be driven from the porch by the servant, tells the man to give him meat and wine. While he eats and drinks, the wretch sees how freely the rich man handles his gold and resolves to kill him. Fechter's description, with his own knowledge of Lemaître, had so inspired Dickens that he was able to reproduce him again for us.

Wednesday, April 15. — [On returning from a reading in "Steinway Hall, than which nothing could be worse for reading or speaking"]: He soon came up after a little soup, when he called for brandy and lemons and made *such* a burnt brandy punch as has been seldom tasted this side of the "pond." As the punch blazed his spirits rose and he began to sing an old-fashioned comic song such as in the old days was given between the plays at the theatre. One song led to another until we fell into inextinguishable laughter, for anything more comic than his renderings of the chorus cannot be imagined. Surely there is no living actor who could excel him in these things if he chose to exert his ability. His rendering of "Chrush ke lan ne chous-kin!!" or a lingo which sounded like that (the refrain of an old Irish song) was something tremendous. We laughed till I was really afraid he would make himself too hoarse to read the next night. He gave a queer old song full of rhymes, obtained with immense difficulty and circumlocution, to the word "annuity," which it appeared has been sought by an old woman with great *assiduity* and granted with immense *incongruity*. The negro minstrels have in great part supplanted these queer old English, Irish, and Scotch ballads, but they are sure to come up again from time to time. We did not separate until 12, and felt the next morning (as he said) as if we had had a regular orgy. They did not forget, Dolby and he, to pay a proper tribute to "Mary-

land, My Maryland," and "Dixie" as very stirring
ballads.

[After another reading, from which Dickens came
home extremely tired]: We ran in at once to talk with
him and he soon cheered up. When I first pushed open
the door he was a perfect picture of prostration, his
head thrown back without support on the couch, the
blood suffusing his throat and temples again where he
had been very white a few minutes before. This is a
physical peculiarity with Dickens which I have never
seen before in a man, though women are very subject
to that thing. Excitement and exercise of reading will
make the blood rush into his hands until they become
at times almost black, and his face and head (especially
since he has become so fatigued) will turn from red to
white and back to red again without his being conscious
of it.

Friday, April 17. — Weather excessively warm, sky
often overcast. Last evening Mr. Dickens read again
and for the last time "Copperfield" and "Bob Sawyer."
He was much exhausted and said he watched a man
who was carried out in a fainting condition to see how
they managed it, with the lively interest of one who was
about to go through the same scene himself. The heat
from the gas around him was intolerable. After the
reading we went into his room to have a little soup,
"broiled bones," and a sherry cobbler. His spirits were
good in spite of fatigue, the thought of home and the
memories of England coming back vividly. We, finally,
from talk of English scenery, found ourselves in Strat-

ford. He says there is an inn at Rochester, very old, which he has no doubt Shakespeare haunted. This conviction came forcibly upon him one night as he was walking that way and discovered Charles's Wain setting over the chimney just as Shakespeare has described. "When you come to Gad's Hill, please God, I will show you Charles's Wain setting over the old roof."

We left him early, hoping he would sleep, but he hardly closed his eyes all night. Whether he was haunted by visions of home, or what the cause was, we cannot discover, but whatever it may be, his strength fails under such unnatural and continual excitement.

Saturday, April 18. — Mr. Dickens has a badly sprained foot. We like our rooms at his hotel — 47 is the number. Last night was "Marigold" and "Gamp" for the last time. He threw in a few touches for our amusement and a great deal of vigor into the whole. Afterward we took supper together, when he told us some remarkable things. Among others he rehearsed a scene described to him years ago by Dr. Eliotson of London of a man about to be hanged. His last hour had approached as the doctor entered the cell of the criminal, who was as justly sentenced as ever a wretch was for having cut off the end of his own illegitimate child. The man was rocking miserably in his chair back and forth in a weak, maudlin condition, while the clergyman in attendance, who had spoken of him as repentant and religious in his frame of mind, was administering the sacrament. The wine stood in a cup at one side until the sacred words were said, when at the proper moment the clergyman gave it to the man, who was still rocking backward and forward, muttering, "What will my poor mother think of this?" Finding the cup in his hands, he looked into it for a moment as if trying to collect himself, and then, putting on his regular old pothouse manner, he said, "Gen'lemen, I drink your health," and drained the cup in a drunken way. "I think," said C. D., "it is thirty years since I heard Dr. Eliotson tell me this, but I shall never forget the horror that scene inspired in my mind." The talk had taken this turn from the fact of a much-dreaded Press dinner which is to come off tonight and which jocosely assumed the idea of a hanging to their minds. C. D. said he had often thought how restricted one's conversation must become with a man who was to be hanged in half an hour. "You could not say, if it rains, 'We shall have fine weather tomorrow!' for what would that be to him? For my part, I think I should confine my remarks to the times of Julius Cæsar and King Alfred!!" He then related a story of a condemned man out of whom no evidence could be elicited. He would not speak. At last he was seated before a fire for a few moments, just before his execution, when a servant entered and smothered what fire there was with a huge hodful of coal. "*In half an hour that will be a good fire,*" he was heard to murmur.

Mr. Dickens has now read 76 times. It seems like a dream.

Sunday, April 19.—Last night the great New York Press dinner came off. It was a close squeeze with Mr. Dickens to get there at all. He had been taken

lame the night before, his foot becoming badly swollen
and painful. In spite of a skilful physician he grew worse
and worse every hour, and when the time for the dinner
arrived he was unable to bear anything upon his foot.
So long as he was above ground, however, it was a
necessity he should go, and an hour and a half after the
time appointed, with his foot sewed up in black silk, he
made his way to Delmonico's. Poor man! Nothing
could be more unfortunate, but he bore this difficult
part off in a stately and composed manner as if it were a
sign of the garter he were doffing for the first time instead of a badge of ill health. The worst of it is that the
papers will telegraph news of his illness to England.
This seems to disturb him more than anything else.
Ah! What a mystery these ties of love are — such pain,
such ineffable happiness — the only happiness. After
his return he repeated to me from memory every word
of his speech without dropping one. He never thinks of
such a thing as writing his speeches, but simply turns it
over in his mind and "balances the sentences," when he
is all right. He produced an immense effect on the Press
of New York, tremendous applause responding to every
sentence. Curtis's speech was very beautiful. "I think
him the very best speaker I ever heard," said C. D. "I
am sure he would produce a great effect in England from
the sympathetic quality he possesses." I have seldom
seen a finer exercise of energy of will than Mr. Dickens's
attendance on this dinner. It brought its own reward,
too, for he returned with his foot feeling better. He
made a rum punch in his room, where we sat until one

o'clock. After repeating his speech, he gave us an imitation of old Rogers as he would repeat a quatrain : —

> "The French have sense in what they do
> Which we are quite without,
> For what in Paris they call *goût*
> In England we call *gout*."

Mr. Dolby sat at dinner near a poor bohemian of great keenness of mind, Henry Clapp, by name, who said some things worthy of Rivarol or any other wittiest Frenchman we might choose to select. Speaking of Horace Greeley (the chairman at the dinner), he said : "He was a self-made man and worshipped his creator." Of Dr. O——, a vain and popular clergyman, that "he was continually looking for a vacancy in the Trinity." Of Mr. Dickens, that "nothing gave him so high an idea of Mr. Dickens's genius as the fact that he created Uriah Heep without seeing a certain Mr. Young (who sat near them), and Wilkins Micawber without being acquainted with himself (Henry Clapp)." Of Henry T—— that "he aimed at nothing and always hit the mark precisely." . . .

This speech of Mr. Dickens will make a fine effect, a reactionary effect, in the country. The enthusiasm for him knew no bounds. Charles Norton spoke for New England. I had a visit from him this morning as well as from Mr. Osgood, Dolby, etc. C. D. lunched at the Jockey Club with Dr. Barker and Donald Mitchell and returned to dine with us. He talked of actors, artists, and the clergy — church and religion — but was evidently suffering more or less all the time with his foot, yet kept up a good heart until nine o'clock, when he retired to the privacy of his own room. He feels bitterly the wrong under which English dissenters have labored for years in being obliged not only to support their own church interests in which they *do* believe, but also the abuses of the English Church against which their whole lives are a continual protest. He spoke of the beauty of the landscape through which we had both been walking and driving under a grey sky, with the eager spring looking out among leafless branches and dancing in the red and yellow sap. He said it had always been a fancy of his to write a story, keeping the whole thing in the same landscape, but picturing its constantly varying effects upon men and things and chiefly, of course, upon the minds of men. He asked me if I had ever read Crabbe's "Lover's Ride." We became indignant over a tax of five per cent which had just been laid upon the entire proceeds of his Readings, telegraphed to Washington, and found that it was unjust and had been taken off.

Monday, April 20. — Attended a meeting of a new "institution" just on foot, first called "Sorosis" and afterwards "Woman's League" for the benefit and mutual support of women. It was the first official meeting, but it proved so unofficial that I was entertained, and amused as well, and was able on my return to make Mr. Dickens laugh until he declared if anything could make him feel better for the evening that account of the Woman's League would.

Tuesday. — I find it very difficult today to write at

all. Mr. Dickens is on his bed and has been unable to
rise, in spite of efforts all day long. . . . Mr. Norton
has been here and we have been obliged to go out, but
our hearts have been in that other room all the time
where our dear friend lies suffering. . . . Oh! these
last times — what heartbreak there is in the words. I
lay awake since early this morning (though we did not
leave him until half-past twelve) feeling as if when I
arose we must say good-bye. How relieved I felt to
brush the tears away and know there was one more day,
but even that gain was lessened when I found he could
not rise and even this must be a day of separation too.
When Jamie told him last night he felt like erecting a
statue to him because of his heroism in doing his duty
so well, he laughed and said, "No, don't; take down one
of the old ones instead!"

The diary goes on to express the genuine sorrow of
Mrs. Fields and her husband at parting from a friend
who had so completely absorbed their affection, but in
terms which the diarist herself would have been the
first to regard as more suitable for manuscript than for
print. The pages that contain them throw more light
upon Mrs. Fields — a warm and tender light it is —
than upon Dickens. There is, however, one paragraph,
written after the Fieldses had returned to Boston from
New York, which tells something both of Dickens and
of Queen Victoria, in whose personality the public interest appears to be perpetual; and with this passage
the quotations from the diary shall end.

Friday, April 24. — After the Press dinner in New
York Mr. Dickens repeated all his speech to me, as I
believe I have said above, never dropping a word. "I
feel," he said, "as if I were listening to the sound of my
own voice as I recall it. A very curious sensation."
Jamie asked him if Curtis was quite right in the facts of
his speech. He said, "Not altogether, as, for instance,
in that matter about the Queen and our little play,
'Frozen Deep.' We had played it many times with considerable success, when the Queen heard of it and
Colonel Phipps (?) called upon me and said he wished
the Queen could see the play. Was there no hall which
would be appropriate for the occasion? What did I
think of Buckingham Palace? I replied that could not
be, for my daughters played in the piece and I had never
asked myself to be presented at court nor had I ever
taken the proper steps to introduce them there, and of
course they could not go as amateur performers where
they had never been as visitors. This seemed to trouble
him a good deal, so I said I would find some hall which
would be appropriate for the purpose and would appoint an evening, which I did immediately, taking the
Gallery of Illustration and having it fitted up for the
purpose. I then drew up a list of the company, chiefly
of artists, literary and scientific men, and interesting
ladies, which I caused to be submitted to the Queen,
begging her to reject or add as she thought proper, setting aside forty seats for the royal party. The whole
thing went off finely until after the first play was over,
when the Queen sent round a request that I would come

TAVISTOCK HOUSE THEATRE.

UNDER THE MANAGEMENT OF MR. CHARLES DICKENS.

On *Twelfth Night, Tuesday, January 6th,* 1857, AT A QUARTER BEFORE 8 O'CLOCK, *will be presented*

AN ENTIRELY NEW

ROMANTIC DRAMA, IN THREE ACTS, BY MR. WILKIE COLLINS,

CALLED

THE FROZEN DEEP.

The Machinery and Properties by MR. IRELAND, *of the Theatre Royal, Adelphi.   The Dresses by* MESSRS. NATHAN, *of Titchbourne Street, Haymarket.   Perruquier,* MR. WILSON, *of the Strand.*

THE PROLOGUE WILL BE DELIVERED BY MR. JOHN FORSTER.

CAPTAIN EBSWORTH, *of The Sea Mew*	MR. EDWARD PIGOTT.
CAPTAIN HELDING, *of The Wanderer*	MR. ALFRED DICKENS.
LIEUTENANT CRAYFORD	MR. MARK LEMON.
FRANK ALDERSLEY	MR. WILKIE COLLINS.
RICHARD WARDOUR	MR. CHARLES DICKENS.
LIEUTENANT STEVENTON	MR. YOUNG CHARLES.
JOHN WANT, *Ship's Cook*	MR. AUGUSTUS EGG, A.R.A.
BATESON ⎫ *Two of The Sea Mew's People*	MR. EDWARD HOGARTH.
DARKER ⎭	MR. FREDERICK EVANS.
(OFFICERS AND CREWS OF THE SEA MEW AND WANDERER.)	
MRS. STEVENTON	MISS HELEN.
ROSE EBSWORTH	MISS KATE.
LUCY CRAYFORD	MISS HOGARTH.
CLARA BURNHAM	MISS MARY.
NURSE ESTHER	MRS. WILLS.
MAID	MISS MARTHA.

THE SCENERY AND SCENIC EFFECTS OF THE FIRST ACT, BY MR. TELBIN.
THE SCENERY AND SCENIC EFFECTS OF THE SECOND AND THIRD ACTS, BY **Mr. STANFIELD, R.A.**
ASSISTED BY MR. DANSON.
THE ACT-DROP, ALSO BY **Mr. STANFIELD, R.A.**

AT THE END OF THE PLAY, HALF-AN-HOUR FOR REFRESHMENT.

To Conclude with MRS. INCHBALD's Farce, in Two Acts, of

ANIMAL MAGNETISM.

(THE SCENE IS LAID IN SEVILLE.)

THE DOCTOR	MR. CHARLES DICKENS.
PEDRILLO	MR. MARK LEMON.
THE MARQUIS DE LA GUARDIA	MR. YOUNG CHARLES.
GREGORIO	MR. WILKIE COLLINS.
CAMILLA	MISS KATE.
JACINTHA	MISS HOGARTH.

Musical Composer and Conductor of the Orchestra—Mr. **FRANCESCO BERGER**, who will preside at the Piano.

CARRIAGES MAY BE ORDERED AT HALF-PAST ELEVEN.

GOD SAVE THE QUEEN!

FACSIMILE PLAY–BILL OF "THE FROZEN DEEP," WITH DICKENS AS
ACTOR–MANAGER

and see her. This was considered an act of immense con-
descension and kindness on her part, and the little party
behind the scenes were delighted. Unfortunately, I had
just prepared myself for the farce which was to follow
and was already standing in motley dress with a red
nose. I knew I could not appear in that plight, so I
begged leave to be excused on that ground. However,
that was forgiven and all passed off well, although the
large expense of the whole thing of course fell on me,
which amounted to one hundred and fifty or two hundred pounds. Several years after, when Prince Albert
died, the Queen sent to me for a copy of the play. I told
Colonel Phipps the play had never been printed and
was the property of a gentleman, Mr. Wilkie Collins.
Then would I have it copied? So I had a very beautiful
copy made and bound in the most perfect manner, and
presented to her Majesty. Whereupon the Princess of
Prussia, seeing this, asked for another for herself. I said
I would again ask the permission of Mr. Collins and
again I had a beautiful with copy made great labor.
Then the Queen sent to ask the price of the books. I
sent word that my friend, Mr. Wilkie Collins, was a
gentleman who would, I was sure, hear to nothing of the
kind and begged her acceptance of the volumes." "How
has the Queen shown her gratitude for such favors?" I
said. "We have never heard anything more from her
since that time." Good Mr. Dolby said quietly, "You
know in England we call her 'Her Ungracious Majesty.'" Certainly one would not have believed it possible for even a queen's nature to have become so

hardened as this to the kindly acts of any human being, not to speak of the efforts of one of her most noble subjects and perhaps the greatest genius of our time.

If any reader wishes to follow the further course of the friendship between Dickens and the Fieldses, he has only to turn to "Yesterdays with Authors," in which many letters written by Dickens after April, 1868, are quoted, and many remembrances of their intercourse when the Fieldses visited England in 1869, the year before Dickens's death, are presented. Here it will suffice to quote one out of several passages in Mrs. Fields's diary relating to Dickens, and to bring to light a single characteristic little note from Dickens, not hitherto printed.

On Wednesday, May 12, 1869, Mrs. Fields wrote of Dickens: —

He drove us through the Parks in the fashionable afternoon hour and afterward to dine with him at the St. James, where Fechter and Dolby were the only outsiders. Mrs. Collins was like one of Stothard's pictures. I felt this more even after refreshing my memory of Stothard's coloring at the Kensington Museum yesterday. C. D. told me that the book of all others which he read perpetually and of which he never tired, the book which always appeared more imaginative in proportion to the fresh imagination he brings to it, a book for inexhaustiveness to be placed before every other book, is Carlyle's "French Revolution." When he was writing

"A Tale of Two Cities," he asked Carlyle if he might see some book to which he referred in his history. Whereat Carlyle sent down to him all his books, and Dickens read them faithfully; but the more he read the more he was astounded to find how the facts but passed through the alembic of Carlyle's brain and had come out and fitted themselves each as a part of the one great whole, making a compact result, indestructible and un-rivalled, and he always found himself turning away from the books of reference and rereading this marvel-lous new growth from those dry bones with renewed wonder.

The note from Dickens read : —

GAD'S HILL PLACE
HIGHAM BY ROCHESTER, KENT
Wednesday Sixth October, 1869

MY DEAR FIELDS :—

Delighted to enjoy the prospect of seeing you and yours on Saturday. Wish you had been at Birming-ham. Wish you were not going home. Wish you had had nothing to do with the Byron matter.[1] Wish Mrs. Stowe was in the pillory. Wish Fechter had gone over when he ought. Wish he may not go under when he ought n't.

With love,
Ever affectionately yours,
CHARLES DICKENS

[1] Mrs. Stowe's unhappily historic article on "The True Story of Lady Byron's Life" appeared in the *Atlantic Monthly* for September, 1869.

Wednesday Sixth October, 1869.

My Dear Fields

Delighted to enjoy the
prospect of seeing you and yours on
Saturday. Wish you had been at
Birmingham. Wish you were not going
home. Wish you had had nothing to do
with the Byron matter. Wish Mrs
Stowe was in the pillory. Wish
Fechter had gone over when he
ought. Wish he may not go under
when he oughtn't.

With love

Ever affectionately Yours

Charles Dickens

Facsimile note from Dickens to Fields

Among the papers preserved by Mrs. Fields there are, besides the manuscript letters of Dickens himself, many letters written after his death by his sister-in-law, Miss Georgina Hogarth. From bits of these, and especially from a letter written by Dickens's daughter, while his death was still a poignant grief, the affection in which he was held in his own household is touchingly imaged forth.

"All the Old World," wrote Miss Dickens, "all the New World loved him. He never had anything to do with a living soul without attaching them to him. If strangers could so love him, you can tell a little what he must have been to his own flesh and blood. It is a glorious inheritance to have such blood flowing in one's veins. I 'm so glad I have never changed my name."

From one of Miss Hogarth's letters a single passage may be taken, since it adds something of first-hand knowledge to the accessible facts about one piece of Dickens's writing which — in so far as the editor of these pages is aware — has never seen the light of print. This letter was written in the September after Dickens's death:

"I must now tell you about the beautiful little New Testament which he wrote for his children. I am sorry to say it is *never to be published*. It happens that he expressed that decided determination only last autumn to me, so we have no alternative. He wrote it years ago when his elder children were quite little. It is about sixteen short chapters, chiefly adapted from St. Luke's Gospel, most beautiful, most touching, most simple, as such a narrative should be. He never would have it printed and I used to read it to the little boys in MS. before they were old enough to read *writing* themselves. When Charley's children became old enough to have this kind of teaching, I promised Bessy (his wife) that I would make her a copy of this History, and I determined to do it as a Christmas Gift for her last year, but before I began my copy I asked Charles if he did not think it would be well for him to have it printed, at all events for *private* circulation, if he would not publish it (though I think it is a pity he would never do that!). He said he would look over the MS. and take a week or two to consider. At the end of the time he gave it back to me and said he had decided *never to publish it — or even have it privately printed*. He said I might make a copy for Bessy, or for any one of his children, *but for no one else*, and that he also begged that we would never even lend the MS., or a copy of it, to any one to take out of the house; so there is no doubt about his *strong feeling* on the subject, and we must obey it. I made my copy for Bessy and gave it to her last Christmas. After his death the original MS. became *mine*. As it was never published, of course it did not count as one of Mr. Forster's MSS., and therefore it was one of his private papers, which were left to me. So I gave it at once to Mamie, who was, I thought, the most natural and proper possessor of it, as being his eldest daughter. You must come to England and read it, dear Friend! as we must not send it to you! We should be glad to see you and to show it to you and Mr. Fields in our own house."

Miss Hogarth must have known full well that, if this manuscript Gospel according to Charles Dickens was to be shown to anybody outside his immediate circle, he himself would have chosen the Charles Street friends from what he called — to them — his "native Boston."

VI

STAGE FOLK AND OTHERS

HAD anyone crossed the Charles Street threshold of the Fieldses with the expectation of encountering within none but the New England Augustans, he would soon have found himself happily disillusioned, even at a time when there was no Dickens in Boston. As it was in reality, so must it be in these pages, if they are to fulfill their purpose of restoring a vanished scene, the variety of which must indeed be counted among its most distinctive characteristics. The pages that follow will accordingly serve to illustrate the familiar fact that the pudding of a "family party" is often rendered the more acceptable by the introduction of a few plums not plucked from the domestic tree.

Mrs. Fields once noted in her diary the circumstance that, when her husband came to Boston from Portsmouth at the age of fourteen, and began to work as a "boy" in the bookshop of Carter & Hendee, the second of these employers had a box at the theatre and, to keep his young employees happy, used constantly to ask one or more of them to see a play in his company. Thus enabled in his youth to see such actors as the elder Booth, Fanny Kemble and her father, and many others of the best players to be seen in America at the time, Fields acquired a love of the theatre and of stage folk which stood him in good stead throughout his life. A

JAMES T. FIELDS AT FIFTEEN
From a drawing by a French painter

certain exuberance in his own nature must have sought a response in social contacts other than those of the straiter sect of his local contemporaries. In men and women of the stage, in authors from beyond the compass of the local horizon, writers with whom he formed relations in his double capacity of editor and publisher, in artists and public men outside the immediate "literary" circle of Boston, Fields took an unceasing delight, shared by his wife, and still communicable through her journals.

From their pages, then, I propose to assemble here a group of passages relating first to stage folk, and then to others, and, since these records so largely explain themselves, to burden them as lightly as possible with explanations. Slender as certain of the entries are, each contributes something to a recovery of the time and of the persons that graced it.

Thomas Bailey Aldrich, says his biographer, used to declare in his later years, "Though I am not genuine Boston, I am Boston-plated." His intimate relation with Boston began in 1865, through the publication of a "Blue and Gold" edition of his poems by the firm of which Fields was a member, and the beginning of his editorship of "Every Saturday," an illustrated journal issued under the same auspices. His range of acquaintance before that time was such that when the "plating" process began, — it was really more like a transmutation of metals, — he sometimes served as a

sympathetic link between his new Boston and his old
New York. It was in New York, only a few weeks
after the assassination of Lincoln, that Aldrich appears
in the diary, fresh from seeing his friend, Edwin
Booth.

May 3, 1865. — An hour before we went to tea,
Aldrich came to see us. He said he and Launt Thompson were staying with Edwin Booth alternate nights
during this season of sorrow; that it was "all right
between himself and the lady he was about to marry."
Then he described to us the first night while Booth was
plunged in agony. He said the gas was left burning low
and the bed stood in the corner, just where he lay sleep-
less, looking at a fearfully good crayon portrait of Wilkes
Booth which glared at him over the gas. Launt Thompson started with the mother from New York for Philadelphia, where she was going to join her daughter the
day that John Wilkes was shot, and an extra containing
the news was brought them by a newsboy as they
stepped on the ferry-boat. The old woman would have
the paper. "He was her 'Johnny' after all," said T. B. A.

Friday. — Have seen a lady who knows the person to
whom Booth is engaged — said that her letter telling
him she was true passed his letter of relinquishment on
its way to Philadelphia. She thinks these two women
have saved Booth. "I have been loved too well," he
said once. . . .

Aldrich said we should not have been more astonished to hear he himself had done the terrible deed than

he was to know Wilkes Booth had done it. "He was so gentle, gentler than I, and very handsome — a slight, beautiful figure," and (as he described the face, it was the Greek Antinous kind of beauty there) I could not but reflect how the deed may deform the man. Nobody said he was beautiful after he was dead, but they laid a cloth upon the face and said how dreadful. It has been a strange experience to come among the people who know the family. I hoped I should be spared this, but the soul of good in things evil God means we should all see.

Sunday, May 7. — A radiant day. Went to hear Dr. Bellows — a grand discourse. After service sat in his drawing-room and talked and then walked together. . . . He too has been to see Edwin Booth. The poor fellow said to him, "Ah! if it had been a fellow like myself who had done this dreadful deed, the world would not have wondered — but Johnny!!"

Wednesday, January 3, 1866. — Dined with the Grahams and went to see Booth upon the occasion of his reappearance. The unmoved sadness of the young man and the unceasing plaudits of the house, half filled with his friends, were impressive and made it an occasion not to be forgotten.

September 23, 1866. — Edwin Booth and the Aldriches came to tea; also Tom Beal and Professor Sterry Hunt of Montreal, the latter late. Booth came in the twilight while a magnificent red and purple and gold sunset was staining the bay. The schooners anchored just off shore had already lighted their lanterns and swung them in the rigging, and the full moon cast a silver sheen over the scene. I hear he passes every Sunday morning while here at the grave of his wife in Mt. Auburn. He seems deeply saddened. He was very pleasant, however, and ready to talk, and gave amusing imitations — in particular of his black boy, Jan, who possesses, he says, the one accomplishment of forgetting everything he ought to remember. One day a man with a deep tragic voice, "Forrestian," he said, came to him with letters of introduction asking Mr. Booth to assist him as he was about to go to England. Mr. B. told him he knew no one in England and could do nothing for him, he was sorry. If he ever found it possible to do him a service he would with pleasure. With that Mr. B. turned, — they were in the vestibule of the theatre — and entered the box-office to speak to someone there; immediately he heard the deep voice addressing Jan with "You are with Mr. Booth." "Yes," responded Jan with real negro accent, "I'm wid Mr. Booth." "In what capacity — are you studying?" "Yaas," returned Jan, unblushingly, "I'se studyin'." "What are you upon now?" "Oh, Richelieu, Hamlet, an' a few of dese yer." "Ah, I should be pleased to enter into correspondence with you while I am abroad. Would you have any objections?" "Oh, no, no objection, no objection at all." "Thank you, sir; good-day, sir." With that they parted and Jan came with his mouth stretched wide with laughter. "Massa, what is 'correspond'? I told him I'd correspond, what'd he mean, correspond?" Then Jan, convulsed with his joke, roared and

Hotel Vendome
June 17ᵗ

My dear Mrs Fields
Although my daughter volunteered to convey my thanks to you for your kindly thoughts of me — I being much hurried at the time that your gift of the quaint old document reached me I must re-iterate my the acknowledgements of that, and the gracious words you wrote regarding my performance of Iago — in the ... of the play which Mr. Barrett & I gave for the actor's benefit

Sincerely & with great respect I am
truly yours
Edwin Booth

Facsimile note from Booth to Mrs. Fields

roared again. They are surely a merry race, but provoking enough sometimes. They are capable of real attachments, however; this man has been several times dismissed but will not go. Booth told everything very dramatically, but I was especially struck with his description of a man travelling with two shaggy terrier pups in the cars. He had them in a basket and hung them up over his head and then composed himself to sleep. Waking up half an hour later, he observed a man on the opposite side of the car, his eyes starting from his head and the very picture of dismay, as if a demon were looking at him. The owner of the pups, following the direction of the man's eyes, looked up and saw the two pups had their heads out of the basket. He quietly made a sign for them to go back and they disappeared. The man's gaze did not apparently slacken, however, but in a moment became still more horrified when the pups again looked out. "What's the matter?" said the owner. "What are those?" said the man, pointing with trembling finger; "pray excuse me, but I have been on a spree and I thought they were demons." He introduced the subject of the stage and talked of points in "Hamlet," which he had made for the first time, but occasionally through accident had omitted. The next day he will be sure to be asked by letter or newspaper why he omits certain points which would be so excellent to make, *the writer thinks*. He has had a life of strange vicissitudes, as almost all actors. He referred last night to his frequent travels during childhood over the Alleghanies with his father, of long nights spent in

BOOTH AS HAMLET

this kind of travel; and once in Nevada he walked fifty miles chiefly through snow. "Why?" said Lilian. "Because I was hard up, Lily," he continued; "I walked it too in stage boots which were too tight — it was misery." . . .

They had all gone by half-past ten, but we lay long awake thinking over poor Booth and his strange sad fortune. Hamlet, indeed!—although Forceythe Willson says, "I have been to see Mr. Hamlet play Booth." Yes, perhaps when he is playing it for the 400th time with a bad cold, it may seem so; indeed I found it dullish myself, or his part, I mean, the other night; but he *did* play it once — the night of his reappearance in New York.

May 18, 1869. — Last Sunday evening Booth, Aldrich and his wife and sister, Dr. Holmes and Amelia and Launt Thompson, Leslie and ourselves took tea here together. In the evening came Mr. and Mrs. Emerson. We did have a rare and delightful symposium. Booth talked little as usual, and the next night went round to Aldrich's and took himself off as he behaves in company!! Nevertheless he was glad to see Holmes, though every time Dr. H. addressed him across the table he seemed to receive an electric shock.

A chance meeting between William Warren and Fields in a lane at the seaside Manchester is recorded, with their talk, in the diary as early as 1865. Two entries in 1872 have to do with Jefferson, first alone and then with Warren. The friendship with Jefferson, begun so long ago, was continued until his death.

Tuesday, March 18, 1872. — Left Boston for a short trip to New York. Jefferson the actor, famous throughout the world for his impersonation of "Rip Van Winkle," was on the train and finding us out (or J. him), came to our compartment car to pass the day. He talked without cessation and without effort. He described his sudden disease of the eyes quite bravely and simply, from the use of too much whiskey. He said the newspapers had said it was the gas, and many other reasons had been assigned first and last; but he firmly believed there was no other reason than too much whiskey. He had taken the habit — when he was somewhat below his ordinary physical and mental condition in the evening and wished to rise to the proper point and "carry the audience" — of taking a small glass of whiskey. This glass was after a time made two, and even three or four. Finally he was stricken down by a trouble of the eyes which threatened the entire extinction of sight. His physician at once suggested that unnatural use of stimulants was the cause, of which he himself is now entirely convinced and no longer touches anything stronger than claret. He has played to a larger variety of audiences probably than almost any other great actor. The immense applause he received in England, where he played 170 consecutive nights at the Adelphi in London, always as "Rip," has only

served to make him more modest, it would seem, more
desirous to uphold himself artistically.   He gave us a
hint of his taste for fishing and described his trout-rais-
ing establishment in Jersey; very curious and wonderful it was.   Nature preserves only one in a hundred of
the eggs of trout to come to maturity.   Mr. Jefferson
in his pond is able to raise 85 out of 100.   There seems
no delight to him so great as that of sitting beside a
stream on a sunny day, line in hand.

Talking of the everlasting repetition of "Rip," he
says he should be thankful to rest himself with another
play, but this has been a growth and it would be a daring thing for him to attempt anything new with a public
who would always compare him with himself in this play
which is the result of years of his best thought and
strength.   I think myself, if he were quite well he would
be almost sure to attempt something else.   He told us
several stories very dramatically.   He is an odd, care-
lessly dressed little mortal, a cross between Charles
Lamb and Grimaldi, but we have seldom passed a more
delightful day of talk than with him.   The hours absolutely fled away.

Wednesday, May 22, 1872. — Mr. Longfellow, Dr.
Holmes, and Jefferson and Warren, the two first come-
dians of our time, dined here.   The hour was three
o'clock, to accommodate the two professional gentlemen.
The hours until three, with the exception of two visits
(Miss Sara Clarke and Miss Wainwright in spite of saying "engaged"), were occupied in making preparations
for the little feast.   I mean the hours after breakfast until

time to dress. (Of hours before breakfast I have now-a-days nothing to say. I am not strong enough to do anything early, but country life this summer is to change all that.) Mr. Jefferson and Mr. Warren arrived first. Finding much to interest them in the pictures of our lower room, they lingered there a few moments before coming to the library, when we talked of Marney's pictures (Mr. J. owns some of his water-colors) and looked about at others. Soon Longfellow came with Jamie. He said he felt like one on a journey. He left home early in the morning, had been sight-seeing in Boston all day, was to dine and go to the theatre with us afterward.

He asked Mr. Warren why a Mr. Inglis was selling his fine library and pictures — a question nobody had been able to solve. Mr. Inglis is, however, in some way connected with the stage, and Warren told us it was because he had been arrested with Mr. Harvey Parker and others and condemned to be thrown in the House of Correction, for selling liquor. His money protected him from the rigor of the law, but the disgrace remained. His children felt it much and he was going to Europe at least for a season. We could not help feeling the injustice of this when we remembered the myriad liquor shops for the poor all over the town, with which no one interferes.

Mr. Jefferson was deeply interested in our pictures of the players by Zanaçois. Dr. Holmes came in, talked a little at my suggestion about Anne Whitney's bust of Keats, which he appears to know nothing about artistically (I observed the same lack of knowledge in Emer-

son), but he criticised the hair. He said he supposed
nothing was known about Keats's hair, so it might as
well be one way as another. I told him on the contrary
I owned some of it; whereat I got it out, and he went
off in a little episode about an essay which he had sometimes thought of writing about hair. He has a machine
by which the size of a hair can be measured and recorded. This he would like to use, and make a note of
comparison between the hairs of "G. W." (as he laughingly called Washington), Jefferson, Milton, and other
celebrities of the earth. He thought it might be very
curious to discover the difference in quality.

We were soon seated at the table (only six all told)
where the conversation never flagged. Longfellow properly began it by saying he thought Mr. Charles Mathews
was entirely unjust to Mr. Forrest as King Lear. He
considered Mr. Forrest's rendering of the part, and he
sat through the whole, as fine and close to nature. He
could not understand Mr. Mathews's underrating it as
he did. Of course the other two gentlemen could say
nothing more than the difficulty Mr. Mathews from
his nature would have in estimating at its proper worth
anything Mr. Forrest might do, their idea of Art being
so dissimilar. Here arose the question if one actor was a
good judge of another. Jefferson said he sometimes
thought actors very bad judges — indeed he preferred
to be judged by an audience inspired by feeling rather
than by one intellectually critical.

Jefferson has a clear blue eye, very fine and bright
and sweet. Longfellow thinks his mouth a very weak

one, and certainly his face is not impressive. Warren appears a man of finer intellect and more wit. He had many witty things to say and his little tales were always dramatically given. Dr. Holmes could not seem to recover from the idea that Jefferson had made a fortune out of one play and that he *never* played but one. "I hear, Mr. Jefferson," he said, when he first came in, "that you have been playing the same play ever since you came here." (He has been playing the same for a dozen years, I believe, nearly — and has been here *three weeks!*) Jefferson could hardly help laughing as he assured him that for the space of three weeks he had given the same every night. Dr. Holmes had a way at the table of talking of "you actors," "you gentlemen of the stage," until I saw Longfellow was quite disturbed at the unsympathetic unmannerliness of it, in appearance, and tried to talk more than ever in a different strain.

After I left the table, which I did because I thought they might like to smoke, Jamie sent for Parsons's poems and read them some of the finest. Of course the talk was wittier and quicker as the time came to separate, but I cannot report upon it. The impression the two actors left upon me, however, was rather that of men who enjoyed coming up to the surface to breathe a natural air seldom vouchsafed to them than of men sparring with their wits — they are affectionate, gentle, subdued gentlemen and a noble contrast to the self-opinionated ignorance which we often meet in society. Dr. Holmes was, however, the wit of the occasion, as he always is, and everybody richly enjoyed his sallies.

JEFFERSON IN THE BETROTHAL SCENE OF "RIP VAN WINKLE"

They stayed until the last moment — indeed I do not see how they got to their two theatres in time to dress. It must have been, as they say of eggs, a "hard scrabble." *We* went afterward — we four — to see a new actor, Raymond, play "Colleen Bawn" at the Globe — pretty play, though very touching and melodramatic, by Boucicault. I must confess to dislike such plays where your feelings are wrought to the highest pitch for nothing.

The name of Fechter is familiar to the middle-aged through the memory of fathers, to the young through that of grandfathers. Readers of these pages will recall that Dickens, soon after reaching America in 1867, spoke of him in terms which caused Mrs. Fields to look forward with confidence to a new friendship. His coming to America was specifically heralded by an article, "On Mr. Fechter's Acting," contributed by Dickens to the "Atlantic" for August, 1869. When Fechter was in Boston, warmly received as Dickens's friend, he often appears in the journals of Mrs. Fields, in conjunction with others.

Friday, February 25, 1870. — Mr. Fechter came to lunch with Mr. Longfellow, Mr. Appleton, Mr. and Mrs. Dorr. He talked freely about his Hamlet, so different from all other impersonations. His audience here he finds wonderfully good, better than any other; fine points which have never been applauded before bring

out a round of applause. On the whole he appears to
enjoy new hearers — does not understand the constant
comparison between himself and Booth. They are already great friends. Booth was in the house the last
night of his performance there; afterward he did not
come to speak to him, and Fechter felt it; but a letter
came yesterday saying he was so observed that he
slipped away as soon as possible, and could not come on
Sunday because visitors prevented him. Better late
than never; it was pleasant to Fechter to hear from
Booth — with one exception : he enclosed a notice from
some newspaper, cutting up himself horribly and prais-
ing Fechter. "Ah! that won't do; I shall send it back
to him and tell him why. We are totally unlike in our
Hamlets, and neither should be praised at the other's
expense."

Mr. Fechter described minutely Mr. Dickens's attack of paralysis last year, and, the year before, his
prompt appearance in the box of the theatre at the last
performance of "No Thoroughfare," which he said he
should do; but as Fechter had not heard of his return
from America, it was a great shock. "If it had been
'Hamlet,' or any difficult play, I could not have gone on !
He should not have done such a thing." He told us a
strange touching story of M'lle Mars, during her last
years. She came upon the stage one night to give one
of the youthful parts in which she had once been so
famous. When she appeared, some heartless wretch
threw her a wreath of immortelles, as if for her grave.
She was so shocked that the drops stood on her brow,

A NAST CARTOON OF DICKENS AND FECHTER

the rouge fell from her cheeks, and she stood motionless before the audience, a picture of age and misery. She could not continue her part.

He spoke with intense enthusiasm of Frédérick Lemaître, much as I have heard Mr. Dickens do. "The second-class actors were always arguing with him (only second-class people argue) and saying, 'Why do you wish me to stand here, Frédérick?' 'I don't know,' he would say, 'only do it.'"

Mr. Appleton was deeply interested in the fact that Shakespeare proved himself such a believer in ghosts, as "Hamlet" shows, and would like to push the subject farther, Mr. Fechter evidently finding much to say on this topic also. Mr. Longfellow was interested to ask about the Dumas, *père et fils*. Mr. Fechter has known them well and has many queer stories to tell of their relation to each other. *Le fils* calls *mon père*, "my youngest child born many years ago," and the father usually introduces the son as M. Dumas, *mon père*. The motto on Fechter's note paper is very curious and a type of the man — "*Faiblesse vaut vice*." Mr. Longfellow spoke again of Mr. Dickens's restlessness, of his terrible sadness. "Yes, yes," said Fechter, "all his fame goes for nothing." . . .

Jamie is so weak that he went to sleep almost as soon as they were gone. God knows what it all means; I do not.

It is odd that Fechter's eyes should be brown after all. They look so light in the play. He is a round little man, naturally friendly, spontaneous. We do not know what his life has been, and we will not ask; that does not rest with us; but he is a very fine artist. His imitation of Mr. Dickens, as he sat on the lawn watching him at work, or as he joined him coming from his desk at lunch-time with tears on his cheek and a smile on his mouth, was very close to the life and delightful.

Mr. Longfellow did not talk much, not as much as the last time he was here, but he was lovely and kind.[1] He brought a coin of the French Republic which had been touched by French wit, *Liberté* x (point), *Egalité* x (point), *Fraternité* x (point). And more to the same effect, without altering the coin.

Appleton has just bought a new Troyon, which he says he shall lend me for a week.

At the end of the following August there is a record of a talk with Fechter on the boat from Boston to Nahant, where he and the Fieldses dined with Longfellow. Dickens had died in the June just past, and Fechter had much to say of him and his family life. "Day by day," wrote Mrs. Fields, "I am grateful to think of him at rest." The little party at Nahant is described.

[1] On April 20, 1870, Longfellow wrote to Fields (See *Life of Henry Wadsworth Longfellow*, etc., edited by Samuel Longfellow, III, 148) : —
"Some English poet has said or sung:

'At the close of the day, when the hamlet is still,
And mortals the sweets of forgetfulness prove.'

"I wish Hamlet would be still! I wish I could prove the sweets of forgetfulness! I wish Fechter would depart into infinite space, and 'leave, oh, leave me to repose!' When will this disturbing star disappear, and suffer the domestic planetary system to move on in the ordinary course and keep time with the old clock in the corner?"

We found dear Longfellow looking through a glass to espy our approach, and all his dear little girls and Ernest and his wife and Appleton, who whisked me away from the dinner-table to his studio where he had some really good sketches. The conversation at table was half French, Longfellow and Appleton both finding it agreeable to recall the foreign scenes by the foreign tongue. But except a queer imitation of John Forster, by Fechter, I do not remember any quotable talk. F. said Forster always looked at everybody as if regarding their qualifications for a lunatic asylum (he is commissioner of lunacy), saying to himself, "Well, I'll let you off *today*, but tomorrow you must certainly go and be shut up." He describes Forster's present state of health as something very precarious and wretched.

November 14, 1870. — Monday night went to see Fechter in "Claude Melnotte." Longfellow and his daughter Edith sat in the box adjoining ours. It was the stage box where they were sheltered from observation; ours was the box next it, to be sure, but accessible to all eyes. During the curtain Longfellow came into our box; Mrs. Holmes and Mrs. Andrew were with me, both plain ladies dressed in mourning. His advent caused a little rustle of curiosity to ripple over the house. Longfellow was never looking finer than he is today. His white hair and deep blue eyes and kind face make his presence a benediction wherever he goes — of such men one cannot help feeling what Dr. Putnam so well expressed last Sunday in speaking of the presence of our Lord at a feast. "He rewarded the hospitality of his friends by his presence."

Longfellow brought an illegible scrawl in his hand which Parsons had written from London to Lunt. He told me also of having lately received a photograph from Virginia of a young woman, and written under it were the words, "What fault can be found with this?" He said he thought of replying, "The fault of too great youth." It certainly could not be agreeable to him to sit in the eye of the audience as he did; but he was very talkative and pleasant, expressed his disappointment at not having us at his Nilsson dinner, but his family were too many for him; said how he liked her for her frankness; told me of the old impressario Garrett, the Jew, coming without invitation and certainly without being wanted (as it sent "his children upstairs to dine"); and then, as the play was about to begin, he withdrew. He was much amused and disgusted by the platitudes of the play. Returned to his own box, Jamie said he laughed immoderately over the absurdities of it as it continued. He tooted as the instruments tooted and spouted as the second-rate actors spouted, all of which was highly amusing to Edith, who was weeping over the unhappy lovers, utterly absorbed in the play. Mrs. Holmes and Mrs. Andrew, too, were full of tears, and I found it no use attempting to say anything more during the evening.

Fechter was indeed marvellous. He raised the play into something human, something exquisite whenever he was upon the stage. His terrible earnestness sweeps the audience utterly away. But he is not the player for the million.

Sunday evening, December 11, 1870. — Went to Mr. Bartol's and met Mr. Collyer. He was pleased to hear what Fechter said of him Saturday night (by the by we met Fechter at Mrs. Dorr's dinner on Saturday), that he singled him out, found him a capital audience, and played to him. It was a fine house on Saturday and Fechter played "Don Cæsar." It was never played better. Curtis was there, and fine company. Fechter was graceful and saucy too in talk at dinner — just right for the occasion.

Monday, December 19. — I have just returned from seeing Fechter in "Ruy Blas." The public has just received the news that he is to leave the Globe Theatre and Boston in four weeks. The result was an enormous house, and the most fashionable house I have seen this season. He played with great fire and ease, but he has a wretched cold and his pronunciation was so thick and French (as it is apt to be when he is excited) that I could often hardly catch a word. But his audience was determined to be pleased and they caught and applauded all his good points. I saw but one dissenting spirit, that was a spoiled queen of fashion just returned from Europe, who saw nobody and nothing but herself. . . .

Saturday, January 7, 1871. — Dined at Mr. Longfellow's with Mr. Fechter. The poet welcomed us with a cordiality peculiar to himself and his children, with a simple glad-to-see written over their faces which is worth a world of talk. We had a merry table-talk although Fechter was laboring under the unnatural excitement of his position in having lost his season at the Globe, broken with the proprietor Cheney who was his friend, and finding himself without an engagement for the time. Also, so mischance held the day, Miss Leclercq, his only fit support, injured herself in the afternoon and their superb audience went away disappointed. However, the dinner went off beautifully, as it always must with Longfellow at the helm. There was some talk of poetry and the drama and J. amused them too with anecdotes. Then we adjourned to the room of Charles the East-India man, where we saw many curiosities and had a very pleasant hour before leaving. Passing through the dressing-room of our dear Longfellow, I was struck with seeing how like the house of a German student it was — a Goethean aspect of simplicity and largeness everywhere — books too are put on all the walls. It is surely a most attractive house.

January 13, 1871. — Today Jamie lunched with Appleton. We passed the evening at Mrs. Quincy's. It is the great benefit to Fechter, but in consequence of the tickets being sold unjustly at auction, we shall not go. Unhappily there are rumors about town that Fechter is to be insulted in the theatre. I wish I could get word to him. I shall wait until J. gets home and then ask him to drive up to put F. on his guard.

January 23. — It proved an unnecessary alarm! The evening went off well enough but unenthusiastically, and at last Fechter gave all the money to the poor!

When Mrs. Fields first met that representative of
the once alluring art of "elocution," James E. Murdoch, he was already a veteran who had twice, at
an interval of nearly twenty years, retired from the
stage.   Two notes about him recall his robust personality.

January 13, 1867. — I never met James E. Murdoch,
the actor, to hear any talk until Sunday night. The
knowledge of his patriotism, of his son who died in the
war, and of the weary miles the father had travelled to
comfort the soldiers by reading to them, and afterwards
the large sums of money he had given to the country's
cause gathered up laboriously night by night by public
"readings" — all this I had known. Of course no introduction could have been better, yet I liked the man even
more than I had fancied was possible. He was so modest
and talked in such a free generous way, purely for the
entertainment of others, I fancied, because we saw he
had a severe cold on his chest. The way too in which he
recited "Sheridan's Ride" and anything else for the
children which he thought they would like was quite
beautiful to see in a man of his years, who must have
had quite enough of that kind of thing to do. His hobby
is elocution. He is about to establish a school or college or something of that description, whatever its
honorable title will be, at the West[1] (the money having
been granted in part by legislature, the other half
to be made by his own public efforts) for the pur-

[1] A contemporary definition of Cincinnati.

pose of educating speakers and teaching men and women how to read. He has known Grant and Sheridan well, lived in camp with them at the same mess-table, and has the highest opinion of the patriotism and probity of both of them. There is no mistake about one thing. Mr. Murdoch made himself a power during the war, and now that is over does not cease to work, nor does he allow himself to presume upon the laurels he has won nor to brag of his own work.

Saturday morning, November 13, 1875. — After a western journey, left for home. Sunday met James E. Murdoch in the cars at Springfield. It was about six o'clock A.M., but he was bound for Newton. He came in therefore with us, and talked delightfully until we parted. He is an old man but as full of nerve, vigor, and ripened intellect as anyone whom I have seen. His talk of the stage, of his disgust for Macready's book, his disgust at the manner in which Forrest treated his wife, his account of his own experiences, when he was glad to play for $35 a week, were deeply interesting. The better side of Forrest he understood and appreciated thoroughly.

The hospitalities of Charles Street were by no means confined to the men of the theatrical and kindred professions. In later years Miss Ellen Terry, Lady Gregory, and those other ladies associated with the stage who so surely found their way to Mrs. Fields's door when they visited Boston, were but carrying on the

JAMES E. MURDOCH AND WILLIAM WARREN

traditions of the earlier decades. As the visitors came and went, the diary in the sixties and seventies recorded their exits and their entrances. A few passages are typical of many.

A portion of the notes relating to Charlotte Cushman will be the better understood for a preliminary remark upon a Boston event of huge local moment in the autumn of 1863. This was the dedication of the Great Organ, that wonder of the age, in Music Hall. The first public performance on the organ, at the ceremonies on the evening of November 2, were preceded by Charlotte Cushman's reading of a dedicatory ode, contributed, according to the "Advertiser" of the next day, by an "anonymous lady of this city." The secret of Mrs. Fields's authorship of this poem, which the "Advertiser" found somewhat too long in spite of its merits, must have been shared by some of her friends, though it was temporarily kept from the public.

Sunday, September 20, 1863. — In the evening Charlotte Cushman and her niece, Dr. Dewey and Miss McGregor, Miss Mears and Mr. W. R. Emerson, passed a few hours with us. Charlotte, always of athletic but prejudiced mind, talked busily of people and events. She is a Seward-ite in politics and called Dr. Howe and Judge Conway "ass-sy" because they said Charles Sumner had prevented thus far a war with England. She has made money during the war, but believes apparently not at all in the patriotism of the people. She is to give one performance for "the Sanitary" in each of the four northern seacoast cities, also for fun and fame. She can't endure to give up the stage. She is a woman of effects. She lives for effect, and yet doing always good things and possessed of most admirable qualities. She has warm friends. Mrs. Carlyle is extremely fond of her, gives her presents and says flattering things to her. "Cleverer than her husband," says Miss Cushman. I put this quietly into my German pipe and puff peacefully.

Saturday Evening, September 26, 1863. — Charlotte Cushman played Lady Macbeth for the benefit of the Sanitary Commission to a large audience. Her reading of the letter when she first appears is one of her finest points. She moves her feet execrably and succeeds in developing all the devilish nature in the part, but discovers no beauty. Yet it is delightful to hear the wondrous poetry of the play intelligently and clearly rendered. It would be impossible to say this of the man who played Macbeth, who talked of "encarnardine," and "heat-oppre*st* brain," for "oppressèd," besides innumerable other faults and failures, which he mouthed too much for me to discover. Charlotte in the sleeping scene was fine — that deep-drawn breath of sleep is thrilling. . . .

There has been an ode written to be spoken at the organ opening. No one is to know who wrote it. Miss Cushman will speak it if they are speedy enough in their finishing. This is of interest to many. I trust they will be ready for Miss Cushman.

Monday, November 2, 1863. — Miss Dodge and Una

FROM A CRAYON PORTRAIT OF CHARLOTTE CUSHMAN

Hawthorne came to dine. At 7 o'clock we all started for the Music Hall. Miss Cushman read my ode in a most perfect manner. She was very nervous about it and skipped something, but what she did read was perfect. Her dress and manner too were dignified and beautiful. It was a night never to be forgotten. Afterward we had a little supper. Dr. and Mrs. Holmes, Mr. Ogden of New York, Dr. Upham[1] and Judge Putnam and Mrs. Howe were added to our other guests. Charlotte Cushman left early the next day and Gail Hamilton and I sat down and took a long delicious draught of talk.

April 27, 1871. — Charlotte Cushman came to see us yesterday. Her full brain was brimming over, and her rich sympathetic voice is ringing now in my ears. She does not overestimate herself, that woman, which is part of her greatness, for the word *does* apply to her in a certain way because she grows nearer to it every day. J. de Maistre refused the epithet "grand" to Napoleon because he lacked more stature — but this hand-to-hand fight with death over herself (loving life dearly as she does) has strengthened her hold upon her affection for life, insensibly. She grows daily wiser and nobler.

November 13, 1871. — We all went together to Charlotte Cushman's début in Queen Katherine at the Globe Theatre. A house filled with her friends and a noble piece of acting. She spoke to every woman's heart there; by this I felt the high art and the noble sympathetic nature far above art which was in the woman and

---

[1] Dr. J. Baxter Upham, the moving spirit in the building of the Music Hall and the installation of the organ. He presided at its dedication.

radiates from her. Much of the play beside was poor, but Mrs. Hunt was very amusing and we laughed and laughed at her sallies until I was quite ashamed. J. went behind the scenes and talked with C. C. She was in first-rate condition.

For other contacts with the stage, three brief passages may speak: —

November 8, 1866. — Went to see Ristori's "Pia dei Tolomei" in the evening. It was pure and beautiful. Being R.'s benefit, she made a short speech, and exquisitely simple as it was, her fine voice and the slight difficulty of enunciating the English words made her speech one of the most touching features of the time.

Saturday. — Morning at home. Went to see Ristori for the last time, as Elizabeth, perhaps her finest characterization. Longfellow and Whittier had both promised to go with us, but the courage of both failed at the last moment. The house was crowded. Mr. Grau asked Mr. Fields to go and speak with the great actress, but he excused himself.

Whittier had never been inside of a theatre and could not quite feel like breaking the bonds now — besides he said it would cost him many nights of sleep. Longfellow does not face high tragedy before a crowd.

January 16, 1868. — Fanny Kemble read "The Merchant of Venice" in Boston last night — the old way of losing her breath when she appeared, as if totally overcome by the audience. We could not doubt that she

RISTORI AND FANNY KEMBLE

The photograph of Mrs. Kemble was taken in Philadelphia in 1863

felt her return deeply and sincerely, but — however, the feeling was undoubtedly real if short-lived, and we will give her credit for it. Her voice is sadly faded since the brilliant readings of ten years ago; she has had much sorrow since then and shows the marks of it. It is interesting to compare her work with Mr. Dickens's; he is so much the greater artist! You can never mistake one of his characters for another, nor lose a syllable of his perfectly enunciated words. She speaks much more slowly usually, and there is a grand intonation as the verses sway from her lips, but one cannot be sure always if Jessica or Nerissa be speaking, Antonio or Bassanio. Her face is marvellous in tender passages, a serenity falls upon it born of immortal youth. It is beautiful enough for tears. She enjoys the wit too herself thoroughly, and brought out Launcelot Gobbo with great unction. An enormous and enthusiastic audience gave her hearty welcome. Longfellow could not come His wife in the old days enjoyed this play too well when they used to go together for him to trust himself to hear it again.

Monday, May 18, 1868. — Raining like all possessed again today. I was to have done my gardening today but there is no chance yet. Walked over to Roxbury with J. yesterday and found everything gay with the coming loveliness. It has scarcely come, however. Jamie was much entertained by tales Mrs. Kemble's agent told him of that lady: how she watched an Irish scrubbing woman dawdle over her work, who was paid by the hour, and finally called her to her (she was sitting at her own reading-desk in the hall), and said in her stately fashion, "I fear, madam, if you exert yourself so much over your work you will make yourself ill. Your health is seriously endangered by your severe efforts." The woman, not seeing the sarcasm, replied in the strongest possible brogue to the effect that nothing short of the direst necessity would compel such dreadful labor. Whereat Mrs. Kemble, with a look not to be reproduced, and a wink to Mr. Pugh, withdrew. She read "Midsummer Night's Dream" on Saturday P.M. We went, but found the place entirely without air and left after the first part. She did not begin with much spirit, but her voice was exquisite and her fun also, and her dress was an æsthetic pleasure, as a lady's dress should always be, but alas! so seldom is, in this country.

Wednesday, November 9, 1870. — We have had a reception today for Miss Nilsson. Longfellow and Henry Ward Beecher were here, beside Perabo and many excellent or talented people, nearly sixty in all. It was a curious fact to give out seventy invitations and have sixty (or nearly that) present.

Miss Nilsson, Mrs. Richardson (her attendant), Alice Longfellow, and ourselves sat down to lunch afterward, when she sang snatches of her loveliest songs and talked and laughed and was as graceful and merry and sweet as ever a beautiful woman knows how to be. She is now twenty-seven years old. Her light hair, deep blue eyes, full glorious eyes, are of the Northern type, but her broad intellectual brow, her beautiful teeth, and strong character, belong only to the type of genius and beauty. She is not only brave but almost imperious, I fancy, at times; a manner quite necessary, I say, to protect her from vulgar animosity and audacity. We heard her last night sing "Auld Robin Gray" not only with exqui- site feeling, but with a pronunciation of the Scottish dialect that appeared to us very remarkable. When we spoke to her of it she said, "Yes, but there is much like that too in the Swedish dialect. When I first came up a peasant to Stockholm to learn to sing, I had the dialect very bad indeed, and it was a long time before I lost it. Then I went to school in France, and now my accent and dialect are French. When I went back home and talked with the French dialect, they said to me, 'Now Christine, don't be absurd,' but I could not help it. I catch everything. I have never studied English in my life. I am learning American fast. I have learned 'I guess,' and I shall soon say 'I reckon' by the time I come back from the West."

Vieuxtemps, the violinist, she appreciates and en- joys highly as an artist. Of Ole Bull she says, "He is a charlatan. Ah, you will excuse me, but it is true." Of Viardot-Garcia she has the highest admiration. Noth- ing ever gave her higher delight than Viardot's com- pliment after hearing her "Mignon." It was uncalled for, unexpected, and from the heart. She rehearsed what we recall so well, Viardot's plain face, poor figure — and great genius triumphant over all. Well, we hear poor Viardot has lost her fortune by this sad French war.

I have set down nothing which can recall the strong sweet beauty of Nilsson. She is a power to command success — fine and strong and sweet. Her face glowed and responded and originated in a swift yet gentle way, as one person after another was presented, that was a study and a lesson. She neither looked nor seemed tired until the presentation was over, when she said she was hungry. "We have had no breakfast yet, nothing to eat all day; ah, I shall know again what it means when Mrs. Fields asks me to lunch at one o'clock!" with an arch look at me. I was extremely penitent and hurried the lunch, but the people could not go out of the dining-room. However, all was cleaned at last and we had a quiet cosy talk and sit-down, which was delightful.

On Saturday she sang from "Hamlet," the mad scene of Ophelia. As usual, her dress and whole appearance were of the most refined and perfect beauty, and her singing we appreciated even more deeply than ever. She has not the remote *exalté* nature of highest genius, but she is the great singer of this new time, and her realism is in marked sympathy with her period.

It has already been suggested that, when Thomas Bailey Aldrich made his migration to Boston as editor of "Every Saturday," he brought into the circle of the Fieldses many fresh breezes from the outer world. In the diary of Mrs. Fields there are frequent notes revealing a friendship which lasted, indeed, long after the diary ceased, and up to the end of Aldrich's life,

CHRISTINE NILSSON AS OPHELIA

in 1907. Two entries — the first relating to the mete-
oric author of "The Diamond Lens," regarded in its
day as a bright portent in the literary heavens, the second to the Aldriches themselves at the country place
with the name which Aldrich embalmed in his excellent
title, "From Ponkapog to Pesth" — warrant conver-
sion from manuscript into print.

November 9, 1865. — Aldrich told us the story of Fitz-
James O'Brien, the able author of "The Diamond
Lens." He was a handsome fellow, and began his career
by running away with the wife of an English officer.
The officer was in India, and Fitz-James and the guilty
woman had fled to one of the seaports on the south of
England in order to take passage for America, when the
arrival of the woman's husband was announced to them
and O'Brien fled. He concealed himself on board a ship
bound for New York. There he ran a career of dissipation, landing with only sixty dollars. He went to a first-
rate hotel, ordered wines, and left a large bill behind
when the time came to run away. Then he wrote for
Harpers, and one publisher and another, writing little
and over-drawing funds on a large scale. He came and
lived six weeks upon Aldrich in his uncle's house one
summer when the family were away. One day he tried
to borrow money of Harpers, and being refused he
went into the bindery department, borrowed a board,
printed on it, "I am starving," bored holes through
the ends, put in a string, hung it round his neck,
allowed his fawn-colored gloves to depend over each

end, and stood in the doorway where the firm should see him when they went to dinner. A great laugh and more money was the result of this escapade. Finally, when the war broke out, he enlisted, and this was the last A. heard of him for some time; but, being himself called to take a position on General Lander's staff, he was on his way to Richmond and had reached Petersburg, when someone told him Fitz-James O'Brien had been shot dead. Then he went to the hospital and saw him lying there dead.

Shortly after this, when Bayard Taylor and his wife were dining in a hotel restaurant at Dover, I believe, — it was one of the south of England towns, — they saw themselves closely observed by a lady and gentleman sitting near them. Finally the gentleman arose and came to speak to Taylor, said he observed they were Americans, and asked if he had ever heard of F. J. O'Brien. "Oh, yes," said Taylor, "I knew him very well. He was killed in our war." Then the lady burst into tears and the gentleman said, "She is his mother!"

I forgot to say in the course of the story that he borrowed once sixty-five dollars for which A. became responsible, and when it was not paid he sent a letter to O'B. saying he must pay it. In return O'Brien sent him a challenge for a duel, which A. accepted, in the meantime discovering that an honorable fight could not be between a debtor and a creditor. However, when the time appointed arrived, O'Brien had absconded. We could not repress a smile at the idea of A.'s *fighting*, for he is a painfully small gentleman.

May 31, 1876. — Passed the day with the Aldriches at Ponkapog. Aldrich maintained at dinner that the horse railroad injured Charles Street. His wife and J. T. F. took the opposite ground. Finally J. said, "Well, the Philadelphians don't agree with you; they have learned the value of horse railroads in their streets." "Oh, that's because they are such Christians," said A. "They know whom the Lord loveth He chasteneth."

He is a queer, witty creature. When the railroad dropped us at Green Lodge station, a tiny place surrounded by wild green woods and bog, we found him sitting on a corner of the platform where he said he had been "listening to the bullfrog tune his violin. He had been twanging at one string a long time!" Aldrich was in an ecstasy of delight, and in truth it was a day to put the most untuned spirit into tune. In the afternoon we floated on the beautiful pond. The whole day gave us a series of pictures — only thirteen miles from town, yet the beechwoods can be no more retired. Mr. Pierce owns 500 acres, and it must be a pleasure to him, while he is away in Washington, to feel that someone is using and enjoying his beautiful domain; and how could it be half so well used and enjoyed as by the family of a struggling literary man! The house they live in, which was going to decay, may really be considered a creation of Lilian's. Altogether she is very clever and Aldrich most fortunate and our Washington senator is doubtless most content to think of the enjoyment of others in his domain.

Still more exotic a figure in Boston than Aldrich
was William Morris Hunt — in spite of his temporary
association with Harvard College and his Boston marriage.   Both he and his wife are constantly to be met
in the pages of Mrs. Fields's journals, from which they
emerged with some frequency into her published "Biographical Notes," even as they have reappeared, with
others, on earlier pages of this book.

In other places than Charles Street, Fields and Hunt
were often meeting. One brief record of an encounter,
at the end of a Saturday Club meeting, should surely
be preserved, for all that it suggests of Hunt in amused
rebellion against his surroundings.

Sunday, August 26, 1874. — Hunt came to Jamie
when the afternoon was nearly ended and asked him to
go up to his studio. As they went along, he said, "I 've
made a poem ! First time I ever wrote anything in my
life. 'T is n't long, only four lines, but I 've got it written down." Whereat then and there he pulled out his
pocketbook and read :

> "Boston is a hilly place;
> People all are brothers-in-law.
> If you or I want something done
> They treat us then like mothers-in-law.

"This goes to the tune of Yankee Doodle," whereat he
sang it out on the public highway. He looked very handsome, was beautifully dressed in brown velvet with a

My dear Fields.

Send em along -

I mean Painters .

I have had a delightful
day with your friend
& I know he is a painter -
- Why . because he likes
what I do well & hates
what I don't that a into
worth . . . .

Yours
Wm M Hunt

Facsimile letter from Hunt to Fields

gold chain about his neck, but swore like a trooper and was in one of his most lawless moods.

He gave J. for me a photograph of a marvellous picture which he calls his Persian Sybil, Anahita. I see his wife in it as in so many of his best works. "I don't mean to do any more portraits," he said. "When I remember how I have wasted time on an eyebrow because somebody's 14th cousin thought it ought to turn up a little more — it makes me mad!"

When the English painter, Lowes Dickinson, the father of G. Lowes Dickinson, was visiting the Fieldses in Boston, a photograph of Hunt's portrait of Chief Justice Lemuel Shaw so impressed him that he asked to be taken to the painter's studio. In Miss Helen M. Knowlton's "Art Life of William Morris Hunt" this circumstance is related, together with its sequel, which was the publication of Hunt's "Talks on Art" from notes made by Miss Knowlton herself. It is a surmise but slightly hazardous that a characteristic note found among the Fields papers was written apropos of Dickinson's visit to Hunt: "Send 'em along — I mean Painters," he wrote to Fields. "I have had a delightful day with your friend — and I know he is a painter — why? because he likes what I do well and *hates* what I do that ain't worth. . . ."

It has been seen that, as early as November, 1868, James Parton suggested that "a writer named Mark

Twain" be engaged to contribute to the "Atlantic."[1]
In October, 1868, "F. Bret Harte" wrote to the editor
of the "Atlantic" from San Francisco: "As the author
of 'The Luck of Roaring Camp,' I have to thank you for
an invitation to contribute to the 'Atlantic Monthly,'
but as editor of 'The Overland,' my duties claim most
of my spare time outside of the Government office in
which I am employed. . . . But I am glad of this opportunity to thank someone connected with the 'Atlantic' for its very gracious good-will toward me and my
writings, particularly the book which G. W. Carleton
of New York malformed in its birth.   There was an
extra kindness in your taking the deformed brat by the
hand, and trying to recognize some traces of a parent
so far away."

It was in the discharge of his work as editor of the
"Atlantic" that Fields, hospitable to practitioners of all
the arts, entered especially into relations with writers
whose paths might not otherwise have crossed his, and
his wife's. Of all the young Lochinvars of the pen who
came out of the West while Mrs. Fields was keeping her
diary, Bret Harte and Mark Twain were the daring and
dauntless gallants who most captured the imagination
and have longest held it. To each of them Mrs. Fields
devoted a number of pages in her diary. We shall see
first what she had to say about Bret Harte.

Friday, March 10, 1871. — Too many days full of

[1] See *ante*, page 111.

interest have passed unrecorded. Chiefly I should record what I can recall of Francis Bret Harte, who has made his first visit to the East just now, since he went to San Francisco in his early youth. He is now apparently about 35 years old. His mind is full of the grand landscape of the West, and filled also with sympathetic interest in the half-developed natives who are to be seen there, nearer to the surface than in our Eastern cities. He told me of a gambler who had a friend lying dead in the upper room of a gambling house. The man went out to see about having services performed. "Better have it at the grave," said the parson to whom he applied. Jim shook his head as if he feared the proper honors would not be paid his friend. The other then suggested they should find the minister and leave it to him. "Well," said Jim, "yes, I wish you'd do just that, for I ain't much of a funeral 'sharp' myself." He told me also, as a sign of the wonderful recklessness which had pervaded San Francisco, that at one time there was a glut of tobacco in the market and, a block of houses going up at the same period, *the foundations of those houses were laid of boxes of tobacco.* Bret Harte, as the world calls him, is natural, warm-hearted, with a keen relish for fun, disposed to give just value to the strong language of the West, which he is by no means inclined to dispense with; at ease in every society, quick of sense and sight. Jamie, who saw him more than I, finds him lovable above all. We liked his wife too, — not handsome but with good honest sense, appreciative of him, — and two children. She is said to sing

But I am glad of this opportunity to thank some one connected with the *Atlantic* for its very generous good-will toward me and my writings — particularly the book which G.W. Carleton of New York, malformed in its birth. There was an extra kindness in your taking this deformed brat by the hand, and trying to recognize some traces of a parent so far away. For all of which I assure I

The Editor of the
Atlantic Monthly }

Very faithfully Yrs
F. Bret Harte /

Facsimile page from an early letter of Bret Harte's

well, but poor woman! the fatigues of that most distressing journey across the continent, the fêtes, the
heat (for the weather is unusually warm), have been
almost too much for her and she is not certainly at
her best. They dined and took tea here last Friday.

Tuesday, September 5, 1871. — J. went to Boston.
I wrote in the pastures and walked all the morning.
Coming home, after dinner, came a telegram for me
to meet J. and Bret Harte at Beverly station with the
pony carriage. I drove hard to catch the train, but
arrived in season, glad to take up the two good boys
and show them Beverly shore. Stopped at Mrs. Cabot's
returning to see Mrs. ——, etc. They were all glad to
have a glimpse of Bret Harte. The talk turned a little
upon Hawthorne, and I was much amused to hear
Mrs. —— say, drawing herself up, "Yes, he was born
in Salem, but we never knew anything about him."
(The truth was, Mrs. —— was the last person to appreciate him.) . . . Fortunately Miss Howes was present,
whose father was one of Hawthorne's best friends; so
matters were made clear there. We left soon and came
on to Manchester, where, after showing him the shore,
we sat and talked during the evening.

Mr. Harte had much to say of the beautiful flowers of
California, roses being in bloom about his own house
there every month in the year. He found the cloudless
skies and continued drought of California very hard
to bear. For the first time in my life I considered how
terrible perpetual cloudlessness would be! He thinks
there is no beauty in the mountains of California, hard,

bare, snowless peaks. Neither are there trees, nor any green grass.

He is delighted with the fragrant lawns of Newport and has, I believe, put into verse a delightful ghost story which he told us.[1] He has taken a house of some antiquity in Newport, connected with which is the story of a lady who formerly lived there and who was very fond of the odor of mignonette. The flower was always growing in her house, and after her death, at two o'clock every night, a strong odor has always been perceived passing through the house as if wafted along by the garments of a woman. One night at the appointed hour, but entirely unconnected in his thought with the story Mr. Harte had long ago heard, he was arrested in his work by a strong perfume of mignonette which appeared to sweep by him. He looked about, thinking his wife might have placed a vase of flowers in the room, but finding nothing he began to follow the odor, which seemed to flit before him. Then he recalled, for the first time, the story he had heard. He opened the door; the odor was in the hall; he opened the room where the lady died, but there was no odor there; until returning, after making a circuit of the house, he found a faint perfume as if she had passed but not stayed there also. At last, somewhat oppressed perhaps by the ghostliness of the place and hour, he went out and stood upon the porch. There his dream vanished. The sweet lawn and tree flowers were emitting an odor, as is common at

[1] "A Newport Romance," published in the *Atlantic Monthly* for October, 1871.

the hour when dews congeal, more sweet than at any other time of day or night, and the air was redolent of sweets which might easily be construed into mignonette. The story was well told and I shall be glad to see his poem.

Many good stories came off during the evening, some very characteristic of California; ones such as that of an uproar in a theatre and a man about to be killed, when someone shouts, "Don't waste him, but kill a fiddler with him." Also one of the opening nights at the California theatre, the place packed, when a man who has taken too much whiskey wishes a noise; immediately the manager, a strong executive man, catches him up with the help of a policeman, and before anybody knows the thing is done or the disturber what is the matter, he finds himself set down on the sidewalk outside in the street. "Well," said he with an oath, "is this the way you do business here; raise a fellow before he has a chance to draw?" (referring to the game of poker).

Mr. Harte is a very sensitive and nervous man. He struggles against himself all the time. He sat on the piazza with J. and talked till a late hour. This morning at breakfast I found him most interesting. He talked of his early and best-loved books. It appears that at the age of nine he was a lover and reader of Montaigne. Certain writers, he says, seem to him to stand out as friends and brothers side by side in literature. Now Horace and Montaigne are so associated in his mind. Mr. Emerson, he thinks, never in the least approaches a comprehen-

sion of the character of the man. With an admiration
for his great sayings, he has never guessed at the subtle
springs from which they come. The pleasant acceding
to both sides in politics, and other traits of like nature,
gives him affinity with Hawthorne. By the way, he is
a true appreciator of Hawthorne. He was moved to
much merriment yesterday by remembering a passage
in the notes, where he slyly remarks, "Margaret Fuller's
cows hooked the other cows." Speaking of Dr. Bartol, he
said, "What a dear old man he is! A venerable baby,
nothing more!" But Harte is most kindly and tender.
His wife has been very ill and has given him cause for
terrible anxiety. This accounts for much left undone,
but he is an oblivious man oftentimes to his surroundings — leaves things behind!!

January 12, 1872. — Bret Harte was here at breakfast. It is curious to see his feeling with regard to society. For purely literary society, with its affectations
and contempts, he has no sympathy. He has at length
chosen New York as his residence, and among the
Schuylers, Sherwoods, and their friends he appears to
find what he enjoys. There is evidently a *gêne* about
people and life here, and provincialisms which he found
would hurt him. He is very sensitive and keen, with a
love and reverence for Dickens almost peculiar in this
coldly critical age. Bryant he finds very cold and totally
unwilling to lead the conversation, as he should do
when they are together, as he justly remarks, he being
so much younger — but never a word without cart and
horses to fetch it.

Bret Harte has a queer absent-minded way of spending his time, letting the hours slip by as if he had not altogether learned their value yet. It is a miracle to us how he lives, for he writes very little. Thus far I suppose he has had money from J. R. O. & Co., but I fancy they have done with giving out money save for a *quid pro quo.*

February, 1872 [during a visit to New York]. — We had promised to dine with Mr. and Mrs. Harte early and go to the theatre afterward, therefore four o'clock found us at their door. He welcomed us by opening it himself and only this reassured Jamie. We had driven up in a "Crystal," much to my amusement, in which J. had insisted I should sit until he discovered if that was the house. The scene was altogether comic. I shortened the ludicrousness as much as possible by jumping out and running quickly up the steps. Mrs. Harte was not ready to see me, but I found Mr. Barrett the actor with Mr. Harte in the parlor, and soon being invited upstairs, found Mrs. Barrett and Mrs. Harte together. We had a merry dinner together, the young actor evidently quite nervous with respect to the evening's performance. He went an hour before us to the play. We sat in the stage box; the play was "Julius Cæsar." It is useless to deny Edwin Booth great talent, exquisite grace and feeling. Both the young men, the first, Barrett, a man of intellect, and Booth, a man of inherited grace and feeling as well as good mind, have the advantage moreover of being born to the stage. Their stage habits fit them more perfectly than those of the drawing-room and they

walk the stage with the ease that most men do their
own parlors.   During the performance Booth invited us
into his drawing-room; a short carpeted way led from
the box into the small room where he was sitting in
Roman costume, pipe in mouth; he rose and called
"Mary," as we approached, when the tiniest woman
ever called wife made her appearance.   She is an ardent
little spark of human flame and he really looks large
beside her.

But his grace, his grace! His dress too, was as usual
perfect — more, far more than all, both the actors had
such feeling for Shakespeare and for their parts with
which they are filling the stage nightly, that they were
deeply and truly enthusiastic.   It was a sight to warm
Shakespeare.

Saturday, September 18, 1875. — Bret Harte came on
the ½ past 12 train. He came in good health, save a
headache which ripened as the day went on; but he
was bubbling over with fun, full of the most natural and
unexpected sallies. He wished to know if I was acquainted with the Cochin China hen.   They had one at
Cohasset. They had named him Benventuro (after a
certain gay Italian singer of strong self-appreciation who
came formerly to America). He said this hen's state of
mind on finding a half-exploded fire-cracker and her
depressed condition since its explosion was something
extraordinary. His description was so vivid that I still
see this hen perambulating about the house, first with
pride, second with precipitation, fallen into disgrace
among her fellows.

He said Cohasset was not the place to live in the summer if one wanted sea-breezes. They all came straight from Chicago!! He fancied the place, thinking it an old fishing village, not unlike Yarmouth. Instead of which they prided themselves upon never having "any of your sea-smells," and, being five miles from the doctor, could not be considered a cheerful place to live in with sick children. He said he was surprised to find J. T. F. without a sailor's jacket and collar. The actors among whom he had been living rather overdid the business; their collars were wider, their shirts fuller, and their trousers more bulgy than those of any real sailor he had ever observed, and the manner of hitching up the trousers was entirely peculiar to themselves and to the stage.

We went to call upon the Burlingames. In describing Harrisburg, Virginia, where he had lectured, he said a committee-man came to invite him to take a walk, and he was so afflicted with a headache that he was ready to take or give away his life at any moment; so he accepted the invitation and walked out with him. The man observed that Harrisburg was a very healthy place; only one man a day died in that vicinity. "Oh!" said Harte, remembering the dangerous state of his own mind, "has that man died yet today?" The man shook his head gravely, never suspecting a joke, and said he didn't know, but he would try to find out. Whereat Harte, to keep up the joke, said he wished he would. He went to the lecture forgetting all about it and saw this man hanging around without getting a chance to speak. The next morning very early, he managed to get an

BRET HARTE AND MARK TWAIN

From early photographs

opportunity to speak to him. "I could n't find out exactly about that man yesterday," he said. "What man?" said H. "Why, the one we were speaking of; the Coroner said he could n't say precisely who it was, but the one man would average all right."

Harte said in speaking of Longfellow that no one had yet overpraised him. The delicate quality of humor, the exquisite fineness in the choice of words, the breadth and sweetness of his nature were something he could hardly help worshipping. One day after a dinner at Mr. Lowell's he said, "I think I will not have a carriage to return to town. I will walk down to the Square." "I will walk with you," said Longfellow. When they arrived at his gate, he said, he was so beautiful that he could only think of the light and whiteness of the moon, and if he had stayed a moment longer he should have put his arms around him and made a fool of himself then and there. Whereat he said good night abruptly and turned away.

He brought his novel and play [1] with him which are just now finished, for us to read. He has evidently enjoyed the play, and he enjoys the fame and the money they both bring him.

He is a dramatic, lovable creature with his blue silk pocket-handkerchief and red dressing slippers and his quick feelings. I could hate the man who could help loving him — or the woman either.

In the passages touching upon Mark Twain now to be copied from the journals, he is seen, not in Boston, but

[1] Probably *Gabriel Conroy* and *Two Men of Sandy Bar*.

in Hartford. If Mrs. Fields had continued her diary until 1879, there would doubtless have been a faithful contemporaneous account of the humorist's unhappy attempt to be funny both in the presence and at the expense of the "Augustans" assembled in honor of Whittier's seventieth birthday.[1] But Mrs. Fields's reports of talk and observations under his own roof, in the days when his fame rested entirely upon a handful of his earlier books, should take their place in the authentic annals of an extraordinary personality. On the first of the two occasions recorded, Fields went alone to deliver a lecture in Hartford, and in answer to a post-card invitation signed "Mark," stayed in the new house of the Clemenses. On the second occasion, three weeks later, Mrs. Fields accompanied him. After her husband's return from the first visit she wrote: —

April 6, 1876. — He found Mrs. Clemens quite ill. They had been in New York where he had given four lectures hoping to get money for Dr. Brown. He had never lectured there before without making a great deal of money. This time he barely covered his expenses. He was very interesting and told J. the whole story of his life. They sat until midnight after the lecture, Mark drinking ale to make him sleepy. He says he can't sleep as other people do; his kind of sleep is the only sort for him — three or four hours of good solid comfort — more than that makes him ill; he can't afford to sleep all his thoughts away. He described the hunger of his child-

---

[1] See *The Atlantic Monthly and Its Makers*, pp. 73–75.

hood for books, how the "Fortunes of Nigel" was one of the first stories which came to him while he was learning to be a pilot on a Mississippi boat. He hid himself with it behind a barrel where he was found by the master, who read him a lecture upon the ruinous effects of reading. "I 've seen it over and over agin," he said. "You need n't tell me anythin' about it; if ye 're going to be a pilot on this river yer need n't ever think of reading, for it just spiles all. Yer can't remember how high the tides was in Can's Gut three trips before the last now, I 'll wager." "Why no," said Mark, "that was six months ago." "I don't care if 't was," said the man. "If you had n't been spiling yer mind by readin' ye 'd have remembered." So he was never allowed to read any more after that. "And now," says Mark, "not being able to have it when I was hungry for it, I can only read the Encyclopedia nowadays." Which is not true — he reads everything.

The story of his courtship and marriage, too, was very strange and interesting. A portion of this has, however, leaked into the daily papers, so I will not repeat it here. One point interested me greatly, however, as showing the strength of character and rightness of vision in the man. He said he had not been married many months when his wife's father came to him one evening and said, "My son, would n't you like to go to Europe with your wife?" "Why yes, sir," he said, "if I could afford it." "Well then," said he, "if you will leave off smoking and drinking ale you shall have ten thousand dollars this next year and go to

Europe beside." "Thank you, sir," said Mark, "this is very good of you, and I appreciate it, but I can't sell myself. I will do anything I can for you or any of your family, but I can't sell myself." The result was, said Mark, "I never smoked a cigar all that year nor drank a glass of ale; but when the next year came I found I must write a book, and when I sat down to write I found it was n't worth anything. I must have a cigar to steady my nerves. I began to smoke, and I wrote my book; but then I could n't sleep and I had to drink ale to go to sleep. Now if I had sold myself, I could n't have written my book, or I could n't have gone to sleep, but now everything works perfectly well."

He and his wife have wretched health, poor things! And in spite of their beautiful home must often have rather a hard time. He is very eccentric, disturbed by every noise, and it cannot be altogether easy to have care of such a man. It is a very loving household though Mrs. Clemens's mother, Mrs. Langdon, hardly knows what to make of him sometimes, it is quite evident.

Thursday, April 27, 1876. — We lunched and at 3 P.M. were *en route* for Hartford. I slept, and read Mr. Tom Appleton's journal on the Nile, and looked out at the sunset and the torches of spring in the hollows, each in turn, doing more sleeping than either of the others, I fear, because I seem for some unexplained reason to be tired, as Mrs. Hawthorne used to say, far into the future. By giving up to it, however, I felt quite fresh when we arrived, at half-past seven o'clock, Mr. Clemens' (Mark Twain's) carriage waiting for us to take us to the hall where he was to perform for the second night in succession Peter Spyle in the "Loan of a Lover." It is a pretty play, and the girl's part, Gertrude, was well done by Miss Helen Smith; but Mr. Clemens' part was a creation. I see no reason why, if he chose to adopt the profession of actor, he should not be as successful as Jefferson in whatever he might conclude to undertake. It is really amazing to see what a man of genius can do beside what is usually considered his legitimate sphere.

Afterward we went with Mr. Hammersley to the Club for a bit of supper — this I did not wish to do, but I was overruled of course by the decision of our host. We met at supper one of the clever actors who played in a little operetta called "The Artful Mendicants." It was after twelve o'clock when we finally reached Mr. Clemens' house. He believed his wife would have retired, as she is very delicate in health; but there she was expecting us, with a pretty supper table laid. When her husband discovered this, he fell down on his knees in mock desire for forgiveness. His mind was so full of the play, and with the poor figure he felt he had made in it, that he had entirely forgotten all her directions and injunctions. She is a very small, sweet-looking, simple, finished creature, charming in her ways and evidently deeply beloved by him. The house is a brick villa, designed by one of the first New York architects, standing in a lovely lawn which slopes down to a small stream or river at the side. In this spring season the blackbirds are busy in the trees and the air is sweet and vocal. Inside there is

Those Annual Bills.
Air — Those Evening Bells.
By Mark Twain.

Those annual bills! those an-
    nual bills!
How many a host their discontrilly warning
    thrills fills tells swells
Of "truck" consumed, enjoyed,
    forgot
Since New Year last
Since I reviewed received
Since I was floored, strapped,
    fell under, skinned, scalped,
    flayed by last year's lot!

Those joyous beans are past away,
Those   hams
Those onions blithe, O where are they?
Once loved, lost, mourned — now
    vexing ills
Your ghosts return in annual bills

Facsimile verses and letter

aground Cleaned

And so will be when I am broke;

those yearly duns will still go around
that annual

While bards than I more frantic
still

While other bards ~~shall~~
with frantic quills

Shall damn & _damn_ these
annual bills!

Hartford, Jan. 7/74

My Dear Fields:
I send this original rough
draft just as it was when I laid
the pen down to welcome you
two hours ago. If you had only
opened my cheque-book (which
lay under the MS.) you
would have found them.
Your inspiration there for
even a more gifted poem
than this one is.
I am glad! to send
this to you, since you
were complimentary
enough to ask it. Yr ever
Saml. L. Clemens.

T. T. Fields
148 Charles St
Boston

from Mark Twain to Fields

great luxury. Especially I delight in a lovely conservatory opening out of the drawing-room.

Although we had already eaten supper, the gentlemen took a glass of lager beer to keep Mrs. Clemens company while she ate a bit of bread after her long anxiety and waiting. Meantime Mr. Clemens talked. The quiet earnest manner of his speech would be impossible to reproduce, but there is a drawl in his tone peculiar to himself. Also he is much interested in actors and the art of acting just now, and seriously talks of going to Boston next week to the début of Anna Dickinson.

We were a tired company and went soon to bed and to sleep. I slept late, but I found Mr. Clemens had been re-reading Dana's "Two Years before the Mast" in bed early and revolving subjects for his "Autobiography." Their two beautiful baby girls came to pass an hour with us after breakfast — exquisite affectionate children, the very fountain of joy to their interesting parents. . . .

Returning to lunch, I found our host and hostess and eldest little girl in the drawing-room. We fell into talk of the mishaps of the stage and the disadvantage of an amateur under such circumstances. "For instance, on the first night of our little play," said Mr. Clemens, "the trousers of one of the actors suddenly gave way entirely behind, which was very distressing to him, though we did not observe it at all."

I want to stop here to give a little idea of the appearance of our host. He is forty years old, with some color in his cheeks and a heavy light-colored moustache, and

overhanging light eyebrows. His eyes are grey and
piercing, yet soft, and his whole face expresses great
sensitiveness. He is exquisitely neat also, though careless, and his hands are small, not without delicacy.
He is a small man, but his mass of hair seems the one
rugged-looking thing about him. I thought in the play
last night that it was a wig.

To return to our lunch table — he proceeded to speak
of his "Autobiography," which he intends to write as
fully and simply as possible to leave behind him. His
wife laughingly said she should look it over and leave
out objectionable passages. "No," he said, very earnestly, almost sternly, "*you* are not to edit it — it is to
appear as it is written, with the whole tale told as truly
as I can tell it. I shall take out passages from it, and
publish as I go along in the 'Atlantic' and elsewhere,
but I shall not limit myself as to space, and at whatever
age I am writing about, even if I am an infant, and an
idea comes to me about myself when I am forty, I shall
put that in. Every man feels that his experience is unlike that of anybody else, and therefore he should write
it down. He finds also that everybody else has thought
and felt on some points precisely as he has done, and
therefore he should write it down."

The talk naturally branched to education, and thence
to the country. He has lost all faith in our government.
This wicked ungodly suffrage, he said, where the vote
of a man who knew nothing was as good as the vote
of a man of education and industry; this endeavor to
equalize what God had made unequal was a wrong and

a shame. He only hoped to live long enough to see such a wrong and such a government overthrown. Last summer he wrote an article for the "Atlantic," printed without any signature, proposing the only solution of such evil of which he could conceive. "It is too late now," he continued, "to restrict the suffrage; we must increase it — for this let us give every university man, let us say, ten votes, and every man with common-school education two votes, and a man of superior power and position a hundred votes, if we choose. This is the only way I see to get out of the false position into which we have fallen."

At five, the hour appointed for dinner, I returned to the drawing-room where our host lay at full length on the floor with his head on cushions in the bay-window, reading, and taking what he called "delicious comfort." Mrs. Perkins came in to dinner, and we had a cosy good time. Mr. Clemens described the preaching of a Western clergyman, a great favorite, with the smallest possible allowance of idea to the largest possible amount of words. It was so truthfully and vividly portrayed that we all concluded, perhaps, since the man was in such earnest, he moved his audience more than if he had troubled them with too many ideas. This truthfulness of Mr. Clemens, which will hardly allow him to portray anything in a way to make out a case by exaggerating or distorting a truth, is a wondrous and noble quality. This makes art and makes life, and will continue to make him a daily increasing power among us.

He is so unhappy and discontented with our government that he says he is not conscious of the least emotion of patriotism in himself. He is overwhelmed with shame and confusion and wishes he were not an American. He thinks seriously of going to England to live for a while, at least, and I think it not unlikely he may discover away from home a love of his country which is still waiting to be unfolded. I believe hope must dawn for us, that so much earnest endeavor of our statesmen and patriots cannot come to naught; and perhaps the very idea he has dropped, never believing that it can bring forth fruit, will be adopted in the end for our salvation. Certainly women's suffrage and such a change as he proposes should be tried, since we cannot keep the untenable ground of the present. . . .

It is most curious and interesting to watch this growing man of forty — to see how he studies and how high his aims are. His conversation is always earnest and careful, though full of fun. He is just now pondering much upon actors and their ways. Raymond, who is doing the "Gilded Age," is so hopelessly given "to saving at the spigot and losing at the bung-hole" that he is evidently not over-satisfied nor does he count the acting everything it might be.

We sat talking, chiefly we women, after dinner and looking at the sunset. Mr. Clemens lay down with a book and J. went to look over his lecture. I did not go to lecture, but after all were gone I scribbled away at these pages and nearly finished Mr. Appleton's "Nile Journal." They returned rather late, it was after ten, bearing a box of delicious strawberries, Mrs. Colt's gift from her endless greenhouses. They were a sensation; the whole of summer was foreshadowed by their scarlet globes. Some beer was brought for Mr. Clemens (who drinks nothing else, and as he eats but little this seems to answer the double end of nourishment and soothing for the nerves) and he began again to talk. He said it was astonishing what subjects were missed by the Poet Laureate. He thought the finest incident of the Crimean War had been certainly overlooked. That was the going down at sea of the man of war, Berkeley Castle. The ship with a whole regiment, one of the finest of the English army, on board, struck a rock near the Bosphorus. There was no help — the bottom was out and the boats would only hold the crew and the other helpless ones; there was no chance for the soldiers. The Colonel summoned them on deck; he told them the duty of soldiers was to die; they would do their duty as bravely there as if they were on the battle-field. He bade them shoulder arms and prepare for action. The drums beat, flags were flying, the service playing, as they all went down to silent death in the great deep.

Afterward Mr. Clemens described to us the reappearance before his congregation of an old clergyman who had been incapacitated for work during twelve years — coming suddenly into the pulpit just as the first hymn was ended. The younger pastor proposed they should sing the old man's favorite, "Coronation," *omitting* the first verse. He heard nothing of the omission, but beginning at the first verse he sang in a cracked treble the remaining stanza after all the people were still. There

was a mingling of the comic and pathetic in this incident which made it consonant with the genius of our
host. Our dear little hostess complained of want of air,
and I saw she was very tired, so we all went to bed about
eleven.

Saturday morning. — Dear J. was up early and out in
the beautiful sunshine. I read and scribbled until breakfast at half-past nine. It was a lovely morning, and I
had already ventured out of my window and round the
house to hear the birds sing and see the face of spring
before the hour came for breakfast. When I did go to
the drawing-room, however, I found Mr. Clemens alone.
He greeted me apparently as cheerfully as ever, and it
was not until some moments had passed that he told
me they had a very sick child upstairs. From that instant I saw, especially after his wife came in, that they
could think of nothing else. They were half-distracted
with anxiety. Their messenger could not find the doctor,
which made matters worse. However, the little girl did
not really seem very sick, so I could not help thinking
they were unnecessarily excited. The effect on them,
however, was just as bad as if the child were really very
ill. The messenger was hardly despatched the second
time before Jamie and Mr. Clemens began to talk of our
getting away in the next train, whereat he (Mr. C.) said
to his wife, "Why did n't you tell me of that," etc., etc.
It was all over in a moment, but in his excitement he
spoke more quickly than he knew, and his wife felt it.
Nothing was said at the time, indeed we hardly observed
it, but we were intensely amused and could not help

finding it pathetic too afterward, when he came to us and said he spent the larger part of his life on his knees making apologies and now he had got to make an apology to us about the carriage. He was always bringing the blood to his wife's face by his bad behavior, and here this very morning he had said such things about that carriage! His whole life was one long apology. His wife had told him to see how well we behaved (poor we!) and he knew he had everything to learn.

He was so amusing about it that he left us in a storm of laughter, yet at bottom I could see it was no laughing matter to him. He is in dead earnest, with a desire for growth and truth in life, and with such a sincere admiration for his wife's sweetness and beauty of character that the most prejudiced and hardest heart could not fail to fall in love with him. She looked like an exquisite lily as we left her. So white and delicate and tender. Such sensitiveness and self-control as she possesses are very, very rare.

May Day. — Longfellow, Greene, Alexander Agassiz and Dr. Holmes dined with us. This made summer, Longfellow said at table — that this was May Day enough, it was no matter how cold it was outside. (The wind outside had been raging all day and winter seemed to be giving us a last fling.) Jamie recalled one or two things "Mark Twain" had said which I have omitted. When he lectured a few weeks ago in New York, he said he had just reached the middle of his lecture and was going on with flying colors when he saw in the audience just in front of him a noble gray head and beard. "Nobody told me that William Cullen Bryant was there, but I had seen his picture and I knew that was the old man. I was sure he saw the failure I was making, and all the weak points in what I was saying, and I couldn't do anything more — that old man just spoiled my work. Then they told me afterward that my lecture was good and all that; I could only say, 'no, no, that fine old head spoiled all I had to say *that* night.'"

Longfellow was quite like himself again, but the talk was mainly sustained by Dr. Holmes and Mr. Agassiz. When Dr. Holmes first came in he looked earnestly at the portrait of Sydney Smith. "It reminds me of our famous story-teller, Sullivan," he said; "it is full of epicureanism. *The mouth is made for kisses and canvas-backs.*" Later on in the dinner, when Mr. Agassiz was describing the fatigue he suffered after talking Spanish all day while he still understood the language very imperfectly, "Why," said Holmes, "it 's like playing the piano with mittens on."

There was something pathetic in the fact of this young man sitting here among his father's friends, almost in the very place his father had filled so many times — but his speech was manly and wise, from a full brain. They talked of the spectroscope as on the whole the most important discovery the world had known. "Well, what is it?" said Longfellow. "Explain it to us." (I was glad enough to have him ask.) Agassiz explained quite clearly that it was an instrument to discover the elements which compose the sun, and proceeded to unfold its working in some detail. Two men made the discovery simultaneously, one in India and one in England. This spectroscope has been infinitely improved, however, by every living mind brought to bear upon it, almost, since its first so-called discovery. It is so difficult, Dr. H. said, to tell where an invention began; you could go back until it seemed that no man that ever lived really did it — like some verses, whereupon one of Gray's was given as an example. The talk turned somewhat upon the manner of putting things, the English manner being so poor and inexpressive compared with the southern natures — the French being the masters of expression.

Longfellow gave a delightful account of the old artist and spiritualist, Kirkup, the discoverer of the Dante portrait, though Greene undertook to say that a certain Wilde was the man. I never heard anybody else have the credit but Kirkup, and certainly England believes it was he.

I think they all had "a good time"; I am sure I did.

As Mark Twain, in the preceding pages may be said to have led the reader back into the Boston and Cambridge circle, so there were constant excursions of interest from that circle out into the world in which such a man as Sumner stood as the friend of such another as Longfellow. For twenty-three years, from 1851 till his death in 1874, Sumner was a member of the United States Senate, and consequently was much more to be seen in

CHARLES SUMNER

Washington than in the state he represented. He appears from time to time in the pages of Mrs. Fields's diary, and in the two ensuing passages figures first at her Boston dinner-table and then in Washington.

Saturday, November 18, 1865. — Last night Miss Kate Field and Charles Sumner dined with us. Before we went to dinner Charlotte Foster, the young colored girl whom Elizabeth Whittier was so fond of and who is now secretary of the Freedmen's Bureau, came in to call. She is very pretty and good. It is difficult nevertheless for her to find a boarding-place. People do not readily admit a colored woman into their families. I shall help her to find a good home. . . .

Mr. Sumner opened the conversation at dinner by asking Miss Field to tell him something of Mr. Landor. She, smiling, said that was difficult now because she had talked and written so much of him that she hardly knew what was left unsaid. Mr. Sumner described his own first introduction then at the house of his old friend, Mr. Kenyon, in London. He had dropped in there by accident, but was positively engaged elsewhere at dinner; before he left, however, he was able to parry skilfully a remark aimed at the Yankees, which tickled Mr. Landor and made him try to hold on and induce him to stay. He was obliged to go then, however, but he returned a few days after to breakfast, when Landor asked him why the body of Washington did not rest in the Capitol at Washington. "Because," said Mr. Sumner, "his family wished his ashes to remain at Mt.

Vernon." "Ashes," said L., "his body was not burned; why do you say 'ashes,' sir?" "I quoted, 'E'en in our ashes live their wonted fires,' and he said nothing more at the time, but," added Mr. Sumner, "I have never used 'ashes' since."

Kate Field said "his wife was a perfect fiend"; but Mr. Sumner was inclined to doubt the statement. "These marriages with men of genius are hard," he said, "because genius wins the race in the end."

Then Kate brought the authority of Mr. Browning and others to back her statement, but, referring to Mr. Landor's temper, she said that while the Storys were at Siena passing the summer one year, the Brownings took a villa near by and Mr. Landor lived opposite, while she and Miss Isa Blagden went down to make the Brownings a visit. During their stay Mr. Landor fancied that the stock of tea lately purchased for his use was poisoned, and threw it all out of the window. The Contadine reaped the benefit of this; they came and gathered it up like a flock of doves.

Mr. Sumner spoke of the high, very high place he accorded to Mr. Landor as a writer of prose. He had been a source of great admiration to him for years, he said. As long ago as when G. W. Greene was living in Rome and first becoming a writer, he asked Mr. Sumner what masters of prose he should study. "Then," said Mr. S., "you remember his own style was bad; the sentences apt to be jumbled up together. I told him to read Bacon, and Hooker, and all the prose of Dryden he could find in the prefaces and elsewhere, and Walter Savage Landor; and my reverence for Mr. Landor as a writer of prose has never diminished."

Later during the dinner, talking of his life abroad, Mr. Sumner was reminded of a letter he had received from John P. Hale, our minister plenipotentiary to Spain. He said for a number of years, while Mr. Hale was in the Senate, whenever appeals came from our foreign ministers or consuls abroad asking for increase of salary, Mr. Hale would jump up and say, "Gentlemen of the Senate, allow me to say I would engage to live at any point in Europe upon the salary now granted by the Government. It is no economy, indeed it is a great lack of economy, to think of raising these salaries."

"Hereupon comes a letter from Spain urging an increase of salary in terms which would convulse the Senate with laughter after the protestations they have heard so often. I should like nothing better than to read it to them." For the lack of their presence, however, he read it to us, and it was amusing truly, as if the old days and speeches were a blank.

Mr. Sumner easily slipped from this subject into others connected with the Government.

Kate Field said that Judge Russell told her that President Johnson was no better than a sot, and that the head of the Washingtonian Home (a refuge for inebriates here) had been sent for, as a man having skill in such cases, to try to save him. "Is this true, Mr. Sumner?" she asked. Mr. Sumner said not one word at first; then asked, "What authority had Judge Russell for making such an assertion?" Kate did not know, and I thought on the whole Mr. Sumner, who knew the man had really been sent for by the President himself, it is supposed for some other reason, doubted the whole tale. I doubted it sincerely from the first moment, and I wonder a man can be left to say such things.

Sumner then continued to describe very vividly what he had known of Andy Johnson's behavior. When he left Tennessee to come to Washington to be Vice-President, he travelled with a negro servant and two demijohns of whiskey which he dispensed freely, drinking enough himself at the same time to arrive at Washington in a maudlin condition, in which state he remained until after the fourth of March. He was then living at the hotel, and a young Massachusetts officer, who lived on the same floor and was obliged to pass Mr. Johnson's door many times a day, told Mr. S. that during the two days subsequent to Mr. Johnson's arrival he saw, while passing his room, and counted twenty-six glasses of whiskey go in. At length good men interfered; they saw delirium tremens or some other dreadful thing would be the result if this continued, and old Mr. Blair went with Mr. Preston King and persuaded Mr. Johnson to go down and stay at Mr. Blair's house, and he surrendered at discretion. It was a small house and a very quiet family, but they stowed Mr. Johnson away and Mr. King also, who was kind enough to offer to take care of him. Shortly after this Mr. Lincoln and Mr. Sumner had gone down the river in a yacht, and had landed at General Grant's headquarters. They were sitting together at two desks reading the papers for the day when Mr. Sumner observed a figure darken the door, and looking up found Mr. Johnson. "Ah, Mr. Vice-President, how do you do," he said, putting his papers aside. "Mr. President, here is the Vice-President." Mr. Lincoln arose and extended his hand, but as Mr. Sumner thought very coldly, and after a short time they started again for their yacht. Mr. Johnson walked as far as the wharf, talking with Mr. Lincoln, but when they arrived there, Mr. Lincoln did not say, "Come with us and have lunch," or "Come at night and have dinner," but bade him simply "Good-bye" there, where they observed him afterward watching their departure with Mr. King by his side, who had come to rejoin him.

"This," said Mr. Sumner, "is all Mr. Lincoln saw of Mr. Johnson. One week after this time the President was assassinated, and they never met from that hour until his death."

Mr. Sumner thinks Mr. Beecher is making a dangerous and deadly mistake, and told him so. He said further to Mr. B. that his anxieties prevented him from sleeping, that he had not slept for three nights. "I should think so," Mr. Beecher replied, "you talk like a man who had been deprived of his natural rest." The two men have a respect for each other and talk kindly of each other, but they do not see things from the same point of view now at all.

Friday morning, March 21, 1872. — L. W. J. and her daughter met us at the cars [in New York] bound to go with us to Washington. A pleasant day's journey we had of it with their friendly faces to accompany us and with Colonel Winthrop to meet us at the train. The evening of our arrival Jamie went at once to see Charles Sumner who lives in a fine house adjoining our hotel. Nothing could be finer than the situation he has chosen. He kept J. until midnight and tried to detain him still longer, but the knowledge that I was waiting for him made him insist at length upon coming away. He found him better in health than he had supposed from the newspapers, and "the same old Sumner," as Jamie said.

Saturday morning I went in early with J. and passed the entire morning with the Senator. Several colored persons came in as we sat there, and those who were people of eminence were introduced. He talked of literature and showed us his own curiosities which appear to be numberless. Jamie was called away, but he urged me to stay. He said he had sent a message to the Senate which required a reply and he expected every moment to hear the sound of hoofs on the pavement, as he had requested a special messenger to be sent on horseback. The messenger did not arrive, but I stayed on all the same until his carriage came to take him to the Capitol, when he insisted that I should accompany him. He showed me all the wonders of the place, not forgetting the doors which Crawford never lived even to design in clay altogether, but which his wife, desiring to have the money, caused to be finished by her husband's workmen and foisted upon our Government. They are poor enough. Sumner opposed her in what he considered a dishonest attempt to get money, but of

course he could not make an open opposition of this
nature against a lady, the widow of his friend.

Sumner's character is one of the most extraordinary
pictures of opposing elements ever combined in one
person. He is so possessed by Sumner that there is
really no room for the fair existence of another in his
world. Position, popularity, domestic happiness, health,
have one by one been cut away from him, but he still
stands erect, with as large a faith in Sumner and with
as determined a look toward the future as if it beckoned
him to glory and happiness. I suppose he must believe
that the next turn of Fortune's wheel must give him the
favor he has now lost; but were he another man, all the
honors of the state could hardly recompense him in the
least for what he has lost. He has a firm proud spirit
which his terrible bodily suffering does not appear to
make falter. His health is so precarious that doubtless
a few more adverse strokes would finish him; but he
has had all there are to have, one would say. His
friends, however, uphold him most tenderly; letters
from dear Mrs. Child and others lay upon his table urging him to put away all excitement and try to live for
the service of the state. Public honor, probity, the
high service of his country seem to be the passions which
animate him and by which he endures. He has a mania
for collecting rare books and pictures nowadays and it
is almost pitiful to see how this fancy runs away with
him and how he must frequently be deceived. The
tragedy of his marriage would be far more tragic if it
had left any scar (as far as mortal can discover) save

upon his pride. I would not do a man whom I hold in such honor any injustice, but he never *seemed* in love.

Sunday. — Not well — kept to my room in the Arlington Hotel all day, obliged to refuse to see guests also, and dear J. has gone alone to dine with Sumner. I had hoped to see his home once more and to see him among his peers. There is always a doubt of course, but especially in his state of health, whether we may ever meet again. If not, I shall not soon forget his stately carriage at the Capitol yesterday nor the store he sets at present upon his counted friends.

He pointed out the great avenue named Massachusetts, and the school house named after himself, with a just and noble pride yesterday. The trees are all ready to burst into leaf. Read Bayard Taylor's Norwegian story, "Lars" — very sweet and fine it is — just missing "an excuse for being." L. J. fills us with new respect and regard. Her devotion to her daughter is so perfect and so wise.

Jamie returned about 12 o'clock. There had been a gorgeous dinner. The guests were Caleb Cushing, Carl Schurz, Perley Poore, Mr. Hill, J. T. F. The service was worthy of the house of an English nobleman, the feast worthy of Lucullus. It fairly astonished J. to see Sumner eat. He of course sat at S.'s right. Not a wine, nor a dish, was left untasted and even the richest puddings were taken in large quantities. I thought of poor Mrs. Child and other devout admirers of this their Republican (!) leader, then of Charlotte Brontë's story of Thackeray at dinner. Some day, said J., we shall

STAGE FOLK AND OTHERS 267

take up the paper and find Sumner is no more, and it will be after one of these dinners.

The talk astonished J., utterly unused as he is to look behind the scenes of government. Caleb Cushing, a man over 70, who appears to have the vigor of 50, called Stanton "a master of duplicity." Caleb Cushing said Seward was the first man who introduced ungentlemanly bearing into the Cabinet. Until he came there, there was no smoking, no putting up of the feet, but always a fine courtesy and dignity of behavior was preserved.

Before leaving the diaries from which so many pages have already been drawn, before letting the last of the familiar faces which look out from them fade again from sight, it would be a pity not to assemble a few entries recalling notable persons of whom Mrs. Fields made fragmentary but significant record. Here, for instance, are glimpses of Henry Ward Beecher, fresh from the great service he rendered to the Union cause in the Civil War by his speeches in England.

Tuesday, November 17, 1863. — J. T. F. saw Mr. Kennard today and we heard from him the particulars of Mr. Beecher's landing. He came on shore in the warm fog which was the precursor of the heavy rain we have today, at 3 o'clock A.M. of Sunday. He went to the Parker House until day should break and Mr. Kennard could come and take him to the retirement of Brookline, to pass the day until the train should leave for New York. News of his arrival getting abroad, a company of orthodox deacons waited upon him very early to invite him to preach. "Gentlemen, do you take me for a fool," he said, "to jump so readily into the harness of the pulpit even before the fatigue of the voyage has worn away?" He heard of the illness of one of his younger children and therefore hastened as quickly as possible toward home.

The day before the one upon which he was to speak at Exeter Hall he awoke in the morning with a heavy headache; his voice, too, was seriously impaired by over-use. He wanted to speak, his whole heart was in it, yet how in this condition? He shut himself up in the house all that day and hoped for better things and went early to bed that night. The next morning at dawn he awoke, he opened his eyes quickly. "Is God to suffer me to do this work?" He leaped from the bed with a bound. His head was clear and fresh, but his voice — he hardly dared to try that. "I will speak to my sister three thousand miles away," he said, and cried, "Harriet." The tones were clear and strong. "Thank God!" he said — then speedily dressed — trying his voice again and again — then he sat down and wrote off the heads of his address. All he needed to say came freshly and purely to his mind just in the form he wished. The day ebbed away and the carriage came to take him to the hall. When he descended to the street, to his surprise there was a long file of policemen, through whom he was conducted because of the crowds waiting about his door. He was

obliged to descend also at some distance from Exeter
Hall, and he was again conducted through another line
of police before he reached the door. The people pushed
and cried out so that he ran from the carriage towards
the hall; and one of the staid policemen, observing a
man running, cried out and caught him by the coat-tail
saying he must n't run there, that line was preserved
for the great speaker. "Well, my friend," said Mr.
Beecher, "I can tell you one thing. There won't be
much speaking till I get there." While he hurried on,
he felt a woman lay hold of the skirts of his coat. The
police, seeing her, tried to push her away, but she said
to one of them, "I belong to his party." Mr. B. said,
"I overheard the poor thing, but I thought if she chose
to tell a lie I would not push her away; but as I neared
the door she crept up and whispered to me, 'I am one
of your people. Don't you remember ——, a Scotch
woman who used to live in Brooklyn and go to the
Plymouth Church? I have thought of this for weeks
and longed and dreamt of being with you again. Now
my desire is heard.'"

The rest of this wonderful night the public journals
and his own letters can tell us of — have told us. He
has been as it were a man raised up for this dark hour of
our dear Country. May he live to see the promised
land, and not only from the top of Pisgah.

December 10, 1863. — Visit from H. W. Beecher. . . .
Mr. Beecher did not like Mr. Browning. He found him
flippant and worldly. To be sure he had but one interview and could scarcely judge, but had he met the man

by chance in a company he should never have sought him a second time. He said of Charles Lamb that he always reminded him of a honeysuckle growing between and over a rough trellis; it would cover the stakes, it would throw out blossoms and tendrils, it would attract hummingbirds and make corners for their nests and fill the wide air with its fragrance. Such was C. Lamb to him.

He was sure he could have liked Mrs. Browning — so credulous, generous, outspoken. He liked strong outspoken people, yet he liked serene people too; but then, he loved the world in its wide variety.

He said his boy wished to be either a stage-driver or a missionary. His fancy was for stage-driving; he thought perhaps his duty might make him a missionary. . . .

It was such a privilege to see him back and such a privilege to grasp his hand, I could say nothing but be happy and thankful.

A few years later a passing shape from still an earlier generation casts its shadow of tragic outline across the pages of the diary.

Sunday, January 6, 1867. — A driving snow-storm. Last night Jamie went to the Club; met W. Everett, who said that while his father was member of Congress and was at one time returning from Washington to Boston he was stopped in the street as he passed through Philadelphia by a haggard man wrapped in a cloak. "I am Aaron Burr," said the figure, "and I pray you to

ask Congress for an appropriation to aid me in my misery." Mr. E. replied that the member from his own
district was the person to whom to apply. "I know
that," was the sad rejoinder, "but the others are all
strangers to me and I pray you to help me." After some
reflection Mr. Everett promised to try to do something
in his behalf; fortunately, however, he was released by
death before Congress was again in session.

Then soon appears a more cheerful figure, in the
person of the Rev. Elijah Kellogg whose lines of "Spartacus to the Gladiators" have resounded in many a
schoolhouse. His tales of the Stowes and the family
Bible may still divert a generation that knows not
Spartacus.

Thursday, January 10, 1867. — Yesterday J. fell in
with a Mr. Kellogg, a clergyman from Harpswell,
Maine, the author of many noble things, among the
rest, of the "Speech of Spartacus" which is in Sargent's
"School Speaker," a piece of which the boys are very
fond, but the masters are obliged to forbid their speaking it because it always takes the prize. He wrote it
while in college, to speak himself. He went to school
with Longfellow, though he is younger than the poet,
and the latter calls him a man of genius. He is a preacher
of the gospel and for the past ten months has been
speaking every Sunday at the Sailor's Bethel with great
effect. He called to see J. and told him some queer anecdotes regarding his sea-life. He dresses like a fisherman,

red shirt, etc., while at home. He remembers Professor Stowe and his wife well. He says their arrival at Brunswick was looked for with eagerness by many, with some natural curiosity by himself. One day about the time they were expected he was in his boat floating near the pier and preparing to return to his island where he lives, as the tide was going down and if he delayed much longer he would be ashore; but he observed a woman sitting on a cask upon the wharf swinging her heels, with two large holes the size of a dollar each in the back of her stockings, a man standing by her side, and several children playing about. At once he believed it must be the new professor, so he dallied about in his boat observing them. Presently the man cried out, "Hallo there, will you give my wife a sail?" "I can't," he replied, "there's no wind." "Will you give her a row then?" "The tide's too low and I shan't get home." "Oh," said the woman, "we will pay you; you'd better take me out a little way." "No, I can't," he said. Presently he heard somebody say something about that's being the minister and not a fisherman at all. "Do you think so?" said Mrs. Stowe. With that he dropped down into the bottom of his boat and was off before another word.

He told Mr. Fields also of the professor who preceded Professor Stowe. He was an unmarried man with three sisters, all of whom were insane at times and frequently one of them was away from home in an asylum. One day the brother was away, the eldest sister being at home in apparently good health, when another professor came to visit them to whom she wished to be particularly polite. "What will you have for dinner," said she, "today?" "Oh! the best thing you've got," he replied.   So when dinner came she had stewed the family Bible with cabbage for his repast. He speaks with the greatest enthusiasm of the beauty of that Maine coast. We must go there.

Out of what seems a past almost pre-Augustan come these memories of N. P. Willis, a poet who suffered the misfortune of outliving much of his own fame.

Thursday, January 31, 1867. — The papers of last night brought the news of N. P. Willis's death and that he was to be buried in Boston from St. Paul's Church today. Early this morning a note came from Mrs. Willis asking Mr. Fields to see Dr. Howe and Edmund Quincy, to ask them to be pall-bearers with himself and Colonel Trimble. Fortunately last night J. had seen the announcement, and before going to Longfellow's made up his mind to ask Longfellow and Lowell to come in to assist at the ceremony of their brother-author; he had also sent to Professor Holmes before the note came from Mrs. Willis. He then sent immediately for the others whom she mentioned and for a quantity of exquisite flowers. All his plans turned out as he had arranged and hoped and the poet's grave was attended by the noblest America had to offer. The dead face was not exposed, but the people pressed forward to take a sprig from the coffin in memory of one who had strewn many a flower of thought on the hard way of their lives. There are some to speak hardly of Willis, but usually the awe of death ennobles his memory to the grateful world of his appreciators. "Refrain! refrain!" we long to say to the others who would carp. "If you have tears, shed them on the poet's grave."

There had been previously an exquisite and touching service at Idlewild where Octavius Frothingham did all a man could do, inspired by the occasion and the loveliness of the day and scene. The service here would have seemed cold as stone except for the gracious poets who surrounded the body and prevented one thought of chill lack of sympathy from penetrating the flowers with which it was covered. I could not restrain my tears when I remembered a few years, only two, and the same company had borne Hawthorne's body to its burial. Which, which, of that beloved and worshipped few was next to be borne by the weeping remnant!!

Wednesday, July 1, 1868. — In our walk yesterday J. delighted himself and me by rehearsing his memories of Willis. J. was at the Astor House when Willis returned first from Europe with his young bride. He was then the observed of all observers. As in those days travellers crossed in sailing vessels, his coming was not heralded; the first that was known of their arrival was when he walked into the Astor with his beautiful young wife upon his arm. He wore a brown cloak thrown gracefully about his shoulders and was a man to remind one of Lady Blessington's saying, "If Willis had been born to £10,000 a year he would have been a perfect man."

He was then at the head of the world of literature in America; his influence could do anything and his heart and purse were both at the service of the needy asker. Unfortunately from the first he never paid his debts. J. said he never believed the tales of Willis's dissipation. He spent money freely even when he had it not. All the English folk, lords and ladies, who then came to see America were the guests of Willis.

I asked what his wife was like! "Like a seraph. She was lovely with all womanly attractions."

Of the various "causes" to which Mrs. Fields and her husband paid allegiance, the cause of equal opportunity for men and women cannot justly be left unmentioned. They espoused it before its friends were taken with the seriousness they have long commanded, and, as the following passage will suggest, were full of sympathy with those who fought its early battles. The impact of one of these combatants, Mrs. Mary A. Livermore, a reformer in sundry fields, against the rock of conservatism represented by the President of Harvard College, is the subject of a lively bit of record.

September 22, 1876. — At four came Miss Phelps, at six came Mrs. Livermore. Ah! She is indeed a great woman — a strong arm to those who are weak, a new faith in time of trouble. She came to tea as fresh as if she had been calmly sunning herself all the week instead of speaking at a great meeting at Faneuil Hall the previous evening and taking cold in the process.

She talked most wittily and brilliantly, beside laughing most heartily and merrily over all dear J.'s absurd stories and illustrations. He told her of a woman who came to speak to him after one of his lectures, to thank him for what he was trying to do for the education of women. She said, "I was educated at home with my brothers and taught all they were taught, learning my lessons by their side and reciting with them until the time came for them to go to college. Nobody ever told me I was not to go to college! And when the moment arrived and it dawned upon me that I was to be left behind to do nothing, to learn nothing more, I was terribly unhappy."

"I know just how she felt," said Mrs. Livermore; "there was a party of six of us girls, sisters and cousins, who had studied with our brothers up to the time for going to college. We were all ready, but what was to be done? We were told that no girls had entered Harvard thus far. We said to each other, we six girls will go to Cambridge and call upon President Quincy, show him where we stand in our lessons, and ask him to admit us. I was the youngest of the party. I was noted for being rather hot and intemperate in speech in those days, and the girls made me promise before we left the house [not to speak] — 'For as sure as you do,' they said, 'you will spoil all.' So I promised, and we went to Cambridge and found Mr. Quincy. The girls laid their proposition before him as clearly as they dared, by showing him what they had done in their lessons. 'Very smart girls, unusually capable girls,' he said encouragingly; 'but can you cook?' 'Oh, yes, sir,' said one, 'we have kept house for some time.' 'Highly important,' he said; and so on during the space of an hour."

Mrs. Livermore said she found he was toying with them and they were as far away from the subject in their minds as the moment they arrived, and, forgetting her promise of silence, she said: "'But, Mr. Quincy, what we came to ask is, will you allow us to come to college when our brothers do? You say we are sufficiently prepared; is there anything to prevent our admission?' 'Oh, yes, my dear, we never allow girls at Harvard; you know, the place for girls is at home.' 'Yes, but, Mr. Quincy, if we are prepared, we would not ask to recite, but may we not attend the recitations and sit silent in the classes?' 'No, my dear, you may not.' 'Then I wish—' 'What do you wish?' he said. 'I wish I were God for one instant, that I might kill every woman from Eve down and let you have a masculine world all to yourselves and see how you would like that.' Up to this point the girls had been kept up by excitement, but there we broke down. I tried the best I could not to cry, but I found my eyes were getting full, and the only thing for us to do was to leave as soon as we could for home. We lived in the vicinity of Copp's Hill and I can see, as distinctly as if it were yesterday, the room looking out on the burial-ground in which we all sat down together and cried ourselves half-blind. 'I wish I was dead,' said one. 'I wish I had never been born,' said another. 'Martha, get up from that stone seat,' said a third; 'you'll get cold.' 'I don't care if I do,' said Martha; 'I shall perhaps die the sooner.' We were all terribly indignant."

I was deeply interested in this history. I was standing over the cradle of woman's emancipation and seeing it rocked by the hand of sorrow and indignation.

Other passages might be cited merely to illustrate the skill and industry of Mrs. Fields in reducing to narrative form the mass of reported talk of one sort or another which her husband brought home to her. A striking instance of this is found in the full rendering of a story told by R. H. Dana, Jr., to Fields, at a time when they were discussing a new edition of "Two Years before the Mast." It is a long dramatic account of Dana's experience on a burning ship in the Pacific, which he told Fields he had "never yet found time to write down." In Charles Francis Adams's biography of Dana, the bare bones of the story are preserved in a diary Dana was keeping during the voyage in which this calamity occurred. If Adams could but have turned to the diary of Mrs. Fields for 1868, he would have found a detailed description of an episode in Dana's life which might well have been included in his biography.

But the *if's* of bookmaking are hardly less abundant than those of history. If, for a single instance, this were in any real sense a biography of Mrs. Fields, it would be necessary for the reader to explore with the compiler the journals and letters written during two visits the Fieldses made to Europe in 1859 and 1869. But this

would be foreign to the present purpose, which has not
been either to produce a biography, or to evoke all the
interesting persons known to Mrs. Fields, at home and
abroad, but rather to present them and her against her

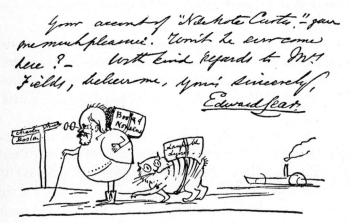

From a letter of Edward Lear's to Fields

own intimate and distinctive background. She herself
has written, in her "Authors and Friends," of Tennyson
and Lady Tennyson, and to the pictures she has drawn
of them it would be easily possible to add fresh lines
from the unprinted records — as it would be, also, to
bring forth passages touching upon many another familiar figure of Victorian England. The roving lover who
justified himself by singing that

They were my visits, but thou art my home,

stated, in essence, the principle to which these pages
have adhered. The frequenters of the house in Charles
Street well knew that something of its color and flavor

was derived from the excursions its hostess made into other scenes. Yet her own color and flavor were not those of the visitor, but of the visited. It is a pity that many who would have been welcome visitors — none more than Edward Lear — never came. Even as it is, there is ample ground for laying the emphasis of this book upon the panorama of a picturesque social life chiefly as seen from within the hospitable walls of Mr. and Mrs. Fields. When he died in 1881, a long and happy chapter in her long and happy life came to its close.

VII

SARAH ORNE JEWETT

Such a statement about Mrs. Fields as that she "was to survive her husband many years and was to flourish as a copious second volume — the connection licenses the figure — of the work anciently issued," almost identifies itself, without remark, as proceeding from the same friend, Henry James, whose words have colored a previous chapter of this book. The many years to which he referred were, indeed, nearly thirty-four in number, about a third of a century, or what is commonly counted a generation. For a longer period than that through which she was the wife of James T. Fields, she was thus his widow. Through nearly all of this period the need of her nature for an absorbing affectionate intimacy was met through her friendship with Sarah Orne Jewett. It was with reference to her that Mrs. Fields, in the preface to a collection of Miss Jewett's letters, published in 1911, two years after her death, wrote of "the power that lies in friendship to sustain the giver as well as the receiver." In the friendship of these two women it would have been impossible to define either one, to the exclusion of the other, as the giver or the receiver. They were certainly both sustained by their relation.

Miss Jewett, born in South Berwick, Maine, in 1849, and continuously identified with that place until her death in 1909, first entered the "Atlantic circle" in

1869, when she was but twenty years old, and Fields was still editor of the magazine. In that year a story by her, called "Mr. Bruce" and credited in the index of the magazine — for contributions then appeared unsigned — to "A. C. Eliot," was printed in the "Atlantic." Four years later, *Consule Howells*, "The Shore House," a second story, appeared over her own name, the practice of printing signatures having meanwhile been instituted. In May, 1875, the "Atlantic" contained a poem by Miss Jewett, which may be quoted, not so much to remind the readers of those stories of New England on which her later fame was based, that in her earlier years she was much given to the writing of verse, as to explain in a way the union — there is no truer word for it — that came later to exist between herself and Mrs. Fields.

Thus it read : —

TOGETHER

I wonder if you really send
  Those dreams of you that come and go!
I like to say, "She thought of me,
  And I have known it."   Is it so?

Though other friends walk by your side,
  Yet sometimes it must surely be,
They wonder where your thoughts have gone,
  Because I have you here with me.

And when the busy day is done
  And work is ended, voices cease,
When every one has said good night,
  In fading firelight, then in peace

SARAH ORNE JEWETT

I idly rest: you come to me, —
   Your dear love holds me close to you.
If I could see you face to face
   It would not be more sweet and true;

I do not hear the words you speak,
   Nor touch your hands, nor see your eyes:
Yet, far away the flowers may grow
   From whence to me the fragrance flies;

And so, across the empty miles
   Light from my star shines.   Is it, dear,
Your love has never gone away?
   I said farewell and — kept you here.

It was not strange that the writer of just such a poem should have seemed to Fields, before his death in 1881, the ideal friend to fill the impending gap in the life of his wife. He must have known that, when the time should come for readjusting herself to life without him, she would need something more than random contacts with friends, no matter how rewarding each such relationship might be. He must have realized that the intensely personal element in her nature would require an outlet through an intensely personal devotion. If he could have foreseen the relation that grew up between Mrs. Fields and Miss Jewett — her junior by about fifteen years — almost immediately upon his death, and continued throughout the life of the younger friend, he would surely have felt a great security of satisfaction in what was yet to be. In all her personal manifestations, and in all her work, Miss Jewett embodied a quality of distinction, a quality of the true *aristophile*, — to employ a term which has seemed to me before to fit that small company of lovers of the best to which these ladies preëminently belonged, — that made them foreordained companions. To Mrs. Fields it meant much to stand in a close relation — apart from all considerations of a completely uniting friendship — with such an artist as Miss Jewett, to feel that through sympathy and encouragement she was furthering a true and permanent contribution to American letters. To Miss Jewett, whose life, before this intimacy began, had been led almost entirely in the Maine village of her birth, — a village of dignity and high traditions that were her own inheritance, — there came an extension of interests and stimulating contacts through finding herself a frequent member of another household than her own, and that a very nucleus of quickening human intercourse. To pursue her work of writing chiefly at South Berwick, to come to Boston, or Manchester, for that freshening of the spirit which the creative writer so greatly needs, and there to find the most sympathetic and devoted of friends, also much occupied herself with the writing of books and with all commerce of vital thoughts — what could have afforded a more delightful arrangement of life?

Even as early as 1881, the year of Fields's death, Miss Jewett published the fourth of her many books, "Country By-Ways," preceded by "Deephaven" (1877), "Play Days" (1878), and "Old Friends and New" (1879). From 1881 onward her production was constant and abundant. In 1881 also began a period of

THE LIBRARY IN CHARLES STREET; MRS. FIELDS AT THE WINDOW, MISS JEWETT AT THE RIGHT

remarkable productiveness on the part of Mrs. Fields. In that very year of her husband's death she published both her "James T. Fields: Biographical Notes and Personal Sketches," and a second edition of "Under the Olive," a small volume in which she had brought together in 1880 a number of poems in which the influence of the Greek and English poets is sometimes manifested — notably in "Theocritus" — to excellent purpose. If Mrs. Fields had been a poet of distinctive power, the fact would long ago have established itself. To make any such claim for her at this late day would be to depart from the purpose of this book. It was for the most part rather as a friend than as a daughter of the Muses that she turned to verse, the medium of utterance for so many of that nest of singing-birds in which her life was passed. In 1883 came her little volume "How to Help the Poor," representing an interest in the less fortunate which prepared her to become one of the founders of the Associated Charities of Boston, kept her long active and influential in the service of that organization, and made her at the last one of its generous benefactors. In 1895 and 1900, respectively, appeared two more volumes of verse, "The Singing Shepherd and Other Poems," assembling the work of earlier and later years, and "Orpheus, a Masque," each strongly touched, like "Under the Olive," with the Grecian spirit. From "The Singing Shepherd" I cannot resist quoting one of the best things it contains — a sonnet, "Flammantis Mœnia Mundi," under which, in my own copy of the book, I find the penciled note, written probably more than twenty years ago: "Mrs. Fields tells me that this sonnet came to her complete, one may almost say; standing on her feet she made it, but for one or two small changes, just as it is, in about fifteen minutes."

> I stood alone in purple space and saw
> The burning walls of the world, like wings of flame,
> Circling the sphere; there was no break nor flaw
> In those vast airy battlements whence came
> The spirits who had done with time and fame
> And all the playthings of earth's little hour;
> I saw them each, I knew them for the same,
> Mothers and brothers and the sons of power.
>
> Yet were they changed; the flaming walls had burned
> Their perishable selves, and there remained
> Only the pure white vision of the soul,
> The mortal part consumed, and swift returned
> Ashes to ashes; while unscathed, unstained,
> The immortal passed beyond the earth's control.

For the rest, her writings may be said to have grown out of the life which the pages of her diary have pictured. The successive volumes were these: "Whittier: Notes of his Life and of his Friendship" (New York, 1893); "A Shelf of Old Books" (New York, 1894); "Letters of Celia Thaxter" (edited with Miss Rose Lamb, Boston, 1895); "Authors and Friends" (Boston, 1896); "Life and Letters of Harriet Beecher Stowe" (Boston, 1897); "Nathaniel Hawthorne" (in the "Beacon Biographies," Boston, 1899); "Charles Dudley Warner" (New York, 1909); and, after the death of the friend whose name appears above this chapter, "Letters of Sarah Orne Jewett" (Boston, 1911).

This catalogue of publications is in itself a dry bit of

reading, and to add the titles of all the books produced by Miss Jewett after 1881 would not enliven the record. But the lists, explicit and implicit, will serve at least to suggest the range and nature of the activities of

I stood, alone, in purple space and saw
The burning walls of the world like wings of flame
Circling the sphere; there was no break nor flaw
In those great fiery battlements whence came
The spirits who had done with time and fame
And all the playthings of earth's little hour;
I saw them pass, I knew them for the same,
Mothers and brothers and the sons of power.

Yet were they changed; the fires of death had burned
Their perishable selves and there remained
Only the pure white vision of the soul,
The mortals part consumed and quick returned
Ashes to ashes ~~Back to earth's bosom~~ while, in flight, unstained
The spirits passed beyond the earth's control.

A. Fields.

An autograph copy of Mrs. Fields's "Flammantis Moenia Mundi"
before its final revision

mind and spirit in which the two friends shared for many years. It is no wonder that Mrs. Fields, who abandoned the regular maintenance of her diary in the face of her husband's failing health, resumed it in later years only under the special provocations of travel. In its place she took up the practice of writing daily missives — sometimes letters, more often the merest notes — to Miss Jewett whenever they were separated. These innumerable little messages of affection contained frequent references to persons and passing events, but rather as memoranda for talk when the two friends should meet than as records at all resembling the earlier journals. Such local friends as Mrs. Pratt and Mrs. Bell, in whom the spirit and wit of their father, Rufus Choate, shone on for later generations; Mrs. Whitman, mistress of the arts of color and of friendship; Miss Guiney, figuring always as "the Linnet," even as Mrs. Thaxter was "the Sandpiper"; Dr. Holmes, Phillips Brooks, "dear Whittier" — these and scores of others, young and old, known and unknown to fame, people the scene which the little notes recall. There are, besides, such visitors from abroad as Matthew Arnold and his wife, Mrs. Humphry Ward and her daughter, M. and Mme. Brunetière, and Mme. Blanc ("Th. Bentzon"), whose article, "Condition de la Femme aux États-Unis," in the "Revue des Deux Mondes" for September, 1894, could not have been written but for the knowledge of Boston acquired through a long visit to the house in Charles Street. Of the salon of her hostess she wrote: "Je voudrais essayer de peindre celui qui se rapproche le plus, par beaucoup de côtés, les salons de France de la meilleure époque, le salon de Mrs. J. T. Fields." She goes on to paint it, and from the picture at least one fragment — apropos of the portraits in the house — should be rescued, if only for the piquancy conferred by Mme. Blanc's native tongue upon a bit of anecdote: "Emerson réalise

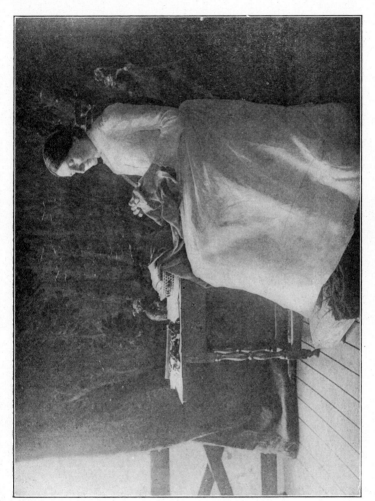

MRS. FIELDS ON HER MANCHESTER PIAZZA

bien, en physique, l'idée d'immatérialité que je me fai-
sais de lui. Mrs. Fields me conte une jolie anecdote :
vers la fin de sa vie, il fut prit d'un singulier accès de
curiosité ; il voulut savoir une fois ce que c'était le whisky et entra dans un bar pour s'en servir : — Vous vou-
lez un verre d'eau, Mr. Emerson ? dit le garçon, sans
lui donner le temps d'exprimer sa criminelle envie.
Et le philosophe but son verre d'eau, . . . et il mourut
sans connaître le goût du whisky."

But if the notes of Mrs. Fields to Miss Jewett, and
Miss Jewett's own letters to her friend in Boston, do
not provide any counterpart to the diaries which make
up the greater portion of this book, there are, in the
journals kept by Mrs. Fields on special occasions of
travel, records of experiences shared by the two friends
which should be given here.

When they went to Europe together, as early as 1882,
the two travellers were happily characterized by Whittier in a sonnet, "Godspeed," as

> her in whom
> All graces and sweet charities unite
> The old Greek beauty set in holier light;
> And her for whom New England's byways bloom,
> Who walks among us welcome as the Spring,
> Calling up blossoms where her light feet stray.

No effort or adventure seemed to daunt the companions in their journeyings. There was an indomitable
quality in Mrs. Fields which Miss Jewett used to as-
cribe to her "May blood," with its strain of aboli-
tionism, and it showed itself when she accepted with

enthusiasm, and successfully urged Miss Jewett to accept, an invitation to make a two months' winter cruise in West Indian waters, in company with Mr. and Mrs. Aldrich, on the yacht Hermione of their friend, Henry L. Pierce. The diary of Mrs. Fields records discomforts and pleasures with an equal hand, and gives lively glimpses of island and ocean scenes. At Santo Domingo, for example, the President of the Republic of Haiti dined on the Hermione on St. Valentine's Day, 1896, and talked in a manner to which the impending liberation of Cuba from the Spanish yoke may now be seen to have added some significance.

Anything more interesting than his conversation [wrote Mrs. Fields] would be impossible to find. He ended just before we left the table by speaking of Cuba. He is inclined to believe that the day of Spain is over. The people are already conquerors in the interior and are approaching Havana. Spain will soon be compelled to retire to her coast defenses and she is sure to be driven thence in two years or sooner. Of course, if the Cubans are recognized by the great powers they will triumph all the sooner.

"Do these island republics take the part of Cuba?" someone asked.

"I will tell you a little tale of a camel," he said, "if you will allow me — a camel greatly overladen who lamented his sad fate. 'I am bent to the earth,' he said; 'everything is heaped upon me and I feel as if I could never rise again under such a load.' Upon his pack was seated a flea, who heard the lament of the camel. Immediately the flea jumped to the ground. 'See!' he said; 'now rise, I have relieved you of my own weight.' 'Thank you, Mr. Elephant,' said the camel, as he glanced at the flea hopping away. The recognition of these islands would help Cuba about as much," he added laughingly.

But the President of Haiti, concerning whom much more might be quoted, is less a part of the present picture than Thomas Bailey Aldrich, of whom Mrs. Fields wrote, February 21 : —

T. B. A.'s wit and pleasant company never fail — he is so natural, finding fault at times, without being a fault-finder, and being crusty like another human creature when out of sorts — but on the whole a most refreshing companion, coming up from below every morning with a shining countenance, his hair curling like a boy's, and ready for a new day. He said yesterday that he should like to live 450 years — "shouldn't you?" "No," I said; "I am on tip-toe for the flight." "Ah," he said with a visible shudder, "we know nothing about it! Oddly enough, I have strange impressions of having lived before — once in London especially — not at St. Paul's, or Pall Mall, or in any of the great places where I might have been deceived by previous imaginations, — not at all, — but among some old streets where I had never been before and where I had no associations." He would have gone on in this vein and would have drawn me into giving some reasons for my faith which would have been none to him, but fortunately we were interrupted. He is full of quips and cranks in talk — is a worshipper of the English language and a good student of Murray's Grammar, in which he faithfully believes. His own training in it he values as much as anything which ever came to him. He picks up the unfortunates, of which I am chief, who say "people" meaning "persons," who say "at length" for "at last," and who use foolish redundancies, but I cannot seem to record his fun. He began to joke Bridget early in the voyage about the necessity of being tattooed when she arrived at the Windward Islands, like the rest of the crew! Fancying that he saw a sort of half idea that he was in earnest, he kept it up and told her that the buttermark of Ponkapog should be the device! The matter had nearly blown over when yesterday he wanted her suddenly and called, "Bridget," at the gangway rather sharply. "Here, sir," said the dear creature running quickly to mount the stairs. "The tattoo-man is here," said T. B. With all seriousness Bridget paused a moment, wavered, looked again, and then came on laughing to do what he really wanted. "That man will be the death of me — so he will," said B. as she went away on her errand. She is his slave; gets his clothes and waits upon him every moment; but his fun and sweetness with her "*désennuie de service*," and more, charges it with pleasantness.

T. B. A. is a most careful reader and a true reporter upon the few good books of which he is cognizant. He has read Froude's history twice through, and Queen Mary's reign three times. He has read a vast number of novels, hundreds and hundreds, — French and English, — but his knowledge of French seems to stop there. He also once knew Spanish, but that seems to have dropped — he never, I think, could speak much of any language save his own. Being a master there is so much more than the rest of us achieve that we feel he has won his laurels.

On a later journey, in 1898, Mrs. Fields and Miss Jewett, visiting England and France in company with Miss Jewett's sister and nephew, were on more familiar and more suitable ground — if indeed that word can be used even figuratively for the unstable deck of a yacht. In London there were many old and new friends to be seen. In Paris Mme. Blanc opened for the travellers the doors of many a salon not commonly accessible to visiting Americans. But from all the abundant chronicle of these experiences, it will be enough to make two selections. The first describes a visit to the Provençal poet, Mistral, with his "Boufflo Beel" dog and hat; the second, a glimpse of Henry James at Rye.

It was in May of 1898, that Mrs. Fields and Miss Jewett, finding Paris cold and rainy, determined to strike for sunshine, and the South. A little journey into Provence, and a visit to Mistral, followed this decision. The following notes record the visit.

A perfect time and perfect weather in which to see the country of Provence. Fields of great white poppies and other flowers planted for seed in this district made the way beautiful on either hand. Olive trees with rows of black cypress and old tiled-roofed farmhouses, and the mountains always on the horizon, filled the landscape. The first considerable house we reached was the home of the poet. A pretty garden which attracted our attention with a rare eglantine called La Reine Joanne, and other charming things hanging over the wall made us suspicious of the poet's vicinity. Turning the corner of this garden and driving up a short road, we found the courtyard and door on the inner side as it were. We heard a barking dog. "Take care," said the driver, "there is a dangerous dog inside." We waited until Mistral himself came to meet us from the garden; he was much amused. There was an old dog tied, half asleep, on a bench and a young one by his side. He said laughing, "These are all, and they could not be less dangerous. The elder" (he let them loose while he spoke and they played about us), "the elder I call Bouffe, from Boufflo Beel" (Mistral does not speak any English, nor does his wife) "and the reason is because I happened to be in the neighborhood of Paris once just after Buffalo Bill had passed on toward Calais with his troupe. I saw a little dog, unlike the dogs of our country, who seemed to be lost, but the moment he saw me, he thought I was 'Boufflo Beel' and adopted me for his master. You see I look like him," he said, putting his wide felt hat a little more on one side! Yes,

MISTRAL, MASTER OF "BOUFFLO BEEL"

we did think so. "Well, the little dog has been with us ever since. He possesses the most wonderful intelligence and understands every word we say. One day I said to him, 'What a pity such a nice dog as you should have no children!' A few days later the servant said to me, 'Bouffe has been away nearly two days, but he has now come back bringing his wife.' 'Ah!' I said, 'take good care of them both.' In due time this other little dog, his son, arrived in the world, and shortly after Bouffe carried his wife away again, but kept the little dog. He is a wonderful fellow, to be sure."

We went into the house and sat down to talk awhile about poetry and books. There was a large book-case full of French and Provençal literature here, but it was rather the parlor and everyday sitting-room than his work-room. Unhappily, they have no children. Evidently they are exceedingly happy together and naturally do not miss what they have never had. She opened the drawing-room for us, which is the room of state. It is full of interesting things connected with Provence and their own life, but perfectly simple, in accord with the country-like fashion of their existence. There is a noble bas-relief of the head of Mistral, the drum or "tambour" of the Félibre, or for the Farandole, and, without overloading, plenty of good things — photographs, one or two pictures, not many, for the house is not that of a rich man, plaster casts, and one or two busts, — perhaps the presents of artists, — illustrations of "Mirèio," and things associated with their individual lives or the life of Provence. Presently Mistral gave me his arm and we went across the hall. Standing in the place of honor opposite the front door and in the large corner made by the staircase, is a fine copy of the bust of Lamartine, crowned with an olive wreath. We paused a moment here while Mistral spoke of Lamartine, and always with the sincere reverence which he has expressed in the poem entitled "*Élégie sur la mort de Lamartine.*" . . .

The dining-room was still more Provençal, if possible, than the rooms we had visited. The walls were white, which, with the closed green blinds, must give a pleasant light when the days are hot, yet bright even on grey days. Specimens of the pottery of the country hang around, decorated with soft colors. The old carved bread-mixing-and-holding affair, which belonged in every well-to-do house of the old time, was there, and one or two other old pieces of furniture, while the chairs, sofa, and table were of quaint shape, painted green with some decorations.

The details are all petty enough, but they proved how sincerely Mistral and his wife love their country and their surroundings and endeavor to ennoble them and make the most of them. After sitting at table and enjoying their hospitality, we went out again into the garden where Madame Mistral gathered "Nerto" (myrtle) for us, beside roses and other more beautiful but more formidable things. "Nerto" is the title of one of his last books (I hear) and the wife doubtless believed that we should cherish a branch of her myrtle especially in memory of the visit. She was quite right, but these things which are "to last" — how frail they are; the things that remain are those which are written on the heart.

We cannot forget these two picturesque beings standing in their garden, filling our hands with flowers and bidding us farewell. As we drove away into the sunny plain once more, we found it speaking to us with a voice of human kindness echoing from that poetic and friendly home. In a more personal vein, the address to Lamartine by Mistral expresses better his mood of the afternoon when we stood together looking at the bust and recalling each our personal remembrance of the man.

An excursion from London, on September 12, devoted to a day with Henry James, gave Mrs. Fields a memorable glimpse of the son of an old friend, and an honest pleasure in learning at first hand of his appreciation of Miss Jewett's writings.

Monday, September 13, 1898. — We left London about 11 o'clock for Rye, to pass the day with Mr. Henry James. He was waiting for us at the station with a carriage, and in five minutes we found ourselves at the top of a silent little winding street, at a green door with a brass knocker, wearing the air of impenetrable respectability which is so well known in England. Another instant and an old servant, Smith (who with his wife has been in Mr. James's service for 20 years), opened the door and helped us from the carriage. It was a pretty interior — large enough for elegance, and simple enough to suit the severe taste of a scholar and private gentleman.

Mr. James was intent on the largest hospitality. We were asked upstairs over a staircase with a pretty balustrade and plain green drugget on the steps; everything was of the severest plainness, but in the best taste, "not at all austere," as he himself wrote us.

We soon went down again after leaving our hats, to find a young gentleman, Mr. McAlpine, who is Mr. James's secretary, with him, awaiting us. This young man is just the person to help Mr. James. He has a bump of reverence and appreciates his position and opportunity. We sat in the parlor opening on a pretty garden for some time, until Mr. James said he could not conceive why luncheon was not ready and he must go and inquire, which he did in a very responsible manner, and soon after Smith appeared to announce the feast. Again a pretty room and table. We enjoyed our talk together sincerely at luncheon and afterward strolled into the garden. The dominating note was dear Mr. James's pleasure in having a home of his own to which he might ask us. From the garden, of course, we could see the pretty old house still more satisfactorily. An old brick wall concealed by vines and laurels surrounds the whole irregular domain; a door from the garden leads into a paved courtyard which seemed to give Mr. James peculiar satisfaction; returning to the garden, and on the other side, at an angle with the house, is a building which he laughingly called the temple of the Muse. This is his own place *par excel-*

P.S. I would for instance with pleasure

address you a Letter, an Editor — a

Letter of reminiscence or appreciation

or making 25 pages of print or so,

which would serve, if you cared,
to your Volume:
as Introduction — a thing very

frank, familiar, as a thorough Friend

&c. — oh so Tender or so admiring —

as I do admire her work!

Reduced facsimile of postscript of a letter from Henry James,
expressing the intention, which he could not fulfill, to provide
an Introduction to the "Letters of Sarah Orne Jewett"

lence. A good writing-table and one for his secretary, a typewriter, books, and a sketch by Du Maurier, with a few other pictures (rather mementoes than works of art), excellent windows with clear light, such is the temple! Evidently an admirable spot for his work.

After we returned to the parlor Mr. James took occasion to tell Sarah how deeply and sincerely he appreciated her work; how he re-reads it with increasing admiration. "It is foolish to ask, I know," he said, "but were you in just such a place as you describe in the 'Pointed Firs'?" "No," she said, "not precisely; the book was chiefly written before I visited the locality itself." "And such an island?" he continued. "Not exactly," she said again. "Ah! I thought so," he said musingly; and the language — "It is so absolutely true —not a word overdone — such elegance and exactness." "And Mrs. Dennet — how admirable she is," he said again, not waiting for a reply. I need not say they were very much at home together after this.

Meanwhile the carriage came again to the door, for he had made a plan to take us on a drive to Winchelsea, a second of the Cinq Portes, Rye itself also being one. The sea has retreated from both these places, leaving about two miles of the Romney Marsh between them and the shore. Nothing could be more like something born of the imagination than the old city of Winchelsea. . . . Just outside the old gate looking towards Rye and the sea from a lonely height is the cottage where Ellen Terry has found a summer resting-place and retirement. It is a true home for an artist — nothing

could be lovelier. Unhappily she was not there, but we
were happy to see the place which she described to us
with so great satisfaction.

From Winchelsea Mr. James drove us to the station,
where we took the train for Hastings. He had brought
his small dog, an aged black and tan terrier, with him
for a holiday. He put on the muzzle, which all dogs
just now must wear, and took it off a great many times
until, having left it once when he went to buy the tickets and recovered it, he again lost it and it could not be
found; so as soon as he reached Hastings, he took a carriage again to drive us along the esplanade, but the first
thing was to buy a new muzzle. This esplanade is three
miles long, but we began to feel like tea, so having
looked upon the sea sufficiently from this decidedly un-
romantic point of view, we went into a small shop and
enjoyed more talk under new conditions. "How many
cakes have you eaten?" "Ten," gravely replied Mr.
James — at which we all laughed. "Oh, I know," said
the girl with a wise look at the desk. "How do you suppose they know?" said Mr. James musingly as he
turned away. "They always do!" And so on again
presently to the train at Hastings, where Mr. McAlpine appeared at the right instant. Mr. James's train
for Rye left a few moments before ours for London. He
took a most friendly farewell and having left us to Mr.
McA. ran for his own carriage. In another five minutes
we too were away, bearing our delightful memories of
this meeting.

Not because they record momentous events and encounters, but merely as little pictures of the life which Mrs. Fields and Miss Jewett led together, these passages are brought to light. They are the last to be presented here. For more than another decade beyond the summer of 1898, Miss Jewett, sorely invalided through the final years as the result of a carriage accident, remained the central personal fact in Mrs. Fields's interest and affections. Soon after her death, in June, 1909, Mrs. Fields wrote about her to a common friend: "Of my dear Sarah—I believe one of her noblest qualities was her great generosity. Others could only guess at this, but I was allowed to know it. Not that she made gifts, but a wide sympathy was hers for every disappointed or incompetent fellow creature. It was a most distinguishing characteristic! Governor Andrew spoke of Judge B—— once as 'A friend to every man who did not need a friend'! Sarah's quick sympathy knew a friend was in need before she knew it herself; she was the spirit of beneficence, and her quick delicate wit was such a joy in daily companionship!"

Of this daily companionship an anonymous contributor to the "Atlantic Monthly" for August, 1909, had been a fortunate witness. I need not ask his permission to repeat a portion of what he then wrote: —

"There is but one familiar portrait of Miss Jewett. It has been so often reprinted that many who have seen it, even without seeing her, must think of her as immune from change, blessed with perpetual youth, with a gracious, sympathetic femininity, with an air of breeding and distinction quite independent of shifting fashions.

"This portrait is intimately symbolic of her work. It typifies with a rare faithfulness the quality of all the products of her pen. In them one found, and finds, the same abiding elements of beauty, sympathy, and distinction. The element of sympathy — perhaps the greatest of these — found its expression in a humor that provoked less of outward laughter than of smiles within, and in a pathos the very counterpart of this delicate quality. The beauty and the distinction may be less capable of brief characterization, but they pervaded her art. . . .

"This work of hers, in dealing with the New England life she knew and loved, was essentially American, as purely indigenous as the pointed firs of her own countryside. The art with which she wrought her native themes was limited, on the contrary, by no local boundaries. At its best it had the absolute quality of the highest art in every quarter of the globe. And the spirit in which she approached her task was as broad in its scope and sympathy as her art in its form. It was precisely this union of what was at once so clearly American and so clearly universal that distinguished her stories, in the eyes of both editor and reader, as the best — so often — in any magazine that contained them.

"Her constant demand upon herself was for the best. There were no compromises with mediocrity, either in her tastes or in her achievement s. It was the best aspect of New England character and tradition on which her vision steadily dwelt. She was satisfied with nothing short of the best in her interpretation of New England life. The form of creative writing in which she won her highest successes — the short story — is the form in which Americans have made their most distinctive contributions to English literature; and her place with the few best of these writers appears to be secure.

"If the familiar portrait typifies her work, it is equally true to the person herself. The quick, responsive spirit of youth, with all its sincerity, all its enjoyment in friendship or whatever else the day might hold, was an immutable possession. So were all the other qualities for which the features spoke. Through the recent years of physical disability, due in the first instance to an accident so gratuitous that it seemed to her friends unendurable, there was a noble patience, a sweet endurance, that could have sprung only from an heroic strain of character."

For nearly six years Mrs. Fields survived Miss Jewett, bereaved as by the loss of half her personal world, yet indomitable of spirit and energy, so long as her physical forces would permit any of the old accustomed exercises of hospitality and friendship. The selection and publication of Miss Jewett's letters was a labor of love which continued the sense of companionship for the first two of the remaining years. Through the four others there was a failing of bodily strength, though not at all of mental and spiritual eagerness; and in her outward mien through all the later years, there was that which must have recalled to many the ancient couplet :—

No Spring, nor summer's beauty hath such grace
As I have seen in one autumnal face.

Towards the end there was a brief return to the keeping of a sporadic diary. Its final words, written January 25, 1913, were these: "The days go on cheerfully. I have just read Mark Twain's life, the life of a man who had greatness in him. I am now reading his 'Joan of Arc.' I hope to wait as cheerfully as he did for the trumpet call and as usefully, but I am ready."

When Mrs. Fields died and the Charles Street door was finally closed, at the beginning of 1915, the world had entered upon its first entire year of a new era. It is an era as sharply separated from that of her intimate contemporaries, the American Victorians, as any new from any old order. The figures of every old order take their places by degrees as "museum pieces," objects of curious and sometimes condescending study. But let us not be too sure that in parting with the past we have let it keep only that which can best be spared. We would not wish them back, those Victorians of ours. They were the product of their own day, and would be hardly at ease — poor things — in our twentieth-century Zion. Even some of us who inhabit it gain a sense of rest in reëntering their quiet, decorous dwelling-places.   As we emerge again from one of them, may it be with a renewed allegiance to those lasting "things that are more excellent," which belong to every generation of civilized men and women.

INDEX

PAGE numbers set in bold-faced type indicate, generally speaking, the more important references to the persons concerned. As a complete list of the pages on which Mr. or Mrs. Fields, or both, are mentioned would include substantially the whole book, only a few of the more significant references to them have been selected for inclusion under their names.

McGrath - Sherrill Press
GRAPHIC ARTS BLDG.
BOSTON